# THE POPES
# AGAINST
# MODERN ERRORS

*"For there shall be a time, when they will not endure sound doctrine; but, according to their own desires, they will heap to themselves teachers, having itching ears: and will indeed turn away their hearing from the truth, but will be turned unto fables."* —2 Timothy 4:3-4

# THE POPES AGAINST MODERN ERRORS

## 16 PAPAL DOCUMENTS

*Arranged and Edited by*
Anthony J. Mioni, Jr.

*"If I say the truth to you, why do you not believe me? He that is of God, heareth the words of God. Therefore you hear them not, because you are not of God."* —John 8:46-47

TAN Books
Charlotte, North Carolina

Copyright © 1999 by TAN Books.

ISBN 978-0-89555-643-1

Library of Congress Catalog Card No.: 98-61396

Cover illustration: Pope Gregory XVI. Detail of monument by Luigi Amici (1854) in St. Peter's, Rome. Photo: Alinari/Art Resource, New York.

Printed and bound in India

TAN Books
Charlotte, North Carolina
www.TANBooks.com
2012

"Thus, Venerable Brethren, it is clear why this Apostolic See has never allowed its subjects to take part in the assemblies of non-Catholics. There is but one way in which the unity of Christians may be fostered, and that is by furthering the return to the one true Church of Christ of those who are separated from it; for from that one true Church they have in the past fallen away."

—Pope Pius XI, *Mortalium Animos,* par. 15
(On Fostering True Religious Unity, p. 301)


"Justice therefore forbids, and reason itself forbids, the State to be godless; or to adopt a line of action which would end in godlessness—namely, to treat the various religions (as they call them) alike, and to bestow upon them promiscuously equal rights and privileges. Since, then, the profession of one religion is necessary in the State, that religion must be professed which alone is true, and which can be recognized without difficulty, especially in Catholic States, because the marks of truth are, as it were, engraven upon it. This religion, therefore, the rulers of the State must preserve and protect, if they would provide—as they should do—with prudence and usefulness for the good of the community."

—Pope Leo XIII, *Libertas Praestantissimum,* par. 21
(On the Nature of True Liberty, p. 96)


"Nations will be reminded by the annual celebration of this feast [of Christ the King] that not only private individuals but also rulers and princes are bound to give public honor and obedience to Christ. It will call to their minds the thought of the Last Judgment, wherein Christ, who has been cast out of public life, despised, neglected and ignored, will most severely avenge these insults; for His kingly dignity demands that the State should take account of the Commandments of God and of Christian principles, both in making laws and in administering justice, and also in providing for the young a sound moral education."

—Pope Pius XI, *Quas Primas,* par. 32
(On the Feast of Christ the King, p. 290)

# CONTENTS

of Public and Private Life—Reign of Christ Would Bring True Peace—
Church Feasts Affect Both Mind and Heart—Feasts Encourage Wide-
spread Devotion—New Feasts Minister to the Needs of Souls—The
Plague of Anti-clericalism—Nations Suppress All Mention of Christ's
Name—Christ's Kingship Recognized in Pious Customs—Fruits of the
Past Holy Year—Feast of Christ the King Established—Crowning Glory
upon the Mysteries of Christ's Life—Blessings We Desire—Reminding
Men of the Rights of the Church—Rulers Bound to Give Public Honor
and Obedience to Christ—None of Our Faculties Exempt from His
Empire—The Apostolic Benediction

# ACKNOWLEDGMENTS

*Mirari Vos.* Translated by Fr. Bernard A. Hausmann, S.J. From *The Papal Encyclicals: 1740-1878,* ed. by Claudia Carlen, I.H.M., McGrath Publishing Company, Wilmington, NC, 1981; The Pierian Press, reprint, c. 1990. Used with the kind permission of Sister Claudia Carlen, I.H.M.

*Quanta Cura.* Originally published by *Catholic Historical Review,* American Catholic Historical Association, Vol. 13, pp. 247-253; copyright July, 1927; from Carlen, *The Papal Encyclicals: 1740-1878.*

*Syllabus of Errors.* Translation authorized by Cardinal McCabe, Archbishop of Dublin. From *Dogmatic Canons and Decrees,* published by Devin-Adair, New York, 1912; TAN, 1977.

*Diuturnum Illud.* From *The Church Speaks to the Modern World,* ed. Etienne Gilson, Doubleday, 1954. Translation originally published by Paulist Press. Courtesy of Paulist Press, Mahwah, NJ.

*Humanum Genus.* From *The Church Speaks to the Modern World,* ed. Etienne Gilson, Doubleday, 1954. Translation originally published by Paulist Press. Courtesy of Paulist Press, Mahwah, NJ.

*Libertas Praestantissimum.* From *The Church Speaks to the Modern World,* ed. Etienne Gilson, Doubleday, 1954. Translation originally published by Paulist Press. Courtesy of Paulist Press, Mahwah, NJ.

*Rerum Novarum.* Translation courtesy of National Catholic Welfare Conference, Washington, D. C.

*Graves de Communi Re.* From *The Church Speaks to the Modern World,* ed. Etienne Gilson, Doubleday, 1954. Translation originally published by Paulist Press. Courtesy of Paulist Press, Mahwah, NJ.

*Lamentabili Sane.* Transl. Rev. Vincent A. Yzermans. From *All Things in Christ,* ed. Rev. Vincent A. Yzermans, Newman Press, 1954. Courtesy of Paulist Press, Mahwah, NJ.

*Pascendi Dominici Gregis.* From *All Things in Christ,* ed. Rev. Vincent A. Yzermans, Newman Press, 1954. Translation of *Pascendi* from *The Doctrines of the Modernists,* published by Burns, Oates & Washbourne, Ltd.

*Our Apostolic Mandate.* Translation by Mr. Yves Dupont, originally published in 1974. Used courtesy of Instauratio Press, Yarra Junction, Australia.

*Oath Against Modernism.* From *The Church Teaches: Documents of the Church in English Translation,* transl. and ed. by Jesuit Fathers of St. Mary's College, St. Mary's, KS; published by B. Herder Book Co., St. Louis, 1995; TAN, 1973.

*Quas Primas.* Originally published by *The Tablet,* Vol. 147, pp. 72-75. Copyright by *The Tablet* January 16, 1926; from Carlen, *The Papal Encyclicals: 1740-1878.*

*Mortalium Animos.* Catholic Truth Society.

*Divini Redemptoris.* Translation courtesy of National Catholic Welfare Conference, Washington, D. C. 1937 Edition.

*Humani Generis.* Translation courtesy of National Catholic Welfare Conference, Washington, D. C.


Subheadings are either from the original English edition or by the present publisher.

Encyclical Letter of Pope Gregory XVI

# ON LIBERALISM
## (*Mirari Vos*)

August 15, 1832

To All Patriarchs, Primates, Archbishops
and Bishops of the Catholic World

Venerable Brethren,
Greetings and Apostolic Benediction

1. We think that you wonder why, from the time of Our assuming the pontificate, We have not yet sent a letter to you as is customary and as Our benevolence for you demanded. We wanted very much to address you by that voice by which We have been commanded, in the person of blessed Peter, to strengthen the brethren. (*Luke* 22:32). You know what storms of evil and toil, at the beginning of Our pontificate, drove Us suddenly into the depths of the sea. If the right hand of God had not given Us strength, We would have drowned as the result of the terrible conspiracy of impious men. The mind recoils from renewing this grief by enumerating so many dangers; instead We bless the Father of consolation who, having overthrown all enemies, snatched Us from the present danger. When He had calmed this violent storm, He gave Us relief from fear. At once We decided to advise you on healing the wounds of Israel; but the mountain of concerns We needed to address in order to restore public order delayed Us.

### Our Duties Are Heavy

2. In the meantime We were again delayed because of the insolent and factious men who endeavored to raise the standard of
treason. Eventually, We had to use Our God-given authority to
restrain the great obstinacy of these men with the rod. (*1 Cor.*
4:21). Before We did, their unbridled rage seemed to grow from
continued impunity and Our considerable indulgence. For these
reasons Our duties have been heavy.

### We Hasten to Help

3. But when We had assumed Our pontificate according to the
custom and institution of Our Predecessors and when all delays
had been laid aside, We hastened to you. So We now present the
letter and testimony of Our good will toward you on this happy
day, the feast of the Assumption of the Virgin. Since she has been
Our patron and saviour amid so many great calamities, We ask her
assistance in writing to you and her counsels for the flock of
Christ.

### Powers of Darkness Dominate

4. We come to you grieving and sorrowful because We know
that you are concerned for the Faith in these difficult times. Now
is truly the time in which the powers of darkness winnow the elect
like wheat. (*Luke* 22:53). "The earth mourned and faded away . . .
And the earth is infected by the inhabitants thereof: because they
have transgressed the laws, they have changed the ordinance, they
have broken the everlasting covenant." (*Is.* 24:4-5).

### The Sacred Is Despised

5. We speak of the things which you see with your own eyes,
which We both bemoan. Depravity exults; science is impudent;
liberty, dissolute. The holiness of the sacred is despised; the
majesty of divine worship is not only disapproved by evil men, but

defiled and held up to ridicule. Hence sound doctrine is perverted and errors of all kinds spread boldly. The laws of the sacred, the rights, institutions and discipline—none are safe from the audacity of those speaking evil. Our Roman See is harassed violently and the bonds of unity are daily loosened and severed. The divine authority of the Church is opposed and her rights shorn off. She is subjected to human reason and with the greatest injustice exposed to the hatred of the people and reduced to vile servitude. The obedience due bishops is denied and their rights are trampled underfoot. Furthermore, academies and schools resound with new, monstrous opinions, which openly attack the Catholic Faith; this horrible and nefarious war is openly and even publicly waged. Thus, by institutions and by the example of teachers, the minds of the youth are corrupted and a tremendous blow is dealt to religion and the perversion of morals is spread. So the restraints of religion are thrown off, by which alone kingdoms stand. We see the destruction of public order, the fall of principalities and the overturning of all legitimate power approaching. Indeed this great mass of calamities had its inception in the heretical societies and sects in which all that is sacrilegious, infamous and blasphemous has gathered as bilge water in a ship's hold, a congealed mass of all filth.

### Shepherds Must Be Watchful

6. These and many other serious things, which at present would take too long to list, but which you know well, cause Our intense grief. It is not enough for Us to deplore these innumerable evils unless We strive to uproot them. We take refuge in your faith and call upon your concern for the salvation of the Catholic flock. Your singular prudence and diligent spirit give Us courage and console Us, afflicted as We are with so many trials. We must raise Our voice and attempt all things lest a wild boar from the woods should destroy the vineyard or wolves kill the flock. It is Our duty to lead the flock only to the food which is healthful. In these evil and dangerous times, the shepherds must never neglect their duty; they must never be so overcome by fear that they abandon the

sheep. Let them never neglect the flock and become sluggish from idleness and apathy. Therefore, united in spirit, let us promote our common cause, or more truly the cause of God; let our vigilance be one and our effort united against the common enemies.

### Preserve Unity with the Holy See

7. Indeed you will accomplish this perfectly if, as the duty of your office demands, you attend to yourselves and to doctrine and meditate on these words: "the universal Church is affected by any and every novelty"[1] and the admonition of Pope Agatho: "Nothing of the things appointed ought to be diminished; nothing changed; nothing added; but they must be preserved both as regards expression and meaning."[2] Therefore may the unity which is built upon the See of Peter as on a sure foundation stand firm. May it be for all a wall and a security, a safe port and a treasury of countless blessings.[3] To check the audacity of those who attempt to infringe upon the rights of this Holy See or to sever the union of the churches with the See of Peter, instill in your people a zealous confidence in the papacy and sincere veneration for it. As St. Cyprian wrote: "He who abandons the See of Peter on which the Church was founded, falsely believes himself to be a part of the Church."[4]

### Bishops Must Guard the Faith

8. In this you must labor and diligently take care that the Faith may be preserved amidst this great conspiracy of impious men who attempt to tear it down and destroy it. May all remember the judgment concerning sound doctrine with which the people are to be instructed. Remember also that the government and administration of the whole Church rests with the Roman Pontiff to whom, in the words of the Fathers of the Council of Florence, "the full power of nourishing, ruling and governing the universal Church was given by Christ the Lord."[5] It is the duty of individual bishops to cling to the See of Peter faithfully, to guard the Faith piously and religiously and to feed their flock. It behooves priests

to be subject to the bishops, whom "they are to look upon as the parents of their souls," as Jerome admonishes.[6] Nor may the priests ever forget that they are forbidden by ancient canons to undertake ministry and to assume the tasks of teaching and preaching "without the permission of their bishop to whom the people have been entrusted; an accounting for the souls of the people will be demanded from the bishop."[7] Finally, let them understand that all those who struggle against this established order disturb the position of the Church.

### Discipline of the Church Must Be Respected

9. Furthermore, the discipline sanctioned by the Church must never be rejected or be branded as contrary to certain principles of natural law. It must never be called crippled, or imperfect or subject to civil authority. In this discipline the administration of sacred rites, standards of morality and the reckoning of the rights of the Church and her ministers are embraced.

### Papal Authority over Canonical Decrees

10. To use the words of the Fathers of Trent, it is certain that the Church "was instructed by Jesus Christ and His Apostles and that all truth was daily taught it by the inspiration of the Holy Spirit."[8] Therefore, it is obviously absurd and injurious to propose a certain "restoration and regeneration" for her as though necessary for her safety and growth, as if she could be considered subject to defect or obscuration or other misfortune. Indeed these authors of novelties consider that a "foundation may be laid of a new human institution," and what Cyprian detested may come to pass, that what was a divine thing "may become a human church."[9] Let those who devise such plans be aware that, according to the testimony of St. Leo, "the right to grant dispensation from the canons is given" only to the Roman Pontiff. He alone, and no private person, can decide anything "about the rules of the Church Fathers." As St. Gelasius writes: "It is the papal responsibility to keep the canonical decrees in their place and to evaluate

the precepts of previous popes so that when the times demand
relaxation in order to rejuvenate the churches, they may be
adjusted after diligent consideration."[10]

## Celibacy Must Be Defended

11. Now, however, We want you to rally to combat the abom-
inable conspiracy against clerical celibacy. This conspiracy
spreads daily and is promoted by profligate philosophers, some
even from the clerical order. They have forgotten their person and
office, and have been carried away by the enticements of pleasure.
They have even dared to make repeated public demands to the
princes for the abolition of that most holy discipline. But it is dis-
gusting to dwell on these evil attempts at length. Rather, We ask
that you strive with all your might to justify and to defend the law
of clerical celibacy as prescribed by the sacred canons, against
which the arrows of the lascivious are directed from every side.

## Marriage Cannot Be Dissolved

12. Now the honorable marriage of Christians, which Paul
calls "a great sacrament . . . in Christ and the Church" (*Eph.* 5:32;
cf. *Heb.* 13:4), demands our shared concern lest anything contrary
to its sanctity and indissolubility is proposed. Our Predecessor
Pius VIII would recommend to you his own letters on the subject.
However, troublesome efforts against this Sacrament still continue to be made. The people therefore must be zealously taught
that a marriage rightly entered upon cannot be dissolved; for those
joined in Matrimony God has ordained a perpetual companion-
ship for life and a knot of necessity which cannot be loosed except
by death. Recalling that Matrimony is a Sacrament and therefore
subject to the Church, let them consider and observe the laws of
the Church concerning it. Let them take care lest for any reason
they permit that which is an obstruction to the teachings of the
canons and the decrees of the councils. They should be aware that
those marriages will have an unhappy end which are entered upon
contrary to the discipline of the Church or without God's favor or

because of concupiscence alone, with no thought of the Sacrament and of the mysteries signified by it.

## Indifferentism Is a Perverse Opinion

13. Now We consider another abundant source of the evils with which the Church is afflicted at present: *indifferentism*. This perverse opinion is spread on all sides by the fraud of the wicked who claim that it is possible to obtain the eternal salvation of the soul by the profession of any kind of religion, as long as morality is maintained. Surely, in so clear a matter, you will drive this deadly error far from the people committed to your care. With the admonition of the Apostle that there is "one Lord, one faith, one baptism" (*Eph.* 4:5), may those fear who contrive the notion that the safe harbor of salvation is open to persons of any religion whatever. They should consider the testimony of Christ Himself who said "He that is not with me, is against me" (*Luke* 11:23), and that they disperse unhappily who do not gather with Him. Therefore "without a doubt, they will perish forever, unless they hold the Catholic faith whole and inviolate."[11] Let them hear Jerome who, while the Church was torn into three parts by schism, tells us that whenever someone tried to persuade him to join his group he always exclaimed: "He who is for the See of Peter is for me."[12] A schismatic flatters himself falsely if he asserts that he, too, has been washed in the waters of regeneration. Indeed Augustine would reply to such a man: "The branch has the same form when it has been cut off from the vine; but of what profit for it is the form, if it does not live from the root?"[13]

## Liberty of Conscience Is an Error

14. This shameful font of indifferentism gives rise to that absurd and erroneous proposition which claims that *liberty of conscience* must be maintained for everyone. It spreads ruin in sacred and civil affairs, though some repeat over and over again with the greatest impudence that some advantage accrues to religion from it. "But the death of the soul is worse than freedom of

error," as Augustine was wont to say.[14] When all restraints are removed by which men are kept on the narrow path of truth, their nature, which is already inclined to evil, propels them to ruin. Then truly "the bottomless pit" (*Apoc.* 9:2) is open from which John saw smoke ascending which obscured the sun, and out of which locusts flew forth to devastate the earth. Thence comes transformation of minds, corruption of youths, contempt of sacred things and holy laws—in other words, a pestilence more deadly to the state than any other. Experience shows, even from earliest times, that cities renowned for wealth, dominion and glory perished as a result of this single evil, namely, immoderate freedom of opinion, license of free speech and desire for novelty.

### False Freedom of Publication

15. Here We must include that harmful and never sufficiently denounced freedom to publish any writings whatever and disseminate them to the people, which some dare to demand and promote with so great a clamor. We are horrified to see what monstrous doctrines and prodigious errors are disseminated far and wide in countless books, pamphlets and other writings which, though small in weight, are very great in malice. We are in tears at the abuse which proceeds from them over the face of the earth. Some are so carried away that they contentiously assert that the flock of errors arising from them is sufficiently compensated by the publication of some book which defends religion and truth. Every law condemns deliberately doing evil simply because there is some hope that good may result. Is there any sane man who would say poison ought to be distributed, sold publicly, stored and even drunk because some antidote is available and those who use it may be snatched from death again and again?

### Action to Destroy the Plague of Bad Books

16. The Church has always taken action to destroy the plague of bad books. This was true even in apostolic times, for we read that the Apostles themselves burned a large number of books.

(*Acts*. 19:19). It may be enough to consult the laws of the fifth Council of the Lateran on this matter and the Constitution which Leo X published afterwards lest "that which has been discovered advantageous for the increase of the faith and the spread of useful arts be converted to the contrary use and work harm for the salvation of the faithful."[15] This also was of great concern to the Fathers of Trent, who applied a remedy against this great evil by publishing that wholesome decree concerning the Index of books which contain false doctrine.[16] "We must fight valiantly," Clement XIII says in an encyclical letter about the banning of bad books, "as much as the matter itself demands and must exterminate the deadly poison of so many books; for never will the material for error be withdrawn, unless the criminal sources of depravity perish in flames."[17] Thus it is evident that this Holy See has always striven, throughout the ages, to condemn and to remove suspect and harmful books. The teaching of those who reject the censure of books as too heavy and onerous a burden causes immense harm to the Catholic people and to this See. They are even so depraved as to affirm that it is contrary to the principles of law, and they deny the Church the right to decree and to maintain it.

## All Authority Comes from God

17. We have learned that certain teachings are being spread among the common people in writings which attack the trust and submission due to princes; the torches of treason are being lit everywhere. Care must be taken lest the people, being deceived, are led away from the straight path. May all recall, according to the admonition of the Apostle, that "there is no power but from God: and those that are, are ordained of God. Therefore he that resisteth the power resisteth the ordinance of God. And they that resist, purchase to themselves damnation." (*Rom.* 13:1-2). Therefore both divine and human laws cry out against those who strive by treason and sedition to drive the people from confidence in their princes and force them from their government.

### Example of the Early Christians

18. And it is for this reason that the early Christians, lest they should be stained by such great infamy, deserved well of the emperors and of the safety of the state even while persecution raged. This they proved splendidly by their fidelity in performing perfectly and promptly whatever they were commanded which was not opposed to their religion, and even more by their constancy and the shedding of their blood in battle. "Christian soldiers," says St. Augustine, "served an infidel emperor. When the issue of Christ was raised, they acknowledged no one but the One who is in Heaven. They distinguished the eternal Lord from the temporal lord, but were also subject to the temporal lord for the sake of the eternal Lord."[18] St. Mauritius, the unconquered martyr and leader of the Theban legion, had this in mind when, as St. Eucharius reports, he answered the emperor in these words: "We are your soldiers, Emperor, but also servants of God, and this we confess freely . . . and now this final necessity of life has not driven us into rebellion: see, we are armed and we do not resist, because we wish rather to die than to be killed."[19] Indeed the faith of the early Christians shines more brightly if with Tertullian we consider that since the Christians were not lacking in numbers and in troops, they could have acted as foreign enemies. "We are but of yesterday," he says, "yet we have filled all your cities, islands, fortresses, municipalities, assembly places, the camps themselves, the tribes, the divisions, the palace, the senate, the forum. . . . For what war should we not have been fit and ready even if unequal in forces—we who are so glad to be cut to pieces—were it not, of course, that in our doctrine we would have been permitted more to be killed rather than to kill? . . . If so great a multitude of people should have deserted to some remote spot on earth, it would surely have covered your domination with shame because of the loss of so many citizens, and it would even have punished you by this very desertion. Without a doubt you would have been terrified at your solitude. . . . You would have sought whom you might rule; more enemies than citizens would have remained for you. Now, however, you have fewer enemies because of the multitude of Christians."[20]

## Promotion of False Liberty

19. These beautiful examples of the unchanging subjection to the princes necessarily proceeded from the most holy precepts of the Christian religion. They condemn the detestable insolence and improbity of those who, consumed with the unbridled lust for freedom, are entirely devoted to impairing and destroying all rights of dominion while bringing servitude to the people under the slogan of liberty. Here surely belong the infamous and wild plans of the Waldensians, the Beghards, the Wycliffites and other such sons of Belial, who were the sores and disgrace of the human race; they often received a richly deserved anathema from the Holy See. For no other reason do experienced deceivers devote their efforts except so that they, along with Luther, might joyfully deem themselves "free of all." To attain this end more easily and quickly, they undertake with audacity any infamous plan whatever.

## Concord between Church and State

20. Nor can We predict happier times for religion and government from the plans of those who desire vehemently to separate the Church from the State, and to break the mutual concord between temporal authority and the priesthood. It is certain that that concord which always was favorable and beneficial for the sacred and the civil order is feared by the shameless lovers of liberty.

## Certain Societies Undermine Authority

21. But for the other painful causes We are concerned about, you should recall that certain societies and assemblages seem to draw up a battle line together with the followers of every false religion and cult. They feign piety for religion; but they are driven by a passion for promoting novelties and sedition everywhere. They preach liberty of every sort; they stir up disturbances in sacred and civil affairs, and pluck authority to pieces.

*God's Help Is Necessary*

22. We write these things to you with grieving mind but trusting in Him who commands the winds and makes them still. Take up the shield of faith and fight the battles of the Lord vigorously. You especially must stand as a wall against every height which raises itself against the knowledge of God. Unsheath the sword of the spirit, which is the word of God, and may those who hunger after justice receive bread from you. Having been called so that you might be diligent cultivators in the vineyard of the Lord, do this one thing, and labor in it together, so that every root of bitterness may be removed from your field, all seeds of vice destroyed and a happy crop of virtues may take root and grow. The first to be embraced with paternal affection are those who apply themselves to the sacred sciences and to philosophical studies. For them may you be exhorter and supporter, lest trusting only in their own talents and strength, they may imprudently wander away from the path of truth onto the road of the impious. Let them remember that God is "the guide of wisdom and the director of the wise." (*Wis.* 7:15). It is impossible to know God without God, who teaches men to know Himself by His word.[21] It is the proud, or rather foolish, men who examine the mysteries of faith which surpass all understanding with the faculties of the human mind, and rely on human reason, which by the condition of man's nature is weak and infirm.

*Enlisting Support from the Princes*

23. May Our dear sons in Christ, the princes, support these Our desires for the welfare of Church and State with their resources and authority. May they understand that they received their authority not only for the government of the world, but especially for the defense of the Church. They should diligently consider that whatever work they do for the welfare of the Church accrues to their rule and peace. Indeed, let them persuade themselves that they owe more to the cause of the Faith than to their kingdom. Let them consider it something very great for them-

selves, as We say with Pope St. Leo, "if in addition to their royal diadem the crown of faith may be added." Placed as if they were parents and teachers of the people, they will bring them true peace and tranquility if they take special care that religion and piety remain safe. God, after all, calls Himself "King of kings and Lord of lords."

### The Virgin Mary Is Our Hope

24. That all of this may come to pass prosperously and happily, let Us raise Our eyes and hands to the most holy Virgin Mary, who alone crushes all heresies, and is Our greatest reliance and the whole reason for Our hope.[22] May she implore by her patronage a successful outcome for Our plans and actions. Let Us humbly ask of the Prince of the Apostles, Peter and his co-Apostle Paul, that all of you may stand as a wall, lest a foundation be laid other than that which has already been laid. Relying on this happy hope, We trust that the Author and Crown of Our faith, Jesus Christ, will console Us in all these Our tribulations. We lovingly impart the Apostolic Benediction to you, Venerable Brethren, and to the sheep committed to your care, as a sign of heavenly aid.

Given in Rome at St. Mary Major, on August 15, the feast of the Assumption of the Virgin, in the year of Our Lord 1832, the second year of Our Pontificate.

Gregory XVI, Pope

### NOTES

1. St. Celestine, Pope, epistle 21 to Bishop Galliar.
2. St. Agatho, Pope, epistle to the emperor, in Labb., ed. Mansi, vol. 2, p. 235.
3. St. Innocent, epistle 11 in Constat.
4. St. Cyprian, *De Unitate Eccles.*
5. Council of Florence, session 25, in definit. in Labb., ed. Venet., vol.

18, col. 527.

6. St. Jerome, epistle 2 to Nepot. a. 1, 24.
7. From canon ap. 38 in Labb., ed Mansi, vol. 1, p. 38.
8. Council of Trent, session 13 on the Eucharist, *pro-oemium*.
9. St. Cyprian, epistle 52, ed. Baluz.
10. St. Gelasius, Pope, in epistle to the bishop of Lucaniae.
11. Symbol S. Athanasius.
12. St. Jerome, epistle 57.
13. St. Augustine, in psalm. contra part. Donat.
14. St. Augustine, epistle 166.
15. Acts of the Lateran Council 5, session 10, where the constitution of Leo X is mentioned; the earlier constitution of Alexander VI, *Inter Multiplices*, ought to be read, in which there are many things on this point.
16. Council of Trent, sessions 18 and 25.
17. Letter of Clement XIII, *Christianae*, 25 November 1766.
18. St. Augustine, in psalt. 124, n. 7.
19. St. Euchenius in Ruinart. Acts of the Holy Martyrs concerning Saint Maurius and his companions, n. 4.
20. Tertullian, in apologet., chap. 37.
21. St. Irenaeus, bk. 14, chap. 10.
22. St. Bernard, *serm. de nat. B.M.V.*, sect. 7.

Encyclical Letter of Pope Pius IX

# ON CURRENT ERRORS
*(Quanta Cura)*

December 8, 1864

To Our Venerable Brethren, all Patriarchs, Primates, Archbishops, and Bishops having favor and Communion of the Holy See

Venerable Brethren, Health and Apostolic Benediction

1. With how great care and pastoral vigilance the Roman Pontiffs, Our Predecessors, fulfilling the duty and office committed to them by the Lord Christ Himself in the person of most Blessed Peter, Prince of the Apostles, of feeding the lambs and the sheep, have never ceased sedulously to nourish the Lord's whole flock with words of faith and with salutary doctrine, and to guard it from poisoned pastures, is thoroughly known to all, and especially to you, Venerable Brethren. And truly the same Our Predecessors, asserters of justice, being especially anxious for the salvation of souls, had nothing ever more at heart than by their most wise Letters and Constitutions to unveil and condemn all those heresies and errors which, being adverse to our Divine Faith, to the doctrine of the Catholic Church, to purity of morals and to the eternal salvation of men, have frequently excited violent tempests, and have miserably afflicted both Church and State. For which cause the same Our Predecessors have, with Apostolic fortitude, constantly resisted the nefarious enterprises of wicked men, who, like raging waves of the sea foaming out their own confusion, and promising liberty whereas they are the slaves of corruption, have

striven by their deceptive opinions and most pernicious writings to raze the foundations of the Catholic religion and of civil society, to remove from among men all virtue and justice, to deprave persons, and especially inexperienced youth, to lead it into the snares of error, and at length to tear it from the bosom of the Catholic Church.

### Grievous Errors Flourish

2. But now, as is well known to you, Venerable Brethren, already scarcely had We been elevated to this Chair of Peter (by the hidden counsel of Divine Providence, certainly by no merit of Our own), when, seeing with the greatest grief of Our soul a truly awful storm excited by so many evil opinions, and (seeing also) the most grievous calamities never sufficiently to be deplored which overspread the Christian people from so many errors, according to the duty of Our Apostolic Ministry, and following the illustrious example of Our Predecessors, We raised Our voice, and in many published Encyclical Letters and Allocutions delivered in Consistory, and other Apostolic Letters, We condemned the chief errors of this most unhappy age, and We excited your admirable episcopal vigilance, and We again and again admonished and exhorted all sons of the Catholic Church, to Us most dear, that they should altogether abhor and flee from the contagion of so dire a pestilence. And especially in Our first Encyclical Letter written to you on November 9, 1846, and in two Allocutions delivered by Us in Consistory, the one on December 9, 1854, and the other on June 9, 1862, We condemned the monstrous portents of opinion which prevail especially in this age, bringing with them the greatest loss of souls and detriment of civil society itself; which are grievously opposed also, not only to the Catholic Church and her salutary doctrine and venerable rights, but also to the eternal natural law engraven by God in all men's hearts, and to right reason; and from which almost all other errors have their origin.

### We Must Maintain Vigilance

3. But, although We have not omitted often to proscribe and reprobate the chief errors of this kind, yet the cause of the Catholic Church, and the salvation of souls entrusted to Us by God, and the welfare of human society itself, altogether demand that We again stir up your pastoral solicitude to exterminate other evil opinions, which spring forth from the said errors as from a fountain. Which false and perverse opinions are on that ground the more to be detested because they chiefly tend to this, that that salutary influence be impeded and (even) removed which the Catholic Church, according to the institution and command of her Divine Author, should freely exercise even to the end of the world—not only over private individuals, but over nations, peoples and their sovereign princes; and (tend also) to take away that mutual fellowship and concord of counsels between Church and State which has ever proved itself propitious and salutary, both for religious and civil interests.[1]

### Liberty of Conscience and Worship a Grave Error

For you well know, Venerable Brethren, that at this time men are found not a few who, applying to civil society the impious and absurd principle of *naturalism,* as they call it, dare to teach that "the best constitution of public society and (also) civil progress altogether require that human society be conducted and governed without regard being had to religion any more than if it did not exist; or, at least, without any distinction being made between the true religion and false ones." And, against the doctrine of Scripture, of the Church and of the Holy Fathers, they do not hesitate to assert that "that is the best condition of civil society in which no duty is recognized, as attached to the civil power, of restraining by enacted penalties, offenders against the Catholic religion, except so far as public peace may require." From which totally false idea of social government they do not fear to foster that erroneous opinion, most fatal in its effects on the Catholic Church and the salvation of souls, called by Our Predecessor, Gregory XVI, *an insanity,*[2] *viz.*, that "liberty of conscience and worship is each man's personal right, which ought to be legally proclaimed and asserted in every rightly constituted society; and that a right resides in the citizens to an absolute liberty, which should be restrained by no authority whether ecclesiastical or civil, whereby they may be able openly and publicly to manifest and declare any of their ideas whatever, either by word of mouth, by the press or in any other way." But, while they rashly affirm this, they do not think and consider that they are preaching *liberty of perdition;*[3] and that "if human arguments are always allowed free room for discussion, there will never be wanting men who will dare to resist truth, and to trust in the flowing speech of human wisdom; whereas we know, from the very teaching of Our Lord Jesus Christ, how carefully Christian faith and wisdom should avoid this most injurious babbling."[4]

### Unjust Civil Law Replaces Church Teaching

4.  And, since where religion has been removed from civil society, and the doctrine and authority of Divine Revelation repudiated, the genuine notion itself of justice and human right is darkened and lost, and the place of true justice and legitimate right is supplied by material force, thence it appears why it is that some, utterly neglecting and disregarding the surest principles of sound reason, dare to proclaim that "the people's will, manifested by what is called public opinion or in some other way, constitutes a supreme law, free from all divine and human control; and that in the political order accomplished facts, from the very circumstance that they are accomplished, have the force of right." But who does not see and clearly perceive that human society, when set loose from the bonds of religion and true justice, can have, in truth, no other end than the purpose of obtaining and amassing wealth, and that (society under such circumstances) follows no other law in its actions except the unchastened desire of ministering to its own pleasure and interests? For this reason, men of the kind pursue with bitter hatred the Religious Orders, although these have deserved extremely well of Christendom, civilization and litera-

ture, and cry out that the same have no legitimate reason for being permitted to exist; and thus (these evil men) applaud the calumnies of heretics. For, as Pius VI, Our Predecessor, taught most wisely, "the abolition of regulars is injurious to that state in which the Evangelical counsels are openly professed; it is injurious to a method of life praised in the Church as agreeable to Apostolic doctrine; it is injurious to the illustrious founders, themselves, whom we venerate on our altars, who did not establish these societies but by God's inspiration."[5] And (these wretches) also impiously declare that permission should be refused to citizens and to the Church, "whereby they may openly give alms for the sake of Christian charity"; and that the law should be abrogated "whereby on certain fixed days servile works are prohibited because of God's worship," and on the most deceptive pretext that the said permission and law are opposed to the principles of the best public economy. Moreover, not content with removing religion from public society, they wish to banish it also from private families. For, teaching and professing the most fatal errors of *Communism* and *Socialism*, they assert that "domestic society or the family derives the whole principle of its existence from the civil law alone; and, consequently, that on civil law alone depend all rights of parents over their children, and especially that of providing for education." By which impious opinions and machinations these most deceitful men chiefly aim at this result, *viz.*, that the salutary teaching and influence of the Catholic Church may be entirely banished from the instruction and education of youth, and that the tender and flexible minds of young men may be infected and depraved by every most pernicious error and vice. For all who have endeavored to throw into confusion things both sacred and secular, and to subvert the right order of society, and to abolish all rights, human and divine, have always (as We above hinted) devoted all their nefarious schemes, devices and efforts to deceiving and depraving incautious youth and have placed all their hope in its corruption. For which reason they never cease by every wicked method to assail the clergy, both secular and regular, from whom (as the surest monuments of history conspicuously attest) so many great advantages have abundantly flowed to Christianity, civilization and literature, and to proclaim that "the clergy, as being hostile to the true and beneficial advance of science and civilization, should be removed from the whole charge and duty of instructing and educating youth."

### Church Authority Subverted by Civil Authorities

5. Others meanwhile, reviving the wicked and so often condemned inventions of innovators, dare with signal impudence to subject to the will of the civil authority the supreme authority of the Church and of this Apostolic See given to her by Christ Himself, and to deny all those rights of the same Church and See which concern matters of the external order. For they are not ashamed of affirming "that the Church's laws do not bind in conscience unless when they are promulgated by the civil power; that acts and decrees of the Roman Pontiffs, referring to religion and the Church, need the civil power's sanction and approbation, or at least its consent; that the Apostolic Constitutions,[6] whereby secret societies are condemned (whether an oath of secrecy be or be not required in such societies), and whereby their frequenters and favorers are smitten with anathema—have no force in those regions of the world wherein associations of the kind are tolerated by the civil government; that the excommunication pronounced by the Council of Trent and by Roman Pontiffs against those who assail and usurp the Church's rights and possessions rests on a confusion between the spiritual and temporal orders, and (is directed) to the pursuit of a purely secular good; that the Church can decree nothing which binds the conscience of the faithful in regard to their use of temporal things; that the Church has no right of restraining by temporal punishments those who violate her laws; that it is conformable to the principles of sacred theology and public law to assert and claim for the civil government a right of property in those goods which are possessed by the Church, by the Religious Orders and by other pious establishments." Nor do they blush openly and publicly to profess the maxim and principle of heretics from which arise so many perverse opinions and errors. For they repeat that the "ecclesiastical power is not by

divine right distinct from, and independent of, the civil power, and that such distinction and independence cannot be preserved without the civil power's essential rights being assailed and usurped by the Church." Nor can we pass over in silence the audacity of those who, not enduring sound doctrine, contend that "without sin and without any sacrifice of the Catholic profession, assent and obedience may be refused to those judgments and decrees of the Apostolic See whose object is declared to concern the Church's general good and her rights and discipline, so only it does not touch the dogmata of faith and morals." But no one can be found not clearly and distinctly to see and understand how grievously this is opposed to the Catholic dogma of the full power given from God by Christ Our Lord Himself to the Roman Pontiff of feeding, ruling and guiding the Universal Church.

### Formal Condemnation of These Errors

6. Amid, therefore, such great perversity of depraved opinions, We, well remembering Our Apostolic Office, and very greatly solicitous for Our most holy Religion, for sound doctrine and the salvation of souls which is entrusted to Us by God, and (solicitous also) for the welfare of human society itself, have thought it right again to raise up Our Apostolic voice. Therefore, by Our Apostolic Authority, We reprobate, proscribe and condemn all the singular and evil opinions and doctrines severally mentioned in this Letter, and will and command that they be thoroughly held by all children of the Catholic Church as reprobated, proscribed and condemned.

### Many Openly Deny Christ Worldwide

7. And besides these things, you know very well, Venerable Brethren, that in these times the haters of truth and justice and most bitter enemies of our religion, deceiving the people and maliciously lying, disseminate sundry and other impious doctrines by means of pestilential books, pamphlets and newspapers dispersed over the whole world. Nor are you ignorant also that in

this our age some men are found who, moved and excited by the spirit of Satan, have reached to that degree of impiety as not to shrink from denying our Ruler and Lord Jesus Christ, and from impugning His Divinity with wicked pertinacity. Here, however, We cannot but extol you, Venerable Brethren, with great and deserved praise, for not having failed to raise with all zeal your episcopal voice against impiety so great.

### Kingdoms Rest on the Foundation of Faith

8. Therefore, in this Our Letter We again most lovingly address you, who, having been called unto a part of Our solicitude, are to Us, among Our grievous distresses, the greatest solace, joy and consolation because of the admirable religion and piety wherein you excel and because of that marvelous love, fidelity and dutifulness whereby, bound as you are to Us and to this Apostolic See in most harmonious affection, you strive strenuously and sedulously to fulfill your most weighty episcopal ministry. For from your signal pastoral zeal We expect that, taking up the sword of the spirit which is the word of God, and strengthened by the grace of Our Lord Jesus Christ, you will, with redoubled care, each day more anxiously provide that the faithful entrusted to your charge "abstain from noxious verbiage, which Jesus Christ does not cultivate because it is not His Father's plantation."[7] Never cease also to inculcate on the said faithful that all true felicity flows abundantly upon man from our august religion and its doctrine and practice; and that "happy is that people whose God is the Lord." (*Ps.* 143:15). Teach that "kingdoms rest on the foundation of the Catholic Faith;"[8] and that "nothing is so deadly, so hastening to a fall, so exposed to all danger (as that which exists) if, believing this alone to be sufficient for us, that we receive free will at our birth, we seek nothing further from the Lord; that is, if forgetting our Creator we abjure His power that we may display our freedom."[9] And again, do not fail to teach "that the royal power was given not only for the governance of the world, but most of all for the protection of the Church";[10] and that there is nothing which can be of greater advantage and glory to Princes and Kings than

if, as another most wise and courageous Predecessor of Ours, St. Felix, instructed the Emperor Zeno, they "permit the Catholic Church to practice her laws, and allow no one to oppose her liberty. For it is certain that this mode of conduct is beneficial to their interests, *viz.*, that where there is question concerning the causes of God, they study, according to His appointment, to subject the royal will to Christ's priests, not to raise it above theirs."[11]

### *Pray to the Sacred Heart for World Peace*

9. But if always, Venerable Brethren, now most of all amid such great calamities both of the Church and of civil society, amid so great a conspiracy against Catholic interests and this Apostolic See, and so great a mass of errors, it is altogether necessary to approach with confidence the throne of grace, that we may obtain mercy and find grace in timely aid. Wherefore, We have thought it well to excite the piety of all the faithful in order that, together with Us and you, they may unceasingly pray and beseech the most merciful Father of light and pity with most fervent and humble prayers, and in the fullness of faith flee always to Our Lord Jesus Christ, who redeemed us to God in His Blood, and earnestly and constantly supplicate His most sweet Heart, the Victim of most burning love toward us, that He would draw all things to Himself by the bonds of His love, and that all men, inflamed by His most holy love, may walk worthily according to His Heart, pleasing God in all things, bearing fruit in every good work. But since without doubt men's prayers are more pleasing to God if they reach Him from minds free from all stain, therefore We have determined to open to Christ's faithful, with Apostolic liberality, the Church's heavenly treasures committed to Our charge, in order that the said faithful, being more earnestly enkindled to true piety, and cleansed through the Sacrament of Penance from the defilement of their sins, may with greater confidence pour forth their prayers to God and obtain His mercy and grace.

### Proclamation of a Jubilee

10. By these Letters, therefore, in virtue of Our Apostolic authority, We concede to all and singular the faithful of the Catholic world, a Plenary Indulgence in the form of Jubilee, during the space of one month only for the whole coming year 1865, and not beyond; to be fixed by you, Venerable Brethren, and other legitimate Ordinaries of places, in the very same manner and form in which we granted it at the beginning of Our supreme Pontificate by Our Apostolic Letters in the form of a Brief dated November 20, 1846, and addressed to all your episcopal Order, beginning, "*Arcano Divinae Providentiae consilio,*" and with all the same faculties which were given by Us in those Letters. We will, however, that all things be observed which were prescribed in the aforesaid Letters, and those things be excepted which We there so declared. And We grant this, notwithstanding anything whatever to the contrary, even things which are worthy of individual mention and derogation. In order, however, that all doubt and difficulty be removed, We have commanded a copy of said Letters be sent you.

### Appeal for God's Mercy through the Virgin Mary

11. "Let us implore," Venerable Brethren, "God's mercy from our inmost heart and with our whole mind; because He has Himself added, 'I will not remove my mercy from them.' Let us ask and we shall receive; and if there be delay and slowness in our receiving because we have gravely offended, let us knock, because to him that knocketh it shall be opened, if only the door be knocked by our prayers, groans and tears, in which we must persist and persevere, and if the prayer be unanimous . . . let each man pray to God, not for himself alone, but for all his brethren, as the Lord hath taught us to pray."[12] But in order that God may the more readily assent to the prayers and desires of Ourselves, of you and of all the faithful, let us with all confidence employ as our advocate with Him the Immaculate and most holy Virgin Mary, Mother of God, who has slain all heresies throughout the world,

and who, the most loving Mother of us all, "is all sweet . . . and full of mercy . . . shows herself to all as easily entreated; shows herself to all as most merciful; pities the necessities of all with a most large affection";[13] and standing as a Queen at the right hand of her only-begotten Son, Our Lord Jesus Christ, in gilded clothing, surrounded with variety, can obtain from Him whatever she will. Let us also seek the suffrages of the Most Blessed Peter, Prince of the Apostles, and of Paul, his fellow Apostle, and of all the Saints in Heaven, who having now become God's friends, have arrived at the heavenly Kingdom, and being crowned, bear their palms, and being secure of their own immortality, are anxious for our salvation.

### The Apostolic Blessing

12. Lastly, imploring from Our great heart for you from God the abundance of all heavenly gifts, We most lovingly impart the Apostolic Benediction from Our inmost heart, a pledge of Our signal love towards you, to yourselves, Venerable Brethren, and to all the clerics and lay faithful committed to your care.

Given at Rome, from St. Peter's, the 8th day of December, in the year 1864, the tenth from the Dogmatic Definition of the Immaculate Conception of the Virgin Mary, Mother of God, in the nineteenth year of Our Pontificate.

Pius IX, Pope

### NOTES

1. Gregory XVI, Encyclical Letter "*Mirari Vos*," 15 August 1832.
2. *Ibid.*
3. St. Augustine, epistle 105 (166).
4. St. Leo, epistle 14 (133), sect. 2, edit. Ball.
5. Epistle to Cardinal De la Rochefoucault, 10 March 1791.
6. Clement XII, *In Eminenti;* Benedict XIV, *Providas Romanorum;*

Pius VII, *Ecclesiam*; Leo XII, *Quo Graviora.*

7. St. Ignatius M. to the Philadelphians, 3.
8. St. Celestine, epistle 22 to Synod. Ephes. in *Const.*, p. 1200.
9. St. Innocent. 1, epistle 29 *ad Episc. conc.* Carthag. in *Coust.*, p. 891.
10. St. Leo, epistle 156 (125).
11. Pius VII, Encyclical Letter, *Diu Satis*, 15 May 1800.
12. St. Cyprian, epist. 11.
13. St. Bernard, Serm. *de duodecim praerogativis B. M. V. ex verbis Apocalyp.*

Issued by Pope Pius IX

# Syllabus of Errors

December 8, 1864

Syllabus of the principal errors of our time, which are censured
in the consistorial Allocutions, Encyclical and other
Apostolical Letters of our Most Holy Lord, Pope Pius IX

## I. PANTHEISM, NATURALISM AND ABSOLUTE RATIONALISM

1. There exists no Supreme, all-wise, all-provident Divine
Being, distinct from the universe, and God is identical with the
nature of things, and is, therefore, subject to changes. In effect,
God is produced in man and in the world, and all things are God
and have the very substance of God, and God is one and the same
thing with the world, and, therefore, spirit with matter, necessity
with liberty, good with evil, justice with injustice. —Allocution
*Maxima Quidem*, June 9, 1862.

2. All action of God upon man and the world is to be denied.—
*Ibid.*

3. Human reason, without any reference whatsoever to God, is
the sole arbiter of truth and falsehood, and of good and evil; it is
law to itself, and suffices, by its natural force, to secure the wel-

fare of men and of nations. —*Ibid.*

4. All the truths of religion proceed from the innate strength of human reason; hence reason is the ultimate standard by which man can and ought to arrive at the knowledge of all truths of every kind.—*Ibid.*, and Encyclical *Qui Pluribus*, Nov. 9, 1846, etc.

5. Divine revelation is imperfect, and therefore subject to a continual and indefinite progress, corresponding with the advancement of human reason.—*Ibid.*

6. The faith of Christ is in opposition to human reason, and divine revelation not only is not useful, but is even hurtful to the perfection of man.—*Ibid.*

7. The prophecies and miracles set forth and recorded in the Sacred Scriptures are the fiction of poets, and the mysteries of the Christian faith the result of philosophical investigations. In the books of the Old and the New Testament there are contained mythical inventions, and Jesus Christ is Himself a myth. —*Ibid.*

## II. MODERATE RATIONALISM

8. As human reason is placed on a level with religion itself, so theological must be treated in the same manner as philosophical sciences.—Allocution *Singulari Quadam*, Dec. 9, 1854.

9. All the dogmas of the Christian religion are indiscriminately the object of natural science or philosophy; and human reason, enlightened solely in an historical way, is able, by its own natural strength and principles, to attain to the true science of even the most abstruse dogmas; provided only that such dogmas be proposed to reason itself as its object.—Letters to the Archbishop of Munich, *Gravissimas Inter*, Dec. 11, 1862, and *Tuas Libenter*, Dec. 21, 1863.

10. As the philosopher is one thing, and philosophy another, so

it is the right and duty of the philosopher to subject himself to the authority which he shall have proved to be true; but philosophy neither can nor ought to submit to any such authority.—*Ibid.*, Dec. 11, 1862.

11. The Church not only ought never to pass judgment on philosophy, but ought to tolerate the errors of philosophy, leaving it to correct itself.—*Ibid.*, Dec. 21, 1863.

12. The decrees of the Apostolic See and of the Roman congregations impede the true progress of science.—*Ibid.*

13. The method and principles by which the old scholastic doctors cultivated theology are no longer suitable to the demands of our times and to the progress of the sciences.—*Ibid.*

14. Philosophy is to be treated without taking any account of supernatural revelation.—*Ibid.*

N.B. To the rationalistic system belong in great part the errors of Anthony Günther, condemned in the letter to the Cardinal Archbishop of Cologne, *Eximiam Tuam*, June 15, 1857, and in that to the Bishop of Breslau, *Dolore Haud Mediocri*, April 30, 1860.

### III. INDIFFERENTISM AND FALSE TOLERANCE

15. Every man is free to embrace and profess that religion which, guided by the light of reason, he shall consider true.— Allocution *Maxima Quidem*, June 9, 1862; Damnatio *Multiplices Inter*, June 10, 1851.

16. Man may, in the observance of any religion whatever, find the way of eternal salvation, and arrive at eternal salvation.— Encyclical *Qui Pluribus*, Nov. 9, 1846.

17. Good hope at least is to be entertained of the eternal salva-

tion of all those who are not at all in the true Church of Christ.—
Encyclical *Quanto Conficiamur*, Aug. 10, 1863, etc.

18. Protestantism is nothing more than another form of the
same true Christian religion, in which form it is given to please
God equally as in the Catholic Church.—Encyclical *Noscitis*,
Dec. 8, 1849.

## IV. SOCIALISM, COMMUNISM, SECRET SOCIETIES, BIBLICAL SOCIETIES, CLERICO-LIBERAL SOCIETIES

Pests of this kind are frequently reprobated in the severest
terms in the Encyclical *Qui Pluribus*, Nov. 9, 1846; Allocution
*Quibus Quantisque*, April 20, 1849; Encyclical *Noscitis et Nobiscum*, Dec. 8, 1849; Allocution *Singulari Quadam*, Dec. 9, 1854;
Encyclical *Quanto Conficiamur*, Aug. 10, 1863.

## V. ERRORS CONCERNING THE CHURCH AND HER RIGHTS

19. The Church is not a true and perfect society, entirely free;
nor is she endowed with proper and perpetual rights of her own,
conferred upon her by her Divine Founder; but it appertains to the
civil power to define what are the rights of the Church, and the
limits within which she may exercise those rights.—Allocution
*Singulari Quadam*, Dec. 9, 1854, etc.

20. The ecclesiastical power ought not to exercise its authority
without the permission and assent of the civil government. —
Allocution *Meminit Unusquisque*, Sept. 30, 1861.

21. The Church has not the power of defining dogmatically that
the religion of the Catholic Church is the only true religion. —
Damnatio *Multiplices Inter*, June 10, 1851.

22. The obligation by which Catholic teachers and authors are
strictly bound is confined to those things only which are proposed

to universal belief as dogmas of faith by the infallible judgment of the Church.—Letter to the Archbishop of Munich, *Tuas Libenter*, Dec. 21, 1863.

23. Roman Pontiffs and ecumenical councils have wandered outside the limits of their powers, have usurped the rights of princes, and have even erred in defining matters of faith and morals.—Damnatio *Multiplices Inter*, June 10, 1851.

24. The Church has not the power of using force, nor has she any temporal power, direct or indirect.—Apostolic Letter *Ad Apostolicae*, Aug. 22, 1851.

25. Besides the power inherent in the episcopate, other temporal power has been attributed to it by the civil authority, granted either explicitly or tacitly, which on that account is revocable by the civil authority whenever it thinks fit.—*Ibid.*

26. The Church has no innate and legitimate right of acquiring and possessing property.—Allocution *Nunquam Fore*, Dec. 15, 1856; Encyclical *Incredibili*, Sept. 7, 1863.

27. The sacred ministers of the Church and the Roman Pontiff are to be absolutely excluded from every charge and dominion over temporal affairs.—Allocution *Maxima Quidem*, June 9, 1862.

28. It is not lawful for bishops to publish even Letters Apostolic without the permission of government.—Allocution *Nunquam Fore*, Dec. 15, 1856.

29. Favors granted by the Roman Pontiff ought to be considered null, unless they have been sought for through the civil government.—*Ibid.*

30. The immunity of the Church and of ecclesiastical persons derived its origin from civil law.—Damnatio *Multiplices Inter*, June 10, 1851.

31. The ecclesiastical forum or tribunal for the temporal causes, whether civil or criminal, of clerics, ought by all means to be abolished, even without consulting and against the protest of the Holy See.—Allocution *Nunquam Fore*, Dec. 15, 1856; Allocution *Acerbissimum*, Sept. 27, 1852.

32. The personal immunity by which clerics are exonerated from military conscription and service in the army may be abolished without violation either of natural right or equity. Its abolition is called for by civil progress, especially in a society framed on the model of a liberal government.—Letter to the Bishop of Monreale, *Singularis Nobisque*, Sept. 29, 1864.

33. It does not appertain exclusively to the power of ecclesiastical jurisdiction by right, proper and innate, to direct the teaching of theological questions.—Letter to the Archbishop of Munich, *Tuas Libenter*, Dec. 21, 1863.

34. The teaching of those who compare the Sovereign Pontiff to a prince, free and acting in the universal Church, is a doctrine which prevailed in the Middle Ages.—Apostolic Letter *Ad Apostolicae*, Aug. 22, 1851.

35. There is nothing to prevent the decree of a general council, or the act of all peoples, from transferring the supreme pontificate from the bishop and city of Rome to another bishop and another city.—*Ibid.*

36. The definition of a national council does not admit of any subsequent discussion, and the civil authority can assume this principle as the basis of its acts.—*Ibid.*

37. National churches, withdrawn from the authority of the Roman Pontiff and altogether separated, can be established.—Allocution *Multis Gravibusque*, Dec. 17, 1860.

38. The Roman Pontiffs have, by their too arbitrary conduct,

contributed to the division of the Church into Eastern and Western.—Apostolic Letter *Ad Apostolicae*, Aug. 22, 1851.

## VI. ERRORS ABOUT CIVIL SOCIETY, CONSIDERED BOTH IN ITSELF AND IN ITS RELATION TO THE CHURCH

39. The State, as being the origin and source of all rights, is endowed with a certain right not circumscribed by any limits.—Allocution *Maxima Quidem*, June 9, 1862.

40. The teaching of the Catholic Church is hostile to the well-being and interests of society.—Encyclical *Qui Pluribus*, Nov. 9, 1846; Allocution *Quibus Quantisque*, April 20, 1849.

41. The civil government, even when in the hands of an infidel sovereign, has a right to an indirect negative power over religious affairs. It therefore possesses not only the right called that of *exsequatur*, but also that of appeal, called *appellatio ab abusu*.—Apostolic Letter *Ad Apostolicae*, Aug. 22, 1851

42. In the case of conflicting laws enacted by the two powers, the civil law prevails.—*Ibid.*

43. The secular power has authority to rescind, declare and render null, solemn conventions, commonly called concordats, entered into with the Apostolic See, regarding the use of rights appertaining to ecclesiastical immunity, without the consent of the Apostolic See, and even in spite of its protest.—Allocution *Multis Gravibusque*, Dec. 17, 1860; Allocution *In Consistoriali*, Nov. 1, 1850.

44. The civil authority may interfere in matters relating to religion, morality and spiritual government: hence, it can pass judgment on the instructions issued for the guidance of consciences, conformably with their mission, by the pastors of the Church. Further, it has the right to make enactments regarding the adminis-

tration of the divine Sacraments and the dispositions necessary for receiving them.—Allocutions *In Consistoriali*, Nov. 1, 1850, and *Maxima Quidem*, June 9, 1862.

45. The entire government of public schools in which the youth of a Christian state is educated, except (to a certain extent) in the case of episcopal seminaries, may and ought to appertain to the civil power, and belong to it so far that no other authority whatsoever shall be recognized as having any right to interfere in the discipline of the schools, the arrangement of the studies, the conferring of degrees, in the choice or approval of the teachers.— Allocutions *Quibus Luctuosissimis*, Sept. 5, 1851, and *In Consistoriali*, Nov. 1, 1850.

46. Moreover, even in ecclesiastical seminaries, the method of studies to be adopted is subject to the civil authority.—Allocution *Nunquam Fore*, Dec. 15, 1856.

47. The best theory of civil society requires that popular schools open to children of every class of the people, and, generally, all public institutes intended for instruction in letters and philosophical sciences and for carrying on the education of youth, should be freed from all ecclesiastical authority, control and interference, and should be fully subjected to the civil and political power at the pleasure of the rulers, and according to the standard of the prevalent opinions of the age.—Epistle to the Archbishop of Freiburg, *Cum Non Sine*, July 14, 1864.

48. Catholics may approve of the system of educating youth unconnected with Catholic faith and the power of the Church, and which regards the knowledge of merely natural things, and only, or at least primarily, the ends of earthly social life.—*Ibid.*

49. The civil power may prevent the prelates of the Church and the faithful from communicating freely and mutually with the Roman Pontiff.—Allocution *Maxima Quidem*, June 9, 1862.

50. Lay authority possesses of itself the right of presenting bishops, and may require of them to undertake the administration of the diocese before they receive canonical institution and the Letters Apostolic from the Holy See.—Allocution *Nunquam Fore*, Dec. 15, 1856.

51. And, further, the lay government has the right of deposing bishops from their pastoral functions, and is not bound to obey the Roman Pontiff in those things which relate to the institution of bishoprics and the appointment of bishops.—Allocution *Acerbissimum*, Sept. 27, 1852; Damnatio *Multiplices Inter*, June 10, 1851.

52. Government can, by its own right, alter the age prescribed by the Church for the religious profession of women and men; and may require of all religious orders to admit no person to take solemn vows without its permission.—Allocution *Nunquam Fore*, Dec. 15, 1856.

53. The laws enacted for the protection of religious orders and regarding their rights and duties ought to be abolished; nay, more, civil government may lend its assistance to all who desire to renounce the obligation which they have undertaken of a religious life, and to break their vows. Government may also suppress the said religious orders, as likewise collegiate churches and simple benefices, even those of advowson and subject their property and revenues to the administration and pleasure of the civil power.—Allocutions *Acerbissimum*, Sept. 27, 1852; *Probe Memineritis*, Jan. 22, 1855; *Cum Saepe*, July 26, 1855.

54. Kings and princes are not only exempt from the jurisdiction of the Church, but are superior to the Church in deciding questions of jurisdiction.—Damnatio *Multiplices Inter*, June 10, 1851.

55. The Church ought to be separated from the State, and the State from the Church.—Allocution *Acerbissimum*, Sept. 27, 1852.

## VII. ERRORS CONCERNING NATURAL AND CHRISTIAN ETHICS

56. Moral laws do not stand in need of the divine sanction, and it is not at all necessary that human laws should be made conformable to the laws of nature and receive their power of binding from God.—Allocution *Maxima Quidem*, June 9, 1862.

57. The science of philosophical things and morals and also civil laws may and ought to keep aloof from divine and ecclesiastical authority.—*Ibid.*

58. No other forces are to be recognized except those which reside in matter, and all the rectitude and excellence of morality ought to be placed in the accumulation and increase of riches by every possible means, and the gratification of pleasure.—*Ibid.*; Encyclical *Quanto Conficiamur*, Aug. 10, 1863.

59. Right consists in the material fact. All human duties are an empty word, and all human facts have the force of right.—Allocution *Maxima Quidem*, June 9, 1862.

60. Authority is nothing else but numbers and the sum total of material forces.—*Ibid.*

61. The injustice of an act when successful inflicts no injury on the sanctity of right.—Allocution *Iamdudum Cernimus*, March 18, 1861.

62. The principle of non-intervention, as it is called, ought to be proclaimed and observed.—Allocution *Novos et Ante*, Sept. 28, 1860.

63. It is lawful to refuse obedience to legitimate princes, and even to rebel against them.—Encyclical *Qui Pluribus*, Nov. 9, 1864; Allocution *Quibusque Vestrum*, Oct. 4, 1847; *Noscitis et Nobiscum*, Dec. 8, 1849; Letter Apostolic *Cum Catholica*.

64. The violation of any solemn oath, as well as any wicked and flagitious action repugnant to the eternal law, is not only not blamable but is altogether lawful and worthy of the highest praise when done through love of country.—Allocution *Quibus Quantisque*, April 20, 1849.

## VIII. ERRORS CONCERNING CHRISTIAN MARRIAGE

65. The doctrine that Christ has raised marriage to the dignity of a Sacrament cannot be at all tolerated.—Apostolic Letter *Ad Apostolicae*, Aug. 22, 1851.

66. The Sacrament of Marriage is only a something accessory to the contract and separate from it, and the Sacrament itself consists in the nuptial benediction alone.—*Ibid.*

67. By the law of nature, the marriage tie is not indissoluble, and in many cases divorce properly so called may be decreed by the civil authority.—*Ibid.*; Allocution *Acerbissimum*, Sept. 27, 1852.

68. The Church has not the power of establishing diriment impediments of marriage, but such a power belongs to the civil authority by which existing impediments are to be removed.— Damnatio *Multiplices Inter*, June 10, 1851.

69. In the dark ages the Church began to establish diriment impediments, not by her own right, but by using a power borrowed from the State.—Apostolic Letter *Ad Apostolicae*, Aug. 22, 1851.

70. The canons of the Council of Trent, which anathematize those who dare to deny to the Church the right of establishing diriment impediments, either are not dogmatic or must be understood as referring to such borrowed power.—*Ibid.*

71. The form of solemnizing marriage prescribed by the Coun-

cil of Trent, under pain of nullity, does not bind in cases where the civil law lays down another form, and declares that when this new form is used the marriage shall be valid.—*Ibid.*

72. Boniface VIII was the first who declared that the vow of chastity taken at ordination renders marriage void.—*Ibid.*

73. In force of a merely civil contract there may exist between Christians a real marriage, and it is false to say either that the marriage contract between Christians is always a Sacrament, or that there is no contract if the Sacrament be excluded.—*Ibid.*; Letter to the King of Sardinia, Sept. 9, 1852; Allocutions *Acerbissimum*, Sept. 27, 1852, *Multis Gravibusque*, Dec. 17, 1860.

74. Matrimonial causes and espousals belong by their nature to civil tribunals.—Encyclical *Qui Pluribus*, Nov. 9, 1846; Damnatio *Multiplices Inter*, June 10, 1851, *Ad Apostolicae*, Aug. 22, 1851; Allocution *Acerbissimum*, Sept. 27, 1852.

N.B.—To the preceding questions may be referred two other errors regarding the celibacy of priests and the preference due to the state of marriage over that of virginity. These have been stigmatized: the first in the Encyclical *Qui Pluribus*, Nov. 9, 1846; the second, in the Letter Apostolic *Multiplices Inter*, June 10, 1851.

## IX. ERRORS REGARDING THE CIVIL POWER OF THE SOVEREIGN PONTIFF

75. The children of the Christian and Catholic Church are divided among themselves about the compatibility of the temporal with the spiritual power.—*Ad Apostolicae*, Aug. 22, 1851.

76. The abolition of the temporal power of which the Apostolic See is possessed would contribute in the greatest degree to the liberty and prosperity of the Church.—Allocutions *Quibus quantisque*, April 20, 1849, *Si Semper Antea*, May 20, 1850.

N.B.—Besides these errors, explicitly censured, very many others are implicitly condemned by the doctrine propounded and established, which all Catholics are bound most firmly to hold touching the temporal sovereignty of the Roman Pontiff. This doctrine is clearly stated in the Allocutions *Quibus Quantisque*, April 20, 1849, and *Si Semper Antea*, May 20, 1850; Letter Apostolic *Cum Catholica Ecclesia*, March 26, 1860; Allocutions, *Noves et Antea*, Sept. 28, 1860; *Iamdudum Cernimus*, March 18, 1861; *Maxima Quidem*, June 9, 1862.

## X. ERRORS HAVING REFERENCE TO MODERN LIBERALISM

77. In the present day it is no longer expedient that the Catholic religion should be held as the only religion of the State, to the exclusion of all other forms of worship.—Allocution *Nemo Vestrum*, July 26, 1855.

78. Hence it has been wisely decided by law, in some Catholic countries, that persons coming to reside therein shall enjoy the public exercise of their own peculiar worship.—Allocution *Acerbissimum*, Sept. 27, 1852.

79. Moreover, it is false that the civil liberty of every form of worship, and the full power, given to all, of overtly and publicly manifesting any opinions whatsoever and thoughts, conduce more easily to corrupt the morals and minds of the people, and to propagate the pest of indifferentism.—Allocution *Nunquam Fore*, Dec. 15, 1856.

80. The Roman Pontiff can, and ought to, reconcile himself and come to terms with progress, Liberalism and modern civilization.—Allocution *Iamdudum Cernimus*, March 18, 1861.

Pius IX, Pope

Encyclical Letter of Pope Leo XIII

# ON GOVERNMENT AUTHORITY
## (Diuturnum Illud)

June 29, 1881

To Our Venerable Brethren, All Patriarchs, Primates,
Archbishops and Bishops of the Catholic World

Venerable Brethren,

1. The long-continued and most bitter war waged against the
divine authority of the Church has reached the culmination to
which it was tending, the common danger, namely, of human society, and especially of the civil power on which the public safety
chiefly reposes. In our own times most particularly this result is
apparent. For popular passions now reject, with more boldness
than formerly, every restraint of authority. So great is the license
on all sides, so frequent are seditions and tumults, that not only is
obedience often refused to those who rule states, but a sufficiently
safe guarantee of security does not seem to have been left to them.

### Rulers of States Attacked

2. For a long time, indeed, pains have been taken to render
rulers the object of contempt and hatred to the multitude. The
flames of envy thus excited have at last burst forth, and attempts
have been several times made, at very short intervals, on the life
of sovereign princes, either by secret plots or by open attacks. The
whole of Europe was lately filled with horror at the horrible mur-

der of a most powerful Emperor.[1] While the minds of men are still filled with astonishment at the magnitude of the crime, abandoned men do not fear publicly to utter threats and intimidations against other European princes.

## Mutual Rights and Duties

3. These perils to commonwealths, which are before Our eyes, fill Us with grave anxiety when We behold the security of rulers and the tranquillity of Empires, together with the safety of nations, put in peril almost from hour to hour. Nevertheless, the divine power of the Christian religion has given birth to excellent principles of stability and order for the State, while at the same time it has penetrated into the customs and institutions of States. And of this power not the least nor last fruit is a just and wise proportion of mutual rights and duties in both princes and peoples. For in the precepts and examples of Christ our Lord there is a wonderful force for restraining in their duty as much those who obey as those who rule; and for keeping between them that agreement which is most according to nature, and that concord of wills, so to speak, from which arises a course of administration tranquil and free from all disturbance. Wherefore, being, by the favor of God, entrusted with the government of the Catholic Church, and made guardian and interpreter of the doctrines of Christ, We judge that it belongs to Our jurisdiction, Venerable Brethren, publicly to set forth what Catholic truth demands of everyone in this sphere of duty; thus making clear also by what way and by what means measures may be taken for the public safety in so critical a state of affairs.

## The Need for Authority

4. Although man, when excited by a certain arrogance and contumacy, has often striven to cast aside the reins of authority, he has never yet been able to arrive at the state of obeying no one. In every association and community of men, necessity itself compels that some should hold pre-eminence; lest society, deprived of a

prince or head, by which it is ruled, should come to dissolution and be prevented from attaining the end for which it was created and instituted. But, if it was not possible that political power should be removed from the midst of states, it is certain that men have used every art to take away its influence and to lessen its majesty, as was especially the case in the sixteenth century, when a fatal novelty of opinions infatuated many. Since that epoch, not only has the multitude striven after a liberty greater than is just, but it has seen fit to fashion the origin and construction of the civil society of men in accordance with its own will.

### *Authority from God*

5.  Indeed, very many men of more recent times, walking in the footsteps of those who in a former age assumed to themselves the name of philosophers,[2] say that all power comes from the people; so that those who exercise it in the State do so not as their own, but as delegated to them by the people, and that, by this rule, it can be revoked by the will of the very people by whom it was delegated. But from these, Catholics dissent, who affirm that the right to rule is from God, as from a natural and necessary principle.

### *Ruler Designated by the People*

6.  It is of importance, however, to remark in this place that those who may be placed over the State may in certain cases be chosen by the will and decision of the multitude, without opposition to or impugning of the Catholic doctrine. And by this choice, in truth, the ruler is designated, but the rights of ruling are not thereby conferred. Nor is the authority delegated to him, but the person by whom it is to be exercised is determined upon.

### *Choice of Government by People*

7.  There is no question here respecting forms of government, for there is no reason why the Church should not approve of the chief power being held by one man or by more, provided only it

be just, and that it tend to the common advantage. Wherefore, so long as justice be respected, the people are not hindered from choosing for themselves that form of government which suits best either their own disposition, or the institutions and customs of their ancestors.

## God the Origin of Political Power

8. But as regards political power, the Church rightly teaches that it comes from God, for it finds this clearly testified in the Sacred Scriptures and in the monuments of antiquity; besides, no other doctrine can be conceived which is more agreeable to reason, or more in accord with the safety of both princes and peoples.

## Scripture Reveals the Source of Authority

9. In truth, that the source of human power is in God the books of the Old Testament in very many places clearly establish. "By me kings reign . . . By me princes rule, and the mighty decree justice." (*Prov.* 8:15-16). And in another place: "Give ear, you that rule the people . . . For power is given you by the Lord, and strength by the most High." (*Wis.* 6:3-4). The same thing is contained in the Book of Ecclesiasticus: "Over every nation he set a ruler." (17:14). These things however, which they had learned of God, men were little by little untaught through heathen superstition, which even as it has corrupted the true aspect and often the very concept of things, so also it has corrupted the natural form and beauty of the chief power. Afterward, when the Christian Gospel shed its light, vanity yielded to truth, and that noble and divine principle whence all authority flows began to shine forth. To the Roman Governor, ostentatiously pretending that he had the power of releasing and of condemning, Our Lord Jesus Christ answered: "Thou shouldst not have any power against me, unless it were given thee from above." (John 19:11). And St. Augustine, in explaining this passage, says, "Let us learn what He said, which also He taught by His Apostle, that there is no power but from God."[3] The faithful voice of the Apostles, as an echo, repeats the

doctrine and precepts of Jesus Christ. The teaching of Paul to the Romans, when subject to the authority of heathen princes, is lofty and full of gravity: "There is no power but from God," from which, as from its cause, he draws this conclusion: "He [the prince] is God's minister to thee." (*Rom.* 13:1, 4).

## *The Teaching of the Fathers of the Church*

10. The Fathers of the Church have taken great care to proclaim and propagate this very doctrine in which they had been instructed. "We do not attribute," says St. Augustine, "the power of giving government and empires to any but the true God."[4] On the same passage St. John Chrysostom says: "That there are kingdoms, and that some rule, while others are subject, and that none of these things are brought about by accident or rashly . . . is, I say, a work of divine wisdom."[5] The same truth is testified by St. Gregory the Great, saying: "We confess that power is given from above to emperors and kings."[6] Verily the holy Doctors have undertaken to illustrate also the same precepts by the natural light of reason in such a way that they must appear to be altogether right and true, even to those who follow reason for their sole guide.

## *Society Needs Authority*

11. And indeed nature, or rather God who is the Author of nature, wills that man should live in a civil society; and this is clearly shown both by the faculty of language, the greatest medium of intercourse, and by numerous innate desires of the mind, and the many necessary things and things of great importance which men isolated cannot procure, but which they can procure when joined and associated with others. But now, a society can neither exist nor be conceived in which there is no one to govern the wills of individuals, in such a way as to make, as it were, one will out of many, and to impel them rightly and orderly to the common good; therefore, God has willed that in a civil society there should be some to rule the multitude. And this also is a pow-

erful argument, that those by whose authority the State is administered must be able so to compel the citizens to obedience that it is clearly a sin in the latter not to obey. But no man has in himself or of himself the power of constraining the free will of others by fetters of authority of this kind. This power resides solely in God, the Creator and Legislator of all things; and it is necessary that those who exercise it should do it as having received it from God. "There is one lawgiver, and judge, that is able to destroy and to deliver." (*James* 4:12). And this is clearly seen in every kind of power. That that which resides in priests comes from God is so acknowledged that among all nations they are recognized as, and called, the ministers of God. In like manner the authority of fathers of families preserves a certain impressed image and form of the authority which is in God, "of whom all paternity in heaven and earth is named." (*Eph.* 3:15). But in this way different kinds of authority have between them wonderful resemblances, since whatever there is of government and authority, its origin is derived from one and the same Creator and Lord of the world, who is God.

### *Free Consent Not the Source of Authority*

12.  Those who believe civil society to have risen from the free consent of men, looking for the origin of its authority from the same source, say that each individual has given up something of his right,[7] and that voluntarily every person has put himself into the power of the one man in whose person the whole of those rights has been centered. But it is a great error not to see, what is manifest, that men, as they are not a nomad race, have been created, without their own free will, for a natural community of life. It is plain, moreover, that the agreement which they allege is openly a falsehood and a fiction, and that it has no authority to confer on political power such great force, dignity and firmness as the safety of the State and the common good of the citizens require. Then only will the government have all those ornaments and guarantees when it is understood to emanate from God as its august and most sacred source.

### The Motive of Obedience

13. And it is impossible that any should be found not only more true but even more advantageous than this opinion. For the authority of the rulers of a State, if it be a certain communication of divine power, will by that very reason immediately acquire a dignity greater than human—not, indeed, that impious and most absurd dignity sometimes desired by heathen emperors when affecting divine honors, but a true and solid one received by a certain divine gift and benefaction. Whence it will behoove citizens to submit themselves and to be obedient to rulers, as to God, not so much through fear of punishment, as through respect for their majesty; nor for the sake of pleasing, but through conscience, as doing their duty. And by this means authority will remain far more firmly seated in its place. For the citizens, perceiving the force of this duty, would necessarily avoid dishonesty and contumacy, because they must be persuaded that they who resist State authority resist the divine Will; that they who refuse honor to rulers refuse it to God Himself.

### Teaching of the Apostles

14. This doctrine the Apostle Paul particularly inculcated on the Romans, to whom he wrote with so great authority and weight on the reverence to be entertained toward the higher powers, that it seems nothing could be prescribed more weightily: "Let every soul be subject to higher powers: for there is no power but from God: and those that are, are ordained of God. Therefore he that resisteth the power, resisteth the ordinance of God. And they that resist, purchase to themselves damnation . . . Wherefore be subject of necessity, not only for wrath, but also for conscience' sake." (*Rom.* 13:1-2, 5). And in agreement with this is the celebrated declaration of Peter, the Prince of the Apostles, on the same subject. "Be ye subject therefore to every human creature for God's sake: whether it be to the king as excelling; or to governors as sent by him for the punishment of evildoers, and for the praise of the good: for so is the will of God." (*1 Peter* 2:13-15).

*Human Authority Must Conform with God's Law*

15. The one only reason which men have for not obeying is when anything is demanded of them which is openly repugnant to the natural or the divine law, for it is equally unlawful to command and to do anything in which the law of nature or the will of God is violated. If, therefore, it should happen to any one to be compelled to prefer one or the other, *viz.*, to disregard either the commands of God or those of rulers, he must obey Jesus Christ, who commands us to "Render therefore to Caesar the things that are Caesar's; and to God, the things that are God's" (*Matt.* 22:21), and must reply courageously after the example of the Apostles, "We ought to obey God, rather than men." (*Acts* 5:29). And yet there is no reason why those who so behave themselves should be accused of refusing obedience; for if the will of rulers is opposed to the will and the laws of God, they themselves exceed the bounds of their own power and pervert justice; nor can their authority then be valid, which, when there is no justice, is null.

*Political Power for the Common Good*

16. But in order that justice may be retained in government it is of the highest importance that those who rule States should understand that political power was not created for the advantage of any private individual; and that the administration of the State must be carried on to the profit of those who have been committed to their care, not to the profit of those to whom it has been committed. Let princes take example from the Most High God, by whom authority is given to them; and, placing before themselves His model in governing the State, let them rule over the people with equity and faithfulness, and let them add to that severity, which is necessary, a paternal charity. On this account they are warned in the oracles of the Sacred Scriptures that they will have themselves some day to render an account to the King of kings and Lord of lords; if they shall fail in their duty, that it will not be possible for them in any way to escape the severity of God: The most High "will examine your works, and search out your

thoughts: because being ministers of his kingdom, you have not judged rightly . . . Horribly and speedily will he appear to you: for a most severe judgment shall be for them that bear rule. . . . For God will not except any man's person, neither will he stand in awe of any man's greatness: for he made the little and the great, and he hath equally care of all. But a greater punishment is ready for the more mighty." (*Wis.* 6:4-6, 8-9).

## *Security of the State and Dignity of the Citizen*

17. And if these precepts protect the State, all cause or desire for seditions is removed; the honor and security of rulers, the quiet and well-being of States will be secure. The dignity also of the citizen is best provided for; for to them it has been permitted to retain even in obedience that greatness which conduces to the excellence of man. For they understand that, in the judgment of God, there is neither slave nor free man; that there is one Lord of all, rich "unto all that call upon Him" (*Rom.* 10:12), but that they on this account submit to and obey their rulers, because these in a certain sort bring before them the image of God, "whom to serve is to reign."

## *Christian Principles of Civic Obedience*

18. But the Church has always so acted that the Christian form of civil government may not only dwell in the minds of men, but that it may be exhibited also in the life and habits of nations. As long as there were at the helm of the States pagan emperors, who were prevented by superstition from rising to that form of imperial government which We have sketched, she studied how to instill into the minds of subjects, immediately on their embracing the Christian institutions, the teaching that they must be desirous of bringing their lives into conformity with them. Therefore, the pastors of souls, after the example of the Apostle Paul, were accustomed to teach the people with the utmost care and diligence "to be subject to princes and powers, to obey at a word" (*Titus* 3:1), and to pray to God for all men and particularly "for kings,

and for all that are in high station . . . For this is good and acceptable in the sight of God our Saviour." (*1 Tim.* 2:2-3). And the
Christians of old left the most striking proofs of this; for when
they were harassed in a very unjust and cruel way by pagan
emperors, they nevertheless at no time omitted to conduct themselves obediently and submissively; so that, in fact, they seemed
to vie with each other, those in cruelty, and these in obedience.

### Christian Loyalty in Pagan Roman Empire

19. This great modesty, this fixed determination to obey, was
so well known that it could not be obscured by the calumny and
malice of enemies. On this account, those who were going to
plead in public before the Emperors for any persons bearing the
Christian name proved by this argument especially that it was
unjust to enact laws against the Christians because they were in
the sight of all men exemplary in their bearing according to the
laws. Athenagoras thus confidently addresses Marcus Aurelius
Antoninus and Lucius Aurelius Commodus, his son: "You allow
us, who commit no evil, yea, who demean ourselves the most
piously and justly of all toward God and likewise toward your
government, to be driven about, plundered and exiled."[8] In like
manner, Tertullian openly praises the Christians because they
were the best and surest friends of all to the Empire: "The Christian is the enemy of no one, much less of the Emperor, whom he
knows to be appointed by God, and whom he must, therefore, of
necessity, love, reverence and honor and wish to be preserved
together with the whole Roman Empire."[9] Nor did he hesitate to
affirm that, within the limits of the Empire, the number of enemies was wont to diminish just in proportion as the number of
Christians increased.[10] There is also a remarkable testimony to the
same point in the Epistle to Diognetus, which confirms the statement that the Christians at that period were not only in the habit
of obeying the laws, but in every office they of their own accord
did more, and more perfectly, than they were required to do by the
laws. "Christians observe these things which have obtained the
sanction of the law, and in the character of their lives they even go

beyond the law."[11]

### The Mark of the Christian Soldier

20. The case, indeed, was different when they were ordered by the edicts of Emperors and the threats of Praetors to abandon the Christian Faith or in any way fail in their duty. At these times, undoubtedly, they preferred to displease men rather than God. Yet, even under these circumstances, they were so far from doing anything seditious or despising the Imperial Majesty, that they took it on themselves only to profess themselves Christians, and declare that they would not in any way alter their faith. But they had no thought of resistance; calmly and joyfully they went to the torture of the rack, in so much that the magnitude of the torments gave place to their magnitude of mind. During the same period the force of Christian principles was observed in like manner in the army. For it was a mark of a Christian soldier to combine the greatest fortitude with the greatest attention to military discipline, and to add to nobility of mind immovable fidelity toward his prince. But, if anything dishonorable was required of him, as, for instance, to break the laws of God, or to turn his sword against innocent disciples of Christ, then, indeed, he refused to execute the orders, yet in such wise that he would rather retire from the army and die for his religion than oppose the public authority by means of sedition and tumult.

### The Majesty of Authority

21. But afterward, when Christian rulers were at the head of States, the Church insisted much more on testifying and preaching how much sanctity was inherent in the authority of rulers. Hence, when people thought of princedom, the image of a certain sacred majesty would present itself to their minds, by which they would be impelled to greater reverence and love of rulers. And on this account she wisely provides that kings should commence their reign with the celebration of solemn rites; which, in the Old Testament, was appointed by divine authority. (*1 Kings* 9:16;

10:1; 16:13).

## The Holy Roman Empire

22. But from the time when the civil society of men, raised from the ruins of the Roman Empire, gave hope of its future Christian greatness, the Roman Pontiffs, by the institution of the Holy Empire, consecrated the political power in a wonderful manner. Greatly, indeed, was the authority of rulers ennobled; and it is not to be doubted that what was then instituted would always have been a very great gain, both to ecclesiastical and civil society, if princes and peoples had ever looked to the same object as the Church. And, indeed, tranquility and a sufficient prosperity lasted so long as there was a friendly agreement between these two powers. If the people were turbulent, the Church was at once the mediator for peace. Recalling all to their duty, she subdued the more lawless passions partly by kindness and partly by authority. So, if, in ruling, princes erred in their government, she went to them and, putting before them the rights, needs and lawful wants of their people, urged them to equity, mercy and kindness. Whence it was often brought about that the dangers of civil wars and popular tumults were stayed.

## False Foundation of Authority

23. On the other hand, the doctrines on political power invented by late writers have already produced great ills among men, and it is to be feared that they will cause the very greatest disasters to posterity. For an unwillingness to attribute the right of ruling to God, as its Author, is no less than a willingness to blot out the greatest splendor of political power and to destroy its force. And they who say that this power depends on the will of the people err in opinion first of all; then they place authority on too weak and unstable a foundation. For the popular passions, incited and goaded on by these opinions, will break out more insolently; and, with great harm to the commonwealth, descend headlong by an easy and smooth road to revolts and to open sedition. In truth,

sudden uprisings and the boldest rebellions immediately followed in Germany the so-called Reformation, the authors and leaders of which, by their new doctrines, attacked at the very foundation religious and civil authority; and this with so fearful an outburst of civil war and with such slaughter, that there was scarcely any place free from tumult and bloodshed. From this heresy there arose in the last century a false philosophy—a new right as it is called, and a popular authority, together with an unbridled license which many regard as the only true liberty. Hence we have reached the limit of horrors, to wit, Communism, Socialism, Nihilism, hideous deformities of the civil society of men and almost its ruin. And yet too many attempt to enlarge the scope of these evils and, under the pretext of helping the multitude, already have fanned no small flames of misery. The things We thus mention are neither unknown nor very remote from Us.

### Fear Is a Weak Foundation for Loyalty

24. This, indeed, is all the graver because rulers, in the midst of such threatening dangers, have no remedies sufficient to restore discipline and tranquility. They supply themselves with the power of laws, and think to coerce, by the severity of their punishment, those who disturb their governments. They are right to a certain extent, but yet should seriously consider that no power of punishment can be so great that it alone can preserve the State. For fear, as St. Thomas admirably teaches, "is a weak foundation; for those who are subdued by fear would, should an occasion arise in which they might hope for immunity, rise more eagerly against their rulers, in proportion to the previous extent of their restraint through fear." And besides, "from too great fear many fall into despair; and despair drives men to attempt boldly to gain what they desire."[12] That these things are so we see from experience. It is therefore necessary to seek a higher and more reliable reason for obedience, and to say explicitly that legal severity cannot be efficacious unless men are led on by duty, and moved by the salutary fear of God. But this is what religion can best ask of them, religion which by its power enters into the souls and bends the

very wills of men, causing them not only to render obedience to their rulers, but also to show their affection and good will, which is in every society of men the best guardian of safety.

### The Popes Are the Defenders of Civil Order

25. For this reason the Roman Pontiffs are to be regarded as having greatly served the public good, for they have ever endeavored to break the turbulent and restless spirit of innovators, and have often warned men of the danger they are to civil society. In this respect we may worthily recall to mind the declaration of Clement VII to Ferdinand, King of Bohemia and Hungary: "In the cause of faith your own dignity and advantage and that of other rulers is included, since the Faith cannot be shaken without your authority being brought down; which has been most clearly shown in several instances." In the same way the supreme forethought and courage of Our Predecessors have been shown, especially of Clement XI, Benedict XIV and Leo XII,[13] who, when in their day the evil of vicious doctrine was more widely spreading and the boldness of the sects was becoming greater, endeavored by their authority to close the door against them. And We Ourselves have several times declared what great dangers are impending, and have pointed out the best ways of warding them off. To princes and other rulers of the State We have offered the protection of religion, and We have exhorted the people to make abundant use of the great benefits which the Church supplies. Our present object is to make rulers understand that this protection, which is stronger than any, is again offered to them; and We earnestly exhort them in Our Lord to defend religion, and to consult the interest of their States by giving that liberty to the Church which cannot be taken away without injury and ruin to the commonwealth.

### The Church Preserves the Balance

26. The Church of Christ indeed cannot be an object of suspicion to rulers, nor of hatred to the people; for it urges rulers to follow justice, and in nothing to decline from their duty; while at

the same time it strengthens and in many ways supports their authority. All things that are of a civil nature the Church acknowledges and declares to be under the power and authority of the ruler: and in things whereof for different reasons the decision belongs both to the sacred and to the civil power, the Church wishes that there should be harmony between the two so that injurious contests may be avoided. As to what regards the people, the Church has been established for the salvation of all men and has ever loved them as a mother. For it is the Church which by the exercise of her charity has given gentleness to the minds of men, kindness to their manners and justice to their laws. Never opposed to honest liberty, the Church has always detested a tyrant's rule. This custom which the Church has ever had of deserving well of mankind is notably expressed by St. Augustine when he says: "The Church teaches kings to study the welfare of their people, and people to submit to their kings, showing what is due to all: and that to all is due charity and to no one injustice."[14]

## Obedience to Authority Is Obedience to God

27. For these reasons, Venerable Brethren, your work will be most useful and salutary if you employ with Us every industry and effort which God has given you in order to avert the dangers and evils of human society. Strive with all possible care to make men understand and show forth in their lives what the Catholic Church teaches on government and the duty of obedience. Let the people be frequently urged by your authority and teaching to fly from the forbidden sects, to abhor all conspiracy, to have nothing to do with sedition, and let them understand that they who for God's sake obey their rulers render a reasonable service and a generous obedience. And as it is God "who gives salvation to kings" (*Ps.* 143:10) and grants to the people to "sit in the beauty of peace, and in the tabernacles of confidence, and in wealthy rest" (*Isaias* 32:18), it is to Him that we must pray, beseeching Him to incline all minds to uprightness and truth, to calm angry passions, to restore the long-wished-for tranquility to the world.

28. That we may pray with greater hope, let us take as our intercessors and protectors of our welfare the Virgin Mary, the Great Mother of God, the Help of Christians and protector of the human race; St. Joseph, her chaste spouse, in whose patronage the whole Church greatly trusts; and the Princes of the Apostles, Peter and Paul, the guardians and protectors of the Christian name.

29. Given at St. Peter's in Rome, the twenty-ninth day of June, 1881, the third year of Our Pontificate.

Leo XIII, Pope

## NOTES

1. An allusion to Alexander II (1818-81), Emperor of Russia.
2. "Philosophers" here refers to a group of eighteenth-century French writers, especially Voltaire, d'Alembert and Diderot.
3. *Tract. 116 in Joan.*, n. 5 (PL 35, 1942).
4. *De civ. Dei*, 5, 21 (PL 41, 167).
5. *In Epist. ad Rom.*, Homil. 23, n. 1 (PG 60, 615).
6. *In Epist. lib. II*, epist. 61.
7. An allusion to the doctrine of "Social contract," developed by Jean-Jacques Rousseau (1712-78). According to this doctrine, all political power comes to rulers from the people. (Note from *The Church Speaks to the Modern World*, edited by Etienne Gilson, Image Books (1954), p. 155, n. 15.)
8. *Legatio pro Christianis*, 1 (PG 6, 891B-894A).
9. *Apolog.*, 35.
10. *Apolog.*, 37 (PL 1, 526A).
11. *Ad Diogn.*, 10 (*A Diognète*, ed. H. I. Marrou, Paris, 1951, pp. 64-65).
12. *On the Governance of Rulers*, 1, 10.
13. Clement XI (1700-21); Benedict XIV (1740-58); Leo XII (1823-29).
14. *De mor. eccl.*, 1, 30, 53 (PL 32, 1236).

# ON FREEMASONRY AND NATURALISM
## *(Humanum Genus)*

### April 20, 1884

To the Patriarchs, Primates, Archbishops, and Bishops of the
Catholic World in Grace and Communion with the
Apostolic See

Venerable Brethren,
Health and Apostolic Benediction

### *Two Kingdoms*

1. The race of man, after its miserable fall from God, the Creator and the Giver of heavenly gifts, "through the envy of the devil," separated into two diverse and opposite parts, of which the one steadfastly contends for truth and virtue, the other for those things which are contrary to virtue and to truth. The one is the kingdom of God on earth, namely, the true Church of Jesus Christ; and those who desire from their heart to be united with it, so as to gain salvation, must of necessity serve God and His only-begotten Son with their whole mind and with an entire will. The other is the kingdom of Satan, in whose possession and control are all whosoever follow the fatal example of their leader and of our first parents, those who refuse to obey the divine and eternal law, and who have many aims of their own in contempt of God, and many aims also against God.

## Two Loves and Two Cities

2. This twofold kingdom St. Augustine keenly discerned and described after the manner of two cities, contrary in their laws because striving for contrary objects; and with a subtle brevity he expressed the efficient cause of each in these words: "Two loves formed two cities: the love of self, reaching even to contempt of God, an earthly city; and the love of God, reaching to contempt of self, a heavenly one."[1] At every period of time each has been in conflict with the other, with a variety and multiplicity of weapons and of warfare, although not always with equal ardor and assault. At this period, however, the partisans of evil seem to be combining together, and to be struggling with united vehemence, led on or assisted by that strongly organized and widespread association called the Freemasons. No longer making any secret of their purposes, they are now boldly rising up against God Himself. They are planning the destruction of holy Church publicly and openly, and this with the set purpose of utterly despoiling the nations of Christendom, if it were possible, of the blessings obtained for us through Jesus Christ our Saviour. Lamenting these evils, We are constrained by the charity which urges Our heart to cry out often to God: "For lo, thy enemies have made a noise: and they that hate thee have lifted up the head. They have taken a malicious counsel against thy people, and have consulted against thy saints. They have said: Come and let us destroy them, so that they be not a nation." (*Ps.* 82:3-5).

## The Pope's Duty

3. At so urgent a crisis, when so fierce and so pressing an onslaught is made upon the Christian name, it is Our office to point out the danger, to mark who are the adversaries and to the best of Our power to make head against their plans and devices, that those may not perish whose salvation is committed to Us, and that the kingdom of Jesus Christ entrusted to Our charge may not only stand and remain whole, but may be enlarged by an ever-increasing growth throughout the world.

### Our Predecessors on the Alert

4. The Roman Pontiffs Our Predecessors, in their incessant watchfulness over the safety of the Christian people, were prompt in detecting the presence and the purpose of this capital enemy immediately it sprang into the light instead of hiding as a dark conspiracy; and, moreover, they took occasion with true foresight to give, as it were the alarm, and to admonish both princes and nations to stand on their guard, and not allow themselves to be caught by the devices and snares laid out to deceive them.

### From Clement XII to Pius IX

5. The first warning of the danger was given by Clement XII in the year 1738,[2] and his constitution was confirmed and renewed by Benedict XIV.[3] Pius VII followed the same path;[4] and Leo XII, by his apostolic constitution, *Quo Graviora*,[5] put together the acts and decrees of former Pontiffs on this subject, and ratified and confirmed them forever. In the same sense spoke Pius VIII,[6] Gregory XVI,[7] and, many times over, Pius IX.[8]

### The Chuch, the State and Masonry

6. For as soon as the constitution and the spirit of the Masonic sect were clearly discovered by manifest signs of its actions, by the investigation of its causes, by the publication of its laws, and of its rites and commentaries, with the addition often of the personal testimony of those who were in the secret, this Apostolic See denounced the sect of the Freemasons, and publicly declared its constitution, as contrary to law and right, to be pernicious no less to Christendom than to the State; and it forbade any one to enter the society, under the penalties which the Church is wont to inflict upon exceptionally guilty persons. The sectaries, indignant at this, thinking to elude or to weaken the force of these decrees, partly by contempt of them, and partly by calumny, accused the sovereign Pontiffs who had passed them either of exceeding the bounds of moderation in their decrees or of decreeing what was

not just. This was the manner in which they endeavored to elude the authority and the weight of the apostolic constitutions of Clement XII and Benedict XIV, as well as of Pius VII and Pius IX.[9] Yet, in the very society itself, there were to be found men who unwillingly acknowledged that the Roman Pontiffs had acted within their right, according to the Catholic doctrine and discipline. The Pontiffs received the same assent, and in strong terms, from many princes and heads of governments, who made it their business either to delate the Masonic society to the Apostolic See, or of their own accord by special enactments to brand it as pernicious, as, for example, in Holland, Austria, Switzerland, Spain, Bavaria, Savoy and other parts of Italy.

### Our Predecessors' Warnings Vindicated

7. But, what is of highest importance, the course of events has demonstrated the prudence of Our Predecessors. For their provident and paternal solicitude had not always and everywhere the result desired; and this, either because of the simulation and cunning of some who were active agents in the mischief, or else of the thoughtless levity of the rest who ought, in their own interest, to have given to the matter their diligent attention. In consequence, the sect of Freemasons grew with a rapidity beyond conception in the course of a century and a half, until it came to be able, by means of fraud or of audacity, to gain such entrance into every rank of the State as to seem to be almost its ruling power. This swift and formidable advance has brought upon the Church, upon the power of princes, upon the public well-being, precisely that grievous harm which Our Predecessors had long before foreseen. Such a condition has been reached that henceforth there will be grave reason to fear, not indeed for the Church—for her foundation is much too firm to be overturned by the effort of men—but for those States in which prevails the power, either of the sect of which we are speaking or of other sects not dissimilar which lend themselves to it as disciples and subordinates.

*The Teaching and Aims of Masonry*

8. For these reasons We no sooner came to the helm of the Church than We clearly saw and felt it to be Our duty to use Our authority to the very utmost against so vast an evil. We have several times already, as occasion served, attacked certain chief points of teaching which showed in a special manner the perverse influence of Masonic opinions. Thus, in Our encyclical letter, *Quod Apostolici Muneris*, We endeavored to refute the monstrous doctrines of the Socialists and Communists; afterwards, in another beginning *"Arcanum,"* We took pains to defend and explain the true and genuine idea of domestic life, of which marriage is the spring and origin; and again, in that which begins *"Diuturnum,"* We described the ideal of political government conformed to the principles of Christian wisdom, which is marvelously in harmony, on the one hand, with the natural order of things, and, on the other, with the well-being of both sovereign princes and of nations. It is now Our intention, following the example of Our Predecessors, directly to treat of the Masonic society itself, of its whole teaching, of its aims and of its manner of thinking and acting, in order to bring more and more into the light its power for evil, and to do what We can to arrest the contagion of this fatal plague.

*Unity of All Secret Societies*

9. There are several organized bodies which, though differing in name, in ceremonial, in form and origin, are nevertheless so bound together by community of purpose and by the similarity of their main opinions, as to make in fact one thing with the sect of the Freemasons, which is a kind of center whence they all go forth, and whither they all return. Now, these no longer show a desire to remain concealed; for they hold their meetings in the daylight and before the public eye, and publish their own newspaper organs; and yet, when thoroughly understood, they are found still to retain the nature and the habits of secret societies. There are many things like mysteries which it is the fixed rule to hide

with extreme care, not only from strangers, but from very many members, also; such as their secret and final designs, the names of the chief leaders and certain secret and inner meetings, as well as their decisions, and the ways and means of carrying them out. This is, no doubt, the object of the manifold difference among the members as to right, office and privilege, of the received distinction of orders and grades, and of that severe discipline which is maintained.

*Secrecy and Deceit*

Candidates are generally commanded to promise—nay, with a special oath, to swear—that they will never, to any person, at any time or in any way, make known the members, the passes, or the subjects discussed. Thus, with a fraudulent external appearance, and with a style of simulation which is always the same, the Freemasons, like the Manichees of old, strive, as far as possible, to conceal themselves, and to admit no witnesses but their own members. As a convenient manner of concealment, they assume the character of literary men and scholars associated for purposes of learning. They speak of their zeal for a more cultured refinement, and of their love for the poor; and they declare their one wish to be the amelioration of the condition of the masses, and to share with the largest possible number all the benefits of civil life. Were these purposes aimed at in real truth, they are by no means the whole of their object. Moreover, to be enrolled, it is necessary that the candidates promise and undertake to be thenceforward strictly obedient to their leaders and masters with the utmost submission and fidelity, and to be in readiness to do their bidding upon the slightest expression of their will; or, if disobedient, to submit to the direst penalties and death itself. As a fact, if any are judged to have betrayed the doings of the sect or to have resisted commands given, punishment is inflicted on them not infrequently, and with so much audacity and dexterity that the assassin very often escapes the detection and penalty of his crime.

### Evil Fruits of Masonry

10. But to simulate and wish to lie hid; to bind men like slaves in the very tightest bonds, and without giving any sufficient reason; to make use of men enslaved to the will of another for any arbitrary act; to arm men's right hands for bloodshed after securing impunity for the crime—all this is an enormity from which nature recoils. Wherefore, reason and truth itself make it plain that the society of which we are speaking is in antagonism with justice and natural uprightness. And this becomes still plainer, inasmuch as other arguments, also, and those very manifest, prove that it is essentially opposed to natural virtue. For, no matter how great may be men's cleverness in concealing and their experience in lying, it is impossible to prevent the effects of any cause from showing, in some way, the intrinsic nature of the cause whence they come. "A good tree cannot bring forth evil fruit, neither can an evil tree bring forth good fruit." (*Matt.* 7:18). Now, the Masonic sect produces fruits that are pernicious and of the bitterest savor. For, from what We have above most clearly shown, that which is their ultimate purpose forces itself into view—namely, the utter overthrow of that whole religious and political order of the world which the Christian teaching has produced, and the substitution of a new state of things in accordance with their ideas, of which the foundations and laws shall be drawn from mere naturalism.

### Masonry and Associated Organizations

11. What We have said, and are about to say, must be understood of the sect of the Freemasons taken generically, and in so far as it comprises the associations kindred to it and confederated with it, but not of the individual members of them. There may be persons among these, and not a few, who, although not free from the guilt of having entangled themselves in such associations, yet are neither themselves partners in their criminal acts nor aware of the ultimate object which they are endeavoring to attain. In the same way, some of the affiliated societies, perhaps, by no means

approve of the extreme conclusions which they would, if consistent, embrace as necessarily following from their common principles, did not their very foulness strike them with horror. Some of these, again, are led by circumstances of times and places either to aim at smaller things than the others usually attempt or than they themselves would wish to attempt. They are not, however, for this reason, to be reckoned as alien to the Masonic federation; for the Masonic federation is to be judged not so much by the things which it has done, or brought to completion, as by the sum of its pronounced opinions.

## The Principles of Naturalism

12. Now, the fundamental doctrine of the naturalists, which they sufficiently make known by their very name, is that human nature and human reason ought in all things to be mistress and guide. Laying this down, they care little for duties to God, or pervert them by erroneous and vague opinions. For they deny that anything has been taught by God; they allow no dogma of religion or truth which cannot be understood by the human intelligence, nor any teacher who ought to be believed by reason of his authority. And since it is the special and exclusive duty of the Catholic Church fully to set forth in words truths divinely received, to teach, besides other divine helps to salvation, the authority of its office, and to defend the same with perfect purity, it is against the Church that the rage and attack of the enemies are principally directed.

## Masonry Upholds Naturalism

13. In those matters which regard religion let it be seen how the sect of the Freemasons acts, especially where it is more free to act without restraint, and then let any one judge whether in fact it does not wish to carry out the policy of the naturalists. By a long and persevering labor, they endeavor to bring about this result—namely, that the teaching office and authority of the Church may become of no account in the civil State; and for this same reason

they declare to the people and contend that Church and State ought to be altogether disunited. By this means they reject from the laws and from the commonwealth the wholesome influence of the Catholic religion; and they consequently imagine that States ought to be constituted without any regard for the laws and precepts of the Church.

### Masonry Attacks Christ's Church

14. Nor do they think it enough to disregard the Church—the best of guides—unless they also injure it by their hostility. Indeed, with them it is lawful to attack with impunity the very foundations of the Catholic religion, in speech, in writing and in teaching; and even the rights of the Church are not spared, and the offices with which it is divinely invested are not safe. The least possible liberty to manage affairs is left to the Church; and this is done by laws not apparently very hostile, but in reality framed and fitted to hinder freedom of action. Moreover, We see exceptional and onerous laws imposed upon the clergy, to the end that they may be continually diminished in number and in necessary means. We see also the remnants of the possessions of the Church fettered by the strictest conditions, and subjected to the power and arbitrary will of the administrators of the State, and the religious orders rooted up and scattered.

### Masonry Assails Christ's Vicar

15. But against the Apostolic See and the Roman Pontiff the contention of these enemies has been for a long time directed. The Pontiff was first, for specious reasons, thrust out from the bulwark of his liberty and of his right, the civil princedom; soon, he was unjustly driven into a condition which was unbearable because of the difficulties raised on all sides; and now the time has come when the partisans of the sects openly declare, what in secret among themselves they have for a long time plotted, that the sacred power of the Pontiffs must be abolished, and that the papacy itself, founded by divine right, must be utterly destroyed.

If other proofs were wanting, this fact would be sufficiently disclosed by the testimony of men well informed, of whom some at other times, and others again recently, have declared it to be true of the Freemasons that they especially desire to assail the Church with irreconcilable hostility, and that they will never rest until they have destroyed whatever the supreme Pontiffs have established for the sake of religion.

### Masonry Undermines All Religion

16. If those who are admitted as members are not commanded to abjure by any form of words the Catholic doctrines, this omission, so far from being adverse to the designs of the Freemasons, is more useful for their purposes. First, in this way they easily deceive the simple-minded and the heedless, and can induce a far greater number to become members. Again, as all who offer themselves are received whatever may be their form of religion, they thereby teach the great error of this age—that a regard for religion should be held as an indifferent matter, and that all religions are alike. This manner of reasoning is calculated to bring about the ruin of all forms of religion, and especially of the Catholic religion, which, as it is the only one that is true, cannot, without great injustice, be regarded as merely equal to other religions.

### Masonic Belief in God

17. But the naturalists go much further; for, having, in the highest things, entered upon a wholly erroneous course, they are carried headlong to extremes, either by reason of the weakness of human nature, or because God inflicts upon them the just punishment of their pride. Hence it happens that they no longer consider as certain and permanent those things which are fully understood by the natural light of reason, such as certainly are—the existence of God, the immaterial nature of the human soul and its immortality. The sect of the Freemasons, by a similar course of error, is exposed to these same dangers; for, although in a general way

they may profess the existence of God, they themselves are witnesses that they do not all maintain this truth with the full assent of the mind or with a firm conviction. Neither do they conceal that this question about God is the greatest source and cause of discords among them; in fact, it is certain that a considerable contention about this same subject has existed among them very lately. But, indeed, the sect allows great liberty to its votaries, so that to each side is given the right to defend its own opinion, either that there is a God, or that there is none; and those who obstinately contend that there is no God are as easily initiated as those who contend that God exists, though, like the pantheists, they have false notions concerning Him: all which is nothing else than taking away the reality, while retaining some absurd representation of the divine nature.

### Loss of Natural Truths

18. When this greatest fundamental truth has been overturned or weakened, it follows that those truths, also, which are known by the teaching of nature must begin to fall—namely, that all things were made by the free will of God the Creator; that the world is governed by Providence; that souls do not die; that to this life of men upon the earth there will succeed another and an everlasting life.

### Effect on Morality

19. When these truths are done away with, which are as the principles of nature and important for knowledge and for practical use, it is easy to see what will become of both public and private morality. We say nothing of those more heavenly virtues, which no one can exercise or even acquire without a special gift and grace of God; of which necessarily no trace can be found in those who reject as unknown the redemption of mankind, the grace of God, the Sacraments and the happiness to be obtained in Heaven. We speak now of the duties which have their origin in natural probity. That God is the Creator of the world and its prov-

ident Ruler; that the eternal law commands the natural order to be maintained, and forbids that it be disturbed; that the last end of men is a destiny far above human things and beyond this sojourning upon the earth: these are the sources and these the principles of all justice and morality.

### No Foundation for Justice

If these be taken away, as the naturalists and Freemasons desire, there will immediately be no knowledge as to what constitutes justice and injustice, or upon what principle morality is founded. And, in truth, the teaching of morality which alone finds favor with the sect of Freemasons, and in which they contend that youth should be instructed, is that which they call "civil," and "independent," and "free," namely, that which does not contain any religious belief. But, how insufficient such teaching is, how wanting in soundness and how easily moved by every impulse of passion, is sufficiently proved by its sad fruits, which have already begun to appear. For, wherever, by removing Christian education, this teaching has begun more completely to rule, there goodness and integrity of morals have begun quickly to perish, monstrous and shameful opinions have grown up and the audacity of evil deeds has risen to a high degree. All this is commonly complained of and deplored; and not a few of those who by no means wish to do so are compelled by abundant evidence to give not infrequently the same testimony.

### Weakness of Our Nature

20. Moreover, human nature was stained by original sin, and is therefore more disposed to vice than to virtue. For a virtuous life it is absolutely necessary to restrain the disorderly movements of the soul, and to make the passions obedient to reason. In this conflict human things must very often be despised, and the greatest labors and hardships must be undergone, in order that reason may always hold its sway. But the naturalists and Freemasons, having no faith in those things which we have learned by the revelation

of God, deny that our first parents sinned, and consequently think that free will is not at all weakened and inclined to evil.[10] On the contrary, exaggerating rather the power and the excellence of nature, and placing therein alone the principle and rule of justice, they cannot even imagine that there is any need at all of a constant struggle and a perfect steadfastness to overcome the violence and rule of our passions.

### A Gospel of Pleasure

Wherefore we see that men are publicly tempted by the many allurements of pleasure; that there are journals and pamphlets with neither moderation nor shame; that stage-plays are remarkable for license; that designs for works of art are shamelessly sought in the laws of a so-called verism; that the contrivances of a soft and delicate life are most carefully devised; and that all the blandishments of pleasure are diligently sought out by which virtue may be lulled to sleep. Wickedly, also, but at the same time quite consistently, do those act who do away with the expectation of the joys of Heaven, and bring down all happiness to the level of mortality, and, as it were, sink it in the earth. Of what We have said the following fact, astonishing not so much in itself as in its open expression, may serve as a confirmation. For, since generally no one is accustomed to obey crafty and clever men so submissively as those whose soul is weakened and broken down by the domination of the passions, there have been in the sect of the Freemasons some who have plainly determined and proposed that, artfully and of set purpose, the multitude should be satiated with a boundless license of vice, as, when this had been done, it would easily come under their power and authority for any acts of daring.

### Teachings on Marriage

21. What refers to domestic life in the teaching of the naturalists is almost all contained in the following declarations: that marriage belongs to the genus of commercial contracts, which can

rightly be revoked by the will of those who made them, and that the civil rulers of the State have power over the matrimonial bond; that in the education of youth nothing is to be taught in the matter of religion as of certain and fixed opinion; and each one must be left at liberty to follow, when he comes of age, whatever he may prefer. To these things the Freemasons fully assent; and not only assent, but have long endeavored to make them into a law and institution. For in many countries, and those nominally Catholic, it is enacted that no marriages shall be considered lawful except those contracted by the civil rite; in other places the law permits divorce; and in others every effort is used to make it lawful as soon as may be. Thus, the time is quickly coming when marriages will be turned into another kind of contract—that is, into changeable and uncertain unions which fancy may join together, and which the same when changed may disunite.

## Educational Principles

With the greatest unanimity the sect of the Freemasons also endeavors to take to itself the education of youth. They think that they can easily mold to their opinions that soft and pliant age, and bend it whither they will; and that nothing can be more fitted than this to enable them to bring up the youth of the State after their own plan. Therefore, in the education and instruction of children they allow no share, either of teaching or of discipline, to the ministers of the Church; and in many places they have procured that the education of youth shall be exclusively in the hands of laymen, and that nothing which treats of the most important and most holy duties of men to God shall be introduced into the instructions on morals.

## Political Doctrines

22. Then come their doctrines of politics, in which the naturalists lay down that all men have the same right, and are in every respect of equal and like condition; that each one is naturally free; that no one has the right to command another; that it is an act of

violence to require men to obey any authority other than that which is obtained from themselves. According to this, therefore, all things belong to the free people; power is held by the command or permission of the people, so that, when the popular will changes, rulers may lawfully be deposed; and the source of all rights and civil duties is either in the multitude or in the governing authority when this is constituted according to the latest doctrines. It is held also that the State should be without God; that in the various forms of religion there is no reason why one should have precedence of another; and that they are all to occupy the same place.

### Communism the Sequel

23. That these doctrines are equally acceptable to the Freemasons, and that they would wish to constitute States according to this example and model, is too well known to require proof. For some time past they have openly endeavored to bring this about with all their strength and resources; and in this they prepare the way for not a few bolder men who are hurrying on even to worse things, in their endeavor to obtain equality and community of all goods by the destruction of every distinction of rank and property.

### Masonry Means Paganism

24. What, therefore, the sect of the Freemasons is, and what course it pursues, appears sufficiently from the summary We have briefly given. Their chief dogmas are so greatly and manifestly at variance with reason that nothing can be more perverse. To wish to destroy the religion and the Church which God Himself has established, and whose perpetuity He insures by His protection, and to bring back after a lapse of eighteen centuries the manners and customs of the pagans, is signal folly and audacious impiety. Neither is it less horrible nor more tolerable that they should repudiate the benefits which Jesus Christ so mercifully obtained, not only for individuals, but also for the family and for civil society, benefits which, even according to the judgment and testimony of

enemies of Christianity, are very great. In this insane and wicked endeavor we may almost see the implacable hatred and spirit of revenge with which Satan himself is inflamed against Jesus Christ.—So also the studious endeavor of the Freemasons to destroy the chief foundations of justice and honesty, and to co-operate with those who would wish, as if they were mere animals, to do what they please, tends only to the ignominious and disgraceful ruin of the human race.

## Dangers to Society

The evil, too, is increased by the dangers which threaten both domestic and civil society. As We have elsewhere shown,[11] in marriage, according to the belief of almost every nation, there is something sacred and religious; and the law of God has determined that marriages shall not be dissolved. If they are deprived of their sacred character, and made dissoluble, trouble and confusion in the family will be the result, the wife being deprived of her dignity and the children left without protection as to their interests and well being. To have in public matters no care for religion, and in the arrangement and administration of civil affairs to have no more regard for God than if He did not exist, is a rashness unknown to the very pagans; for in their heart and soul the notion of a divinity and the need of public religion were so firmly fixed that they would have thought it easier to have city without foundation than a city without God. Human society, indeed, for which by nature we are formed, has been constituted by God the Author of nature; and from Him, as from their principle and source, flow in all their strength and permanence the countless benefits with which society abounds. As we are each of us admonished by the very voice of nature to worship God in piety and holiness, as the Giver unto us of life and of all that is good therein, so also and for the same reason, nations and States are bound to worship Him; and therefore it is clear that those who would absolve society from all religious duty act not only unjustly but also with ignorance and folly.

## Foundation of Civic Obedience

25. As men are by the will of God born for civil union and society, and as the power to rule is so necessary a bond of society that, if it be taken away, society must at once be broken up, it follows that from Him who is the Author of society has come also the authority to rule; so that whosoever rules, he is the minister of God. Wherefore, as the end and nature of human society so requires, it is right to obey the just commands of lawful authority, as it is right to obey God who ruleth all things; and it is most untrue that the people have it in their power to cast aside their obedience whensoever they please.

## True and False Equality

26. In like manner, no one doubts that all men are equal one to another, so far as regards their common origin and nature, or the last end which each one has to attain, or the rights and duties which are thence derived. But, as the abilities of all are not equal, as one differs from another in the powers of mind or body, and as there are very many dissimilarities of manner, disposition and character, it is most repugnant to reason to endeavor to confine all within the same measure, and to extend complete equality to the institutions of civil life. Just as a perfect condition of the body results from the conjunction and composition of its various members, which, though differing in form and purpose, make, by their union and the distribution of each one to its proper place, a combination beautiful to behold, firm in strength and necessary for use; so, in the commonwealth, there is an almost infinite dissimilarity of men, as parts of the whole. If they are to be all equal, and each is to follow his own will, the State will appear most deformed; but if, with a distinction of degrees of dignity, of pursuits and employments, all aptly conspire for the common good, they will present the image of a State both well constituted and conformable to nature.

## A Threat to States

27. Now, from the disturbing errors which We have described the greatest dangers to States are to be feared. For, the fear of God and reverence for divine laws being taken away, the authority of rulers despised, sedition permitted and approved and the popular passions urged on to lawlessness, with no restraint save that of punishment, a change and overthrow of all things will necessarily follow. Yea, this change and overthrow is deliberately planned and put forward by many associations of Communists and Socialists; and to their undertakings the sect of Freemasons is not hostile, but greatly favors their designs, and holds in common with them their chief opinions. And if these men do not at once and everywhere endeavor to carry out their extreme views, it is not to be attributed to their teaching and their will, but to the virtue of that divine religion which cannot be destroyed; and also because the sounder part of men, refusing to be enslaved to secret societies, vigorously resist their insane attempts.

## People and Rulers Deceived

28. Would that all men would judge of the tree by its fruits, and would acknowledge the seed and origin of the evils which press upon us, and of the dangers that are impending! We have to deal with a deceitful and crafty enemy, who, gratifying the ears of people and of princes, has ensnared them by smooth speeches and by adulation. Ingratiating themselves with rulers under a pretense of friendship, the Freemasons have endeavored to make them their allies and powerful helpers for the destruction of the Christian name; and that they might more strongly urge them on, they have, with determined calumny, accused the Church of invidiously contending with rulers in matters that affect their authority and sovereign power. Having, by these artifices, insured their own safety and audacity, they have begun to exercise great weight in the government of States; but nevertheless they are prepared to shake the foundations of empires, to harass the rulers of the State, to accuse and to cast them out, as often as they appear to govern otherwise

than they themselves could have wished. In like manner, they have by flattery deluded the people. Proclaiming with a loud voice liberty and public prosperity, and saying that it was owing to the Church and to sovereigns that the multitude were not drawn out of their unjust servitude and poverty, they have imposed upon the people and, exciting them by a thirst for novelty, they have urged them to assail both the Church and the civil power. Nevertheless, the expectation of the benefits which was hoped for is greater than the reality; indeed, the common people, more oppressed than they were before, are deprived in their misery of that solace which, if things had been arranged in a Christian manner, they would have had with ease and in abundance. But, whoever strive against the order which Divine Providence has constituted pay usually the penalty of their pride, and meet with affliction and misery where they rashly hoped to find all things prosperous and in conformity with their desires.

### Benefit of the Church's Teaching

29. The Church, if she directs men to render obedience chiefly and above all to God the sovereign Lord, is wrongly and falsely believed either to be envious of the civil power or to arrogate to herself something of the rights of sovereigns. On the contrary, she teaches that what is rightly due to the civil power must be rendered to it with a conviction and consciousness of duty. In teaching that from God Himself comes the right of ruling, she adds a great dignity to civil authority, and no small help towards obtaining the obedience and good will of the citizens. The friend of peace and sustainer of concord, she embraces all with maternal love, and, intent only upon giving help to mortal man, she teaches that to justice must be joined clemency, equity to authority and moderation to lawgiving; that no one's right must be violated; that order and public tranquillity are to be maintained and that the poverty of those who are in need is, as far as possible, to be relieved by public and private charity. "But for this reason," to use the words of St. Augustine, "men think, or would have it believed, that Christian teaching is not suited to the good of the State; for

they wish the State to be founded not on solid virtue, but on the impunity of vice."[12] Knowing these things, both princes and people would act with political wisdom, and according to the needs of general safety, if, instead of joining with Freemasons to destroy the Church, they joined with the Church in repelling their attacks.

### The Popes' Warning Reiterated

30. Whatever the future may be, in this grave and widespread evil it is Our duty, Venerable Brethren, to endeavor to find a remedy. And because We know that Our best and firmest hope of a remedy is in the power of that divine religion which the Freemasons hate in proportion to their fear of it, We think it to be of chief importance to call that most saving power to Our aid against the common enemy. Therefore, whatsoever the Roman Pontiffs Our Predecessors have decreed for the purpose of opposing the undertakings and endeavors of the Masonic sect, and whatsoever they have enacted to deter or withdraw men from societies of this kind, We ratify and confirm it all by our apostolic authority: and trusting greatly to the good will of Christians, We pray and beseech each one, for the sake of his eternal salvation, to be most conscientiously careful not in the least to depart from what the Apostolic See has commanded in this matter.

### No Compromise with Masonry

31. We pray and beseech you, Venerable Brethren, to join your efforts with Ours, and earnestly to strive for the extirpation of this foul plague, which is creeping through the veins of the body politic. You have to defend the glory of God and the salvation of your neighbor; and with the object of your strife before you, neither courage nor strength will be wanting. It will be for your prudence to judge by what means you can best overcome the difficulties and obstacles you meet with. But, as it befits the authority of Our office that We Ourselves should point out some suitable way of proceeding, We wish it to be your rule first of all to tear away the mask from Freemasonry, and to let it be seen as

it really is; and by sermons and pastoral letters to instruct the people as to the artifices used by societies of this kind in seducing men and enticing them into their ranks, and as to the depravity of their opinions and the wickedness of their acts. As Our Predecessors have many times repeated, let no man think that he may for any reason whatsoever join the Masonic sect, if he values his Catholic name and his eternal salvation as he ought to value them. Let no one be deceived by a pretense of honesty. It may seem to some that Freemasons demand nothing that is openly contrary to religion and morality; but, as the whole principle and object of the sect lies in what is vicious and criminal, to join with these men or in any way to help them cannot be lawful.

### Sound Religious Instruction Needed

32. Further, by assiduous teaching and exhortation, the multitude must be drawn to learn diligently the precepts of religion; for which purpose we earnestly advise that by opportune writings and sermons they be taught the elements of those sacred truths in which Christian philosophy is contained. The result of this will be that the minds of men will be made sound by instruction, and will be protected against many forms of error and inducements to wickedness, especially in the present unbounded freedom of writing and insatiable eagerness for learning.

### United Effort of Clergy and Laity

33. Great, indeed, is the work; but in it the clergy will share your labors, if, through your care, they are fitted for it by learning and a well-trained life. This good and great work requires to be helped also by the industry of those among the laity in whom a love of religion and of country is joined to learning and goodness of life. By uniting the efforts of both clergy and laity, strive, Venerable Brethren, to make men thoroughly know and love the Church; for, the greater their knowledge and love of the Church, the more will they be turned away from clandestine societies.

## Ideal of St. Francis

34. Wherefore, not without cause do We use this occasion to state again what We have stated elsewhere, namely, that the Third Order of St. Francis, whose discipline We a little while ago prudently mitigated,[13] should be studiously promoted and sustained; for the whole object of this Order, as constituted by its founder, is to invite men to an imitation of Jesus Christ, to a love of the Church and to the observance of all Christian virtues; and therefore it ought to be of great influence in suppressing the contagion of wicked societies. Let, therefore, this holy sodality be strengthened by a daily increase. Among the many benefits to be expected from it will be the great benefit of drawing the minds of men to liberty, fraternity and equality of right; not such as the Freemasons absurdly imagine, but such as Jesus Christ obtained for the human race and St. Francis aspired to: the liberty, We mean, of *sons of God*, through which we may be free from slavery to Satan or to our passions, both of them most wicked masters; the fraternity whose origin is in God, the common Creator and Father of all; the equality which, founded on justice and charity, does not take away all distinctions among men, but, out of the varieties of life, of duties and of pursuits, forms that union and that harmony which naturally tend to the benefit and dignity of society.

## Restore Catholic Guilds

35. In the third place, there is a matter wisely instituted by Our forefathers, but in course of time laid aside, which may now be used as a pattern and form of something similar. We mean the associations or guilds of workmen, for the protection, under the guidance of religion, both of their temporal interests and of their morality. If our ancestors, by long use and experience, felt the benefit of these guilds, our age perhaps will feel it the more by reason of the opportunity which they will give of crushing the power of the sects. Those who support themselves by the labor of their hands, besides being, by their very condition, most worthy above all others of charity and consolation, are also especially

exposed to the allurements of men whose ways lie in fraud and deceit. Therefore, they ought to be helped with the greatest possible kindness, and to be invited to join associations that are good, lest they be drawn away to others that are evil. For this reason, We greatly wish, for the salvation of the people, that, under the auspices and patronage of the bishops, and at convenient times, these guilds may be generally restored. To Our great delight, sodalities of this kind and also associations of masters have in many places already been established, having, each class of them, for their object to help the honest workman, to protect and guard his children and family and to promote in them piety, Christian knowledge and a moral life. And in this matter We cannot omit mentioning that exemplary society, named after its founder, St. Vincent, which has deserved so well of the lower classes. Its acts and its aims are well known. Its whole object is to give relief to the poor and miserable. This it does with singular prudence and modesty; and the less it wishes to be seen, the better is it fitted for the exercise of Christian charity, and for the relief of suffering.

## Special Guidance of Youth

36. In the fourth place, in order more easily to attain what We wish, to your fidelity and watchfulness We commend in a special manner the young, as being the hope of human society. Devote the greatest part of your care to their instruction; and do not think that any precaution can be great enough in keeping them from masters and schools whence the pestilent breath of the sects is to be feared. Under your guidance, let parents, religious instructors and priests having the care of souls use every opportunity, in their Christian teaching, of warning their children and pupils of the infamous nature of these societies, so that they may learn in good time to beware of the various and fraudulent artifices by which their promoters are accustomed to ensnare people. And those who instruct the young in religious knowledge will act wisely if they induce all of them to resolve and to undertake never to bind themselves to any society without the knowledge of their parents, or the advice of their parish priest or director.

## A Call to Prayer and Action

37. We well know, however, that our united labors will by no means suffice to pluck up these pernicious seeds from the Lord's field, unless the Heavenly Master of the vineyard shall mercifully help us in our endeavors. We must, therefore, with great and anxious care, implore of Him the help which the greatness of the danger and of the need requires. The sect of the Freemasons shows itself insolent and proud of its success, and seems as if it would put no bounds to its pertinacity. Its followers, joined together by a wicked compact and by secret counsels, give help one to another, and excite one another to an audacity for evil things. So vehement an attack demands an equal defense—namely, that all good men should form the widest possible association of action and of prayer. We beseech them, therefore, with united hearts, to stand together and unmoved against the advancing force of the sects; and in mourning and supplication to stretch out their hands to God, praying that the Christian name may flourish and prosper, that the Church may enjoy its needed liberty, that those who have gone astray may return to a right mind, that error at length may give place to truth, and vice to virtue. Let us take as our helper and intercessor the Virgin Mary, Mother of God, so that she, who from the moment of her conception overcame Satan, may show her power over these evil sects, in which is revived the contumacious spirit of the demon, together with his unsubdued perfidy and deceit. Let us beseech Michael, the prince of the heavenly Angels, who drove out the infernal foe; and Joseph, the spouse of the most holy Virgin, and heavenly patron of the Catholic Church; and the great Apostles, Peter and Paul, the fathers and victorious champions of the Christian faith. By their patronage, and by perseverance in united prayer, we hope that God will mercifully and opportunely succor the human race, which is encompassed by so many dangers.

38. As a pledge of heavenly gifts and of Our benevolence, We lovingly grant in the Lord, to you, Venerable Brethren, and to the clergy and all the people committed to your watchful care, Our Apostolic Benediction.

Given at St. Peter's in Rome, the twentieth day of April, 1884, the sixth year of Our pontificate.

Leo XIII, Pope

## NOTES

1. *De civ. Dei*, 14, 28 (PL 41, 436).
2. Const. *In Eminenti*, April 24, 1738.
3. Const. *Providas*, May 18, 1751.
4. Const. *Ecclesiam a Jesu Christo*, Sept. 13, 1821.
5. Const. given March 13, 1825.
6. Encyc. *Traditi*, May 21, 1829.
7. Encyc. *Mirari*, August 15, 1832.
8. Encyc. *Qui Pluribus*, Nov. 9, 1846; address *Multiplices Inter*, Sept. 25, 1865, etc.
9. Clement XII (1730-40); Benedict XIV (1740-58); Pius VII (1800-23); Pius IX (1846-78).
10. Trid., sess. vi, *De justif.*, c. 1. Text of the Council of Trent: "*tametsi in eis* (sc. Judaeis) *liberum arbitrium minime extinctum esset, viribus licet attenuatum et inclinatum.*"
11. See *Arcanum*, no. 81.
12. *Epistola 137, ad Volusianum*, c. v, n. 20 (PL 33, 525).
13. The text here refers to the encyclical letter *Auspicato Concessum* (Sept. 17, 1882), in which Pope Leo XIII had recently glorified St. Francis of Assisi on the occasion of the seventh centenary of his birth. In this encyclical, the Pope had presented the Third Order of St. Francis as a Christian answer to the social problems of the times. The constitution *Misericors Dei Filius* (June 23, 1883) expressly recalled that the neglect in which Christian virtues are held is the main cause of the evils that threaten societies. In confirming the rule of the Third Order and adapting it to the needs of modern times, Pope Leo XIII had intended to bring back the largest possible number of souls to the practice of these virtues.

Encyclical Letter of Pope Leo XIII

# ON THE NATURE OF TRUE LIBERTY
## *(Libertas Praestantissimum)*

June 20, 1888

To the Patriarchs, Primates, Archbishops, and Bishops of the
Catholic World in Grace and Communion with the
Apostolic See

1. Liberty, the highest of natural endowments, being the portion only of intellectual or rational natures, confers on man this dignity—that he is "in the hand of his counsel" *(Ecclus.* 15:14) and has power over his actions. But the manner in which such dignity is exercised is of the greatest moment, inasmuch as on the use that is made of liberty the highest good and the greatest evil alike depend. Man, indeed, is free to obey his reason, to seek moral good and to strive unswervingly after his last end. Yet he is free also to turn aside to all other things; and, in pursuing the empty semblance of good, to disturb rightful order and to fall headlong into the destruction which he has voluntarily chosen. The Redeemer of mankind, Jesus Christ, having restored and exalted the original dignity of nature, vouchsafed special assistance to the will of man; and by the gifts of His grace here, and the promise of heavenly bliss hereafter, He raised it to a nobler state. In like manner, this great gift of nature has ever been, and always will be, deservingly cherished by the Catholic Church, for to her alone has been committed the charge of handing down to all ages the benefits purchased for us by Jesus Christ. Yet there are many who

imagine that the Church is hostile to human liberty. Having a false and absurd notion as to what liberty is, either they pervert the very idea of freedom, or they extend it at their pleasure to many things in respect of which man cannot rightly be regarded as free.

### Modern Liberties Are Disorders

2. We have on other occasions, and especially in Our Encyclical Letter *Immortale Dei*, in treating of the so-called *modern liberties*, distinguished between their good and evil elements; and We have shown that whatsoever is good in those liberties is as ancient as truth itself, and that the Church has always most willingly approved and practiced that good: but whatsoever has been added as new is, to tell the plain truth, of a vitiated kind, the fruit of the disorders of the age, and of an insatiate longing after novelties. Seeing, however, that many cling so obstinately to their own opinion in this matter as to imagine these modern liberties, cankered as they are, to be the greatest glory of our age and the very basis of civil life, without which no perfect government can be conceived, We feel it a pressing duty, for the sake of the common good, to treat separately of this subject.

### Reason Is the Foundation of Natural Liberty

3. It is with *moral* liberty, whether in individuals or in communities, that We proceed at once to deal. But, first of all, it will be well to speak briefly of *natural* liberty; for, though it is distinct and separate from moral liberty, natural freedom is the fountainhead from which liberty of whatsoever kind flows, *sua vi suaque sponte*. The unanimous consent and judgment of men, which is the trusty voice of nature, recognizes this natural liberty in those only who are endowed with intelligence or reason; and it is by his use of this that man is rightly regarded as responsible for his actions. For, while other animate creatures follow their senses, seeking good and avoiding evil only by instinct, man has reason to guide him in each and every act of his life. Reason sees that whatever things that are held to be good upon earth may exist or

may not, and discerning that none of them are of necessity for us, it leaves the will free to choose what it pleases. But man can judge of this contingency, as We say, only because he has a soul that is simple, spiritual and intellectual—a soul, therefore, which is not produced by matter, and does not depend on matter for its existence; but which is created immediately by God, and, far surpassing the condition of things material, has a life and action of its own—so that, knowing the unchangeable and necessary reasons of what is true and good, it sees that no particular kind of good is necessary to us. When, therefore, it is established that man's soul is immortal and endowed with reason and not bound up with things material, the foundation of natural liberty is at once most firmly laid.

### Freedom of the Soul

4. As the Catholic Church declares in the strongest terms the simplicity, spirituality and immortality of the soul, so with unequaled constancy and publicity she ever also asserts its freedom. These truths she has always taught, and has sustained them as a dogma of faith, and whensoever heretics or innovators have attacked the liberty of man, the Church has defended it and protected this noble possession from destruction. History bears witness to the energy with which she met the fury of the Manicheans and others like them; and the earnestness with which in later years she defended human liberty at the Council of Trent, and against the followers of Jansenius, is known to all. At no time, and in no place, has she held truce with *fatalism*.

### The Will Is Enlightened by the Intellect

5. Liberty, then, as We have said, belongs only to those who have the gift of reason or intelligence. Considered as to its nature, it is the faculty of choosing means fitted for the end proposed, for he is master of his actions who can choose one thing out of many. Now, since everything chosen as a means is viewed as good or useful, and since good, as such, is the proper object of our desire,

it follows that freedom of choice is a property of the will, or, rather, is identical with the will in so far as it has in its action the faculty of choice. But the will cannot proceed to act until it is enlightened by the knowledge possessed by the intellect. In other words, the good wished by the will is necessarily good in so far as it is known by the intellect; and this the more, because in all voluntary acts choice is subsequent to a judgment upon the truth of the good presented, declaring to which good preference should be given. No sensible man can doubt that judgment is an act of reason, not of the will. The end, or object, both of the rational will and of its liberty is that good only which is in conformity with reason.

### Liberty Means Acting according to Reason

6. Since, however, both these faculties are imperfect, it is possible, as is often seen, that the reason should propose something which is not really good, but which has the appearance of good, and that the will should choose accordingly. For, as the possibility of error, and actual error, are defects of the mind and attest its imperfection, so the pursuit of what has a false appearance of good, though a proof of our freedom, just as a disease is a proof of our vitality, implies defect in human liberty. The will also, simply because of its dependence on the reason, no sooner desires anything contrary thereto than it abuses its freedom of choice and corrupts its very essence. Thus it is that the infinitely perfect God, although supremely free, because of the supremacy of His intellect and of His essential goodness, nevertheless cannot choose evil; neither can the Angels and Saints, who enjoy the Beatific Vision. St. Augustine and others urged most admirably against the Pelagians that, if the possibility of deflection from good belonged to the essence or perfection of liberty, then God, Jesus Christ, and the Angels and Saints, who have not this power, would have no liberty at all, or would have less liberty than man has in his state of pilgrimage and imperfection. This subject is often discussed by the Angelic Doctor in his demonstration that the possibility of sinning is not freedom, but slavery. It will suffice to quote his subtle

commentary on the words of our Lord: "Whosoever committeth sin is the servant of sin." (*John* 8:34). "Everything," he says, "is that which belongs to it naturally. When, therefore, it acts through a power outside itself, it does not act of itself, but through another, that is, as a slave. But man is by nature rational. When, therefore, he acts according to reason, he acts of himself and according to his free will; and this is liberty. Whereas, when he sins, he acts in opposition to reason, is moved by another, and is the victim of foreign misapprehensions. Therefore, 'Whosoever committeth sin is the servant of sin.'"[1] Even the heathen philosophers clearly recognized this truth, especially they who held that the wise man alone is free; and by the term "wise man" was meant, as is well known, the man trained to live in accordance with his nature, that is, in justice and virtue.

### We Are Bound to Law because We Are Free

7. Such, then, being the condition of human liberty, it necessarily stands in need of light and strength to direct its actions to good and to restrain them from evil. Without this, the freedom of our will would be our ruin. First of all, there must be *law*; that is, a fixed rule of teaching what is to be done and what is to be left undone. This rule cannot affect the lower animals in any true sense, since they act of necessity, following their natural instinct, and cannot of themselves act in any other way. On the other hand, as was said above, he who is free can either act or not act, can do this or do that, as he pleases, because his judgment precedes his choice. And his judgment not only decides what is right or wrong of its own nature, but also what is practically good and therefore to be chosen, and what is practically evil and therefore to be avoided. In other words, the reason prescribes to the will what it should seek after or shun, in order to the eventual attainment of man's last end, for the sake of which all his actions ought to be performed. This ordination of *reason* is called law. In man's free will, therefore, or in the moral necessity of our voluntary acts being in accordance with reason, lies the very root of the necessity of law. Nothing more foolish can be uttered or conceived than

the notion that, because man is free by nature, he is therefore exempt from law. Were this the case, it would follow that to become free we must be deprived of reason; whereas the truth is that we are bound to submit to law precisely because we are free by our very nature. For, law is the guide of man's actions; it turns him toward good by its rewards and deters him from evil by its punishments.

### Natural Law Engraved in Every Man's Mind

8. Foremost in this office comes the *natural law*, which is written and engraved in the mind of every man; and this is nothing but our reason, commanding us to do right and forbidding sin. Nevertheless, all prescriptions of human reason can have force of law only inasmuch as they are the voice and the interpreters of some higher power on which our reason and liberty necessarily depend. For, since the force of law consists in the imposing of obligations and the granting of rights, authority is the one and only foundation of all law—the power, that is, of fixing duties and defining rights, as also of assigning the necessary sanctions of reward and chastisement to each and all of its commands. But all this, clearly, cannot be found in man, if, as his own supreme legislator, he is to be the rule of his own actions. It follows, therefore, that the law of nature is the same thing as the *eternal law*, implanted in rational creatures and inclining them *to their right action and end*, and can be nothing else but the eternal reason of God, the Creator and Ruler of all the world. To this rule of action and restraint of evil God has vouchsafed to give special and most suitable aids for strengthening and ordering the human will. The first and most excellent of these is the power of His divine *grace*, whereby the mind can be enlightened and the will wholesomely invigorated and moved to the constant pursuit of moral good, so that the use of our inborn liberty becomes at once less difficult and less dangerous. Not that the divine assistance hinders in any way the free movement of our will; just the contrary, for grace works inwardly in man and in harmony with his natural inclinations, since it flows from the very Creator of his mind and will, by whom all things are

moved in conformity with their nature. As the Angelic Doctor points out, it is because divine grace comes from the Author of nature that it is so admirably adapted to be the safeguard of all natures, and to maintain the character, efficiency and operations of each.

### Human Law Is Based on Natural Law

9. What has been said of the liberty of individuals is no less applicable to them when considered as bound together in civil society. For, what reason and the natural law do for individuals, that *human law* promulgated for their good does for the citizens of States. Of the laws enacted by men, some are concerned with what is good or bad by its very nature; and they command men to follow after what is right and to shun what is wrong, adding at the same time a suitable sanction. But such laws by no means derive their origin from civil society, because, just as civil society did not create human nature, so neither can it be said to be the author of the good which befits human nature, or of the evil which is contrary to it. Laws come before men live together in society, and have their origin in the natural, and consequently in the eternal, law. The precepts, therefore, of the natural law contained bodily in the laws of men have not merely the force of human law, but they possess that higher and more august sanction which belongs to the law of nature and the eternal law. And within the sphere of this kind of laws the duty of the civil legislator is, mainly, to keep the community in obedience by the adoption of a common discipline and by putting restraint upon refractory and viciously inclined men, so that, deterred from evil, they may turn to what is good, or at any rate may avoid causing trouble and disturbance to the State. Now, there are other enactments of the civil authority which do not follow directly, but somewhat remotely, from the natural law, and decide many points which the law of nature treats only in a general and indefinite way. For instance, though nature commands all to contribute to the public peace and prosperity, whatever belongs to the manner and circumstances and conditions under which such service is to be rendered must be determined by

the wisdom of men and not by nature herself. It is in the constitution of these particular rules of life, suggested by reason and prudence, and put forth by competent authority, that human law, properly so called, consists, binding all citizens to work together for the attainment of the common end proposed to the community, and forbidding them to depart from this end, and, in so far as human law is in conformity with the dictates of nature, leading to what is good and deterring from evil.

### God's Law the Sole Standard

10. From this it is manifest that the eternal law of God is the sole standard and rule of human liberty, not only in each individual man, but also in the community and civil society which men constitute when united. Therefore, the true liberty of human society does not consist in every man doing what he pleases, for this would simply end in turmoil and confusion, and bring on the overthrow of the State; but rather in this, that through the injunctions of the civil law all may more easily conform to the prescriptions of the eternal law. Likewise, the liberty of those who are in authority does not consist in the power to lay unreasonable and capricious commands upon their subjects, which would equally be criminal and would lead to the ruin of the commonwealth; but the binding force of human laws is in this, that they are to be regarded as applications of the eternal law, and incapable of sanctioning anything which is not contained in the eternal law, as in the principle of all law. Thus, St. Augustine most wisely says: "I think that you can see, at the same time, that there is nothing just and lawful in that temporal law, unless what men have gathered from this eternal law."[2] If, then, by anyone in authority, something be sanctioned out of conformity with the principles of right reason, and consequently hurtful to the commonwealth, such an enactment can have no binding force of law, as being no rule of justice, but certain to lead men away from that good which is the very end of civil society.

### Obedience to God's Law Perfects Man's Liberty

11. Therefore, the nature of human liberty, however it be considered, whether in individuals or in society, whether in those who command or in those who obey, supposes the necessity of obedience to some supreme and eternal law, which is no other than the authority of God, commanding good and forbidding evil. And, so far from this most just authority of God over men diminishing, or even destroying their liberty, it protects and perfects it, for the real perfection of all creatures is found in the prosecution and attainment of their respective ends; but the supreme end to which human liberty must aspire is God.

### The Church Protects Civil Liberty

12. These precepts of the truest and highest teaching, made known to us by the light of reason itself, the Church, instructed by the example and doctrine of her divine Author, has ever propagated and asserted; for she has ever made them the measure of her office and of her teaching to the Christian nations. As to morals, the laws of the Gospel not only immeasurably surpass the wisdom of the heathen, but are an invitation and an introduction to a state of holiness unknown to the ancients; and, bringing man nearer to God, they make him at once the possessor of a more perfect liberty. Thus, the powerful influence of the Church has ever been manifested in the custody and protection of the civil and political liberty of the people. The enumeration of its merits in this respect does not belong to our present purpose. It is sufficient to recall the fact that slavery, that old reproach of the heathen nations, was mainly abolished by the beneficent efforts of the Church. The impartiality of law and the true brotherhood of man were first asserted by Jesus Christ; and His apostles re-echoed His voice when they declared that in future there was to be neither Jew, nor Gentile, nor barbarian, nor Scythian, but all were brothers in Christ. So powerful, so conspicuous, in this respect is the influence of the Church that experience abundantly testifies how savage customs are no longer possible in any land where she has once

set her foot; but that gentleness speedily takes the place of cruelty, and the light of truth quickly dispels the darkness of barbarism. Nor has the Church been less lavish in the benefits she has conferred on civilized nations in every age, either by resisting the tyranny of the wicked, or by protecting the innocent and helpless from injury, or, finally, by using her influence in the support of any form of government which commended itself to the citizens at home, because of its justice, or was feared by their enemies without, because of its power.

### Unlawful Obedience

13. Moreover, the highest duty is to respect authority, and obediently to submit to just law; and by this the members of a community are effectually protected from the wrongdoing of evil men. Lawful power is from God, and "he that resisteth the power, resisteth the ordinance of God" (*Rom.* 13:2); wherefore, obedience is greatly ennobled when subjected to an authority which is the most just and supreme of all. But where the power to command is wanting, or where a law is enacted contrary to reason, or to the eternal law, or to some ordinance of God, obedience is unlawful, lest, while obeying man, we become disobedient to God. Thus, an effectual barrier being opposed to tyranny, the authority in the State will not have all its own way, but the interests and rights of all will be safeguarded—the rights of individuals, of domestic society and of all the members of the commonwealth; all being free to live according to law and right reason; and in this, as We have shown, true liberty really consists.

### Liberals Follow in the Footsteps of Lucifer

14. If when men discuss the question of liberty they were careful to grasp its true and legitimate meaning, such as reason and reasoning have just explained, they would never venture to affix such a calumny on the Church as to assert that she is the foe of individual and public liberty. But many there are who follow in the footsteps of Lucifer, and adopt as their own his rebellious cry,

"I will not serve," and consequently substitute for true liberty what is sheer and most foolish license. Such, for instance, are the men belonging to that widely spread and powerful organization, who, usurping the name of liberty, style themselves *liberals*.

## Denial of Divine Authority

15. What *naturalists* or *rationalists* aim at in philosophy, that the supporters of *Liberalism*, carrying out the principles laid down by naturalism, are attempting in the domain of morality and politics. The fundamental doctrine of rationalism is the supremacy of the human reason, which, refusing due submission to the divine and eternal reason, proclaims its own independence, and constitutes itself the supreme principle and source and judge of truth. Hence, these followers of Liberalism deny the existence of any divine authority to which obedience is due, and proclaim that every man is the law to himself; from which arises that ethical system which they style *independent* morality, and which, under the guise of liberty, exonerates man from any obedience to the commands of God, and substitutes a boundless license. The end of all this it is not difficult to foresee, especially when society is in question. For, when once man is firmly persuaded that he is subject to no one, it follows that the efficient cause of the unity of civil society is not to be sought in any principle external to man, or superior to him, but simply in the free will of individuals; that the authority in the State comes from the people only; and that, just as every man's individual reason is his only rule of life, so the collective reason of the community should be the supreme guide in the management of all public affairs. Hence the doctrine of the supremacy of the greater number, and that all right and all duty reside in the majority. But, from what has been said, it is clear that all this is in contradiction to reason. To refuse any bond of union between man and civil society, on the one hand, and God the Creator and consequently the supreme Law-giver, on the other, is plainly repugnant to the nature, not only of man, but of all created things; for, of necessity, all effects must in some proper way be connected with their cause; and it belongs to the perfec-

tion of every nature to contain itself within that sphere and grade which the order of nature has assigned to it, namely, that the lower should be subject and obedient to the higher.

### The Results of this Denial

16. Moreover, besides this, a doctrine of such character is most hurtful both to individuals and to the State. For, once ascribe to human reason the only authority to decide what is true and what is good, and the real distinction between good and evil is destroyed; honor and dishonor differ not in their nature, but in the opinion and judgment of each one; pleasure is the measure of what is lawful; and, given a code of morality which can have little or no power to restrain or quiet the unruly propensities of man, a way is naturally opened to universal corruption. With reference also to public affairs: authority is severed from the true and natural principle whence it derives all its efficacy for the common good; and the law determining what it is right to do and avoid doing is at the mercy of a majority. Now, this is simply a road leading straight to tyranny. The empire of God over man and civil society once repudiated, it follows that religion, as a public institution, can have no claim to exist, and that everything that belongs to religion will be treated with complete indifference. Furthermore, with ambitious designs on sovereignty, tumult and sedition will be common among the people; and when duty and conscience cease to appeal to them, there will be nothing to hold them back but force, which of itself alone is powerless to keep their covetousness in check. Of this we have almost daily evidence in the conflict with *Socialists* and members of other seditious societies, who labor unceasingly to bring about revolution. It is for those, then, who are capable of forming a just estimate of things to decide whether such doctrines promote that true liberty which alone is worthy of man, or rather, pervert and destroy it.

### Some Liberals Acknowledge Only Natural Law

17. There are, indeed, some adherents of Liberalism who do

not subscribe to these opinions, which we have seen to be fearful in their enormity, openly opposed to the truth and the cause of most terrible evils. Indeed, very many among them, compelled by the force of truth, do not hesitate to admit that such liberty is vicious, nay, is simple license, whenever intemperate in its claims, to the neglect of truth and justice; and therefore they would have liberty ruled and directed by right reason, and consequently subject to the natural law and to the divine eternal law. But here they think they may stop, holding that man as a free being is bound by no law of God except such as He makes known to us through our natural reason. In this they are plainly inconsistent. For if—as they must admit, and no one can rightly deny—the will of the Divine Law-giver is to be obeyed, because every man is under the power of God, and tends toward Him as his end, it follows that no one can assign limits to His legislative authority without failing in the obedience which is due. Indeed, if the human mind be so presumptuous as to define the nature and extent of God's rights and its own duties, reverence for the divine law will be apparent rather than real, and arbitrary judgment will prevail over the authority and providence of God. Man must, therefore, take his standard of a loyal and religious life from the eternal law; and from all and every one of those laws which God, in His infinite wisdom and power, has been pleased to enact and to make known to us by such clear and unmistakable signs as to leave no room for doubt. And the more so because laws of this kind have the same origin, the same author, as the eternal law, are absolutely in accordance with right reason, and perfect the natural law. These laws it is that embody the government of God, who graciously guides and directs the intellect and the will of man lest these fall into error. Let, then, that continue to remain in a holy and inviolable union which neither can nor should be separated; and in all things—for this is the dictate of right reason itself—let God be dutifully and obediently served.

### *Separation of Church and State Is Fatal*

18. There are others, somewhat more moderate though not

more consistent, who affirm that the morality of individuals is to be guided by the divine law, but not the morality of the State, so that in public affairs the commands of God may be passed over, and may be entirely disregarded in the framing of laws. Hence follows the fatal theory of the need of separation between Church and State. But the absurdity of such a position is manifest. Nature herself proclaims the necessity of the State providing means and opportunities whereby the community may be enabled to live properly, that is to say, according to the laws of God. For, since God is the source of all goodness and justice, it is absolutely ridiculous that the State should pay no attention to these laws or render them abortive by contrary enactments. Besides, those who are in authority owe it to the commonwealth not only to provide for its external well-being and the conveniences of life, but still more to consult the welfare of men's souls in the wisdom of their legislation. But, for the increase of such benefits, nothing more suitable can be conceived than the laws which have God for their author; and, therefore, they who in their government of the State take no account of these laws abuse political power by causing it to deviate from its proper end and from what nature itself prescribes. And, what is still more important, and what We have more than once pointed out, although the civil authority has not the same proximate end as the spiritual, nor proceeds on the same lines, nevertheless in the exercise of their separate powers they must occasionally meet. For their subjects are the same, and not infrequently they deal with the same objects, though in different ways. Whenever this occurs, since a state of conflict is absurd and manifestly repugnant to the most wise ordinance of God, there must necessarily exist some order or mode of procedure to remove the occasions of difference and contention, and to secure harmony in all things. This harmony has been not inaptly compared to that which exists between the body and the soul for the well-being of both one and the other, the separation of which brings irremediable harm to the body, since it extinguishes its very life.

### Liberty of Worship Is Erroneous

19. To make this more evident, the growth of liberty ascribed to our age must be considered apart in its various details. And first, let us examine that liberty in individuals which is so opposed to the virtue of religion, namely, the *liberty of worship*, as it is called. This is based on the principle that every man is free to profess, as he may choose, any religion or none.

### Man's Highest Duty Is Worship

20. But, assuredly, of all the duties which man has to fulfill, that, without doubt, is the chiefest and holiest which commands him to worship God with devotion and piety. This follows of necessity from the truth that we are ever in the power of God, are ever guided by His will and providence, and, having come forth from Him, must return to Him. Add to which, no true virtue can exist without religion, for moral virtue is concerned with those things which lead to God as man's supreme and ultimate good; and therefore religion, which (as St. Thomas says) "performs those actions which are directly and immediately ordained for the divine honor,"³ rules and tempers all virtues. And if it be asked which of the many conflicting religions it is necessary to adopt, reason and the natural law unhesitatingly tell us to practice that one which God enjoins, and which men can easily recognize by certain exterior notes whereby Divine Providence has willed that it should be distinguished, because, in a matter of such moment, the most terrible loss would be the consequence of error. Wherefore, when a liberty such as We have described is offered to man, the power is given him to pervert or abandon with impunity the most sacred of duties, and to exchange the unchangeable good for evil; which, as We have said, is no liberty, but its degradation, and the abject submission of the soul to sin.

### The State Must Protect the True Religion

21. This kind of liberty, if considered in relation to the State,

clearly implies that there is no reason why the State should offer any homage to God, or should desire any public recognition of Him; that no one form of worship is to be preferred to another, but that all stand on an equal footing, no account being taken of the religion of the people, even if they profess the Catholic Faith. But, to justify this, it must needs be taken as true that the State has no duties toward God, or that such duties, if they exist, can be abandoned with impunity, both of which assertions are manifestly false. For it cannot be doubted but that, by the will of God, men are united in civil society; whether its component parts be considered; or its form, which implies authority; or the object of its existence; or the abundance of the vast services which it renders to man. God it is who has made man for society, and has placed him in the company of others like himself, so that what was wanting to his nature, and beyond his attainment if left to his own resources, he might obtain by association with others. Wherefore, civil society must acknowledge God as its Founder and Parent, and must obey and reverence His power and authority. Justice therefore forbids, and reason itself forbids, the State to be godless; or to adopt a line of action which would end in godlessness— namely, to treat the various religions (as they call them) alike, and to bestow upon them promiscuously equal rights and privileges. Since, then, the profession of one religion is necessary in the State, that religion must be professed which alone is true, and which can be recognized without difficulty, especially in Catholic States, because the marks of truth are, as it were, engraven upon it. This religion, therefore, the rulers of the State must preserve and protect, if they would provide—as they should do—with prudence and usefulness for the good of the community. For public authority exists for the welfare of those whom it governs; and, although its proximate end is to lead men to the prosperity found in this life, yet, in so doing, it ought not to diminish, but rather to increase, man's capability of attaining to the supreme good in which his everlasting happiness consists: which never can be attained if religion be disregarded.

### Religion Helps the State

22. All this, however, We have explained more fully elsewhere. We now only wish to add the remark that liberty of so false a nature is greatly hurtful to the true liberty of both rulers and their subjects. Religion, of its essence, is wonderfully helpful to the State. For, since it derives the prime origin of all power directly from God Himself, with grave authority it charges rulers to be mindful of their duty, to govern without injustice or severity, to rule their people kindly and with almost paternal charity; it admonishes subjects to be obedient to lawful authority, as to the ministers of God; and it binds them to their rulers, not merely by obedience, but by reverence and affection, forbidding all seditions and venturesome enterprises calculated to disturb public order and tranquility and cause greater restrictions to be put upon the liberty of the people. We need not mention how greatly religion conduces to pure morals, and pure morals to liberty. Reason shows, and history confirms the fact, that the higher the morality of States, the greater are the liberty and wealth and power which they enjoy.

### Liberty of Speech and of the Press

23. We must now consider briefly *liberty of speech*, and liberty of the press. It is hardly necessary to say that there can be no such right as this, if it be not used in moderation, and if it pass beyond the bounds and end of all true liberty. For right is a moral power which—as We have before said and must again and again repeat—it is absurd to suppose that nature has accorded indifferently to truth and falsehood, to justice and injustice. Men have a right freely and prudently to propagate throughout the State what things soever are true and honorable, so that as many as possible may possess them; but lying opinions, than which no mental plague is greater, and vices which corrupt the heart and moral life should be diligently repressed by public authority, lest they insidiously work the ruin of the State. The excesses of an unbridled intellect, which unfailingly end in the oppression of the untutored

multitude, are no less rightly controlled by the authority of the law than are the injuries inflicted by violence upon the weak. And this all the more surely, because by far the greater part of the community is either absolutely unable, or able only with great difficulty, to escape from illusions and deceitful subtleties, especially such as flatter the passions. If unbridled license of speech and of writing be granted to all, nothing will remain sacred and inviolate; even the highest and truest mandates of natures, justly held to be the common and noblest heritage of the human race, will not be spared. Thus, truth being gradually obscured by darkness, pernicious and manifold error, as too often happens, will easily prevail. Thus, too, license will gain what liberty loses; for liberty will ever be more free and secure in proportion as license is kept in fuller restraint. In regard, however, to all matter of opinion which God leaves to man's free discussion, full liberty of thought and of speech is naturally within the right of everyone; for such liberty never leads men to suppress the truth, but often to discover it and make it known.

### Liberty of Teaching

24. A like judgment must be passed upon what is called *liberty of teaching*. There can be no doubt that truth alone should imbue the minds of men, for in it are found the well-being, the end and the perfection of every intelligent nature; and therefore nothing but truth should be taught both to the ignorant and to the educated, so as to bring knowledge to those who have it not, and to preserve it in those who possess it. For this reason it is plainly the duty of all who teach to banish error from the mind, and by sure safeguards to close the entry to all false convictions. From this it follows, as is evident, that the liberty of which We have been speaking is greatly opposed to reason, and tends absolutely to pervert men's minds, in as much as it claims for itself the right of teaching whatever it pleases—a liberty which the State cannot grant without failing in its duty. And the more so because the authority of teachers has great weight with their hearers, who can rarely decide for themselves as to the truth or falsehood of the instruction given to them.

## Natural Truth Is a Common Patrimony

25. Wherefore, this liberty, also, in order that it may deserve the name, must be kept within certain limits, lest the office of teaching be turned with impunity into an instrument of corruption. Now, truth, which should be the only subject matter of those who teach, is of two kinds: natural and supernatural. Of natural truths, such as the principles of nature and whatever is derived from them immediately by our reason, there is a kind of common patrimony in the human race. On this, as on a firm basis, morality, justice, religion and the very bonds of human society rest: and to allow people to go unharmed who violate or destroy it would be most impious, most foolish and most inhuman.

## God Is Man's Best Teacher

26. But with no less religious care must we preserve that great and sacred treasure of the truths which God Himself has taught us. By many and convincing arguments, often used by defenders of Christianity, certain leading truths have been laid down: namely, that some things have been revealed by God; that the only-begotten Son of God was made flesh, to bear witness to the truth; that a perfect society was founded by Him—the Church, namely, of which He is the head, and with which He has promised to abide till the end of the world. To this society He entrusted all the truths which He had taught, in order that it might keep and guard them and with lawful authority explain them; and at the same time He commanded all nations to hear the voice of the Church, as if it were His own, threatening those who would not hear it with everlasting perdition. Thus, it is manifest that man's best and surest teacher is God, the Source and Principle of all truth; and the only-begotten Son, who is in the bosom of the Father, the Way, the Truth and the Life, the true Light which enlightens every man, and to whose teaching all must submit: "And they shall all be taught of God." (*John* 6:45).

## The Church Partakes of God's Authority

27.  In faith and in the teaching of morality, God Himself made the Church a partaker of His divine authority, and through His heavenly gift she cannot be deceived. She is therefore the greatest and most reliable teacher of mankind, and in her swells an inviolable right to teach them. Sustained by the truth received from her divine Founder, the Church has ever sought to fulfill holily the mission entrusted to her by God; unconquered by the difficulties on all sides surrounding her, she has never ceased to assert her liberty of teaching, and in this way the wretched superstition of paganism being dispelled, the wide world was renewed unto Christian wisdom. Now, reason itself clearly teaches that the truths of Divine Revelation and those of nature cannot really be opposed to one another, and that whatever is at variance with them must necessarily be false. Therefore, the divine teaching of the Church, so far from being an obstacle to the pursuit of learning and the progress of science, or in any way retarding the advance of civilization, in reality brings to them the sure guidance of shining light. And for the same reason it is of no small advantage for the perfecting of human liberty, since our Saviour Jesus Christ has said that by truth is man made free: "You shall know the truth, and the truth shall make you free." (*John* 8:32). Therefore, there is no reason why genuine liberty should grow indignant, or true science feel aggrieved, at having to bear the just and necessary restraint of laws by which, in the judgment of the Church and of reason itself, human teaching has to be controlled.

## The Church Promotes Every Kind of Human Learning

28.  The Church, indeed—as facts have everywhere proved— looks chiefly and above all to the defense of the Christian Faith, while careful at the same time to foster and promote every kind of human learning. For learning is in itself good, and praiseworthy, and desirable; and further, all erudition which is the outgrowth of sound reason, and in conformity with the truth of things, serves not a little to confirm what we believe on the authority of God.

The Church, truly, to our great benefit, has carefully preserved the monuments of ancient wisdom; has opened everywhere homes of science, and has urged on intellectual progress by fostering most diligently the arts by which the culture of our age is so much advanced. Lastly, we must not forget that a vast field lies freely open to man's industry and genius, containing all those things which have no necessary connection with Christian faith and morals, or as to which the Church, exercising no authority, leaves the judgment of the learned free and unconstrained.

### Liberals Restrict the Church's Liberty

29. From all this may be understood the nature and character of that liberty which the followers of Liberalism so eagerly advocate and proclaim. On the one hand, they demand for themselves and for the State a license which opens the way to every perversity of opinion; and on the other, they hamper the Church in divers ways, restricting her liberty within narrowest limits, although from her teaching not only is there nothing to be feared, but in every respect very much to be gained.

### True and False Liberty of Conscience

30. Another liberty is widely advocated, namely, *liberty of conscience*. If by this is meant that everyone may, as he chooses, worship God or not, it is sufficiently refuted by the arguments already adduced. But it may also be taken to mean that every man in the State may follow the will of God and, from a consciousness of duty and free from every obstacle, obey His commands. This, indeed, is true liberty, a liberty worthy of the sons of God, which nobly maintains the dignity of man and is stronger than all violence or wrong—a liberty which the Church has always desired and held most dear. This is the kind of liberty the Apostles claimed for themselves with intrepid constancy, which the apologists of Christianity confirmed by their writings, and which the martyrs in vast numbers consecrated by their blood. And deservedly so; for this Christian liberty bears witness to the

absolute and most just dominion of God over man, and to the chief and supreme duty of man toward God. It has nothing in common with a seditious and rebellious mind; and in no tittle derogates from obedience to public authority; for the right to command and to require obedience exists only so far as it is in accordance with the authority of God, and is within the measure that He has laid down. But when anything is commanded which is plainly at variance with the will of God, there is a wide departure from this divinely constituted order, and at the same time a direct conflict with divine authority; therefore, it is right not to obey.

## Liberals Make the State Omnipotent

31. By the patrons of Liberalism, however, who make the State absolute and omnipotent, and proclaim that man should live altogether independently of God, the liberty of which We speak, which goes hand in hand with virtue and religion, is not admitted; and whatever is done for its preservation is accounted an injury and an offense against the State. Indeed, if what they say were really true, there would be no tyranny, no matter how monstrous, which we should not be bound to endure and submit to.

## Christian Teaching Should Penetrate Society

32. The Church most earnestly desires that the Christian teaching, of which We have given an outline, should penetrate every rank of society in reality and in practice; for it would be of the greatest efficacy in healing the evils of our day, which are neither few nor slight, and are the offspring in great part of the false liberty which is so much extolled, and in which the germs of safety and glory were supposed to be contained. The hope has been disappointed by the result. The fruit, instead of being sweet and wholesome, has proved cankered and bitter. If, then, a remedy is desired, let it be sought for in a restoration of sound doctrine, from which alone the preservation of order and, as a consequence, the defense of true liberty can be confidently expected.

### The Common Good May Require the Toleration of Evil

33. Yet, with the discernment of a true mother, the Church weighs the great burden of human weakness, and well knows the course down which the minds and actions of men are in this our age being borne. For this reason, while not conceding any right to anything save what is true and honest, she does not forbid public authority to tolerate what is at variance with truth and justice, for the sake of avoiding some greater evil, or of obtaining or preserving some greater good. God Himself in His providence, though infinitely good and powerful, permits evil to exist in the world, partly that greater good may not be impeded, and partly that greater evil may not ensue. In the government of States it is not forbidden to imitate the Ruler of the world; and, as the authority of man is powerless to prevent every evil, it has (as St. Augustine says) to overlook and leave unpunished many things which are punished, and rightly, by Divine Providence.[4] But if, in such circumstances, for the sake of the common good (and this is the only legitimate reason), human law may or even should tolerate evil, it may not and should not approve or desire evil for its own sake; for evil of itself, being a privation of good, is opposed to the common welfare which every legislator is bound to desire and defend to the best of his ability. In this, human law must endeavor to imitate God, who, as St. Thomas teaches, in allowing evil to exist in the world, "neither wills evil to be done, nor wills it not to be done, but wills only to permit it to be done; and this is good."[5] This saying of the Angelic Doctor contains briefly the whole doctrine of the permission of evil.

### Toleration of Evil to Be Strictly Limited

34. But, to judge aright, we must acknowledge that, the more a State is driven to tolerate evil, the further is it from perfection; and that the tolerance of evil which is dictated by political prudence should be strictly confined to the limits which its justifying cause, the public welfare, requires. Wherefore, if such tolerance would be injurious to the public welfare, and entail greater evils on the

State, it would not be lawful; for in such case the motive of good is wanting. And although in the extraordinary condition of these times the Church usually acquiesces in certain modern liberties, not because she prefers them in themselves, but because she judges it expedient to permit them, she would in happier times exercise her own liberty; and, by persuasion, exhortation and entreaty would endeavor, as she is bound, to fulfill the duty assigned to her by God of providing for the eternal salvation of mankind. One thing, however, remains always true—that the liberty which is claimed for all to do all things is not, as We have often said, of itself desirable, inasmuch as it is contrary to reason that error and truth should have equal rights.

### Liberals Allow Boundless License

35. And as to *tolerance*, it is surprising how far removed from the equity and prudence of the Church are those who profess what is called Liberalism. For, in allowing that boundless license of which We have spoken, they exceed all limits, and end at last by making no apparent distinction between truth and error, honesty and dishonesty. And because the Church, the pillar and ground of truth, and the unerring teacher of morals, is forced utterly to reprobate and condemn tolerance of such an abandoned and criminal character, they calumniate her as being wanting in patience and gentleness, and thus fail to see that, in so doing, they impute to her as a fault what is in reality a matter for commendation. But, in spite of all this show of tolerance, it very often happens that, while they profess themselves ready to lavish liberty on all in the greatest profusion, they are utterly intolerant toward the Catholic Church, by refusing to allow her the liberty of being herself free.

### True Liberty Is Submission to God

36. And now to reduce for clearness' sake to its principal heads all that has been set forth with its immediate conclusions, the summing up is this briefly: that man, by a necessity of his nature, is wholly subject to the most faithful and ever-enduring power of

God; and that, as a consequence, any liberty except that which consists in submission to God and in subjection to His will is unintelligible. To deny the existence of this authority in God, or to refuse to submit to it, means to act, not as a free man, but as one who treasonably abuses his liberty; and in such a disposition of mind the chief and deadly vice of Liberalism essentially consists. The form, however, of the sin is manifold; for in more ways and degrees than one can the will depart from the obedience which is due to God or to those who share the divine power.

### The Worst Kind of Liberalism

37. For, to reject the supreme authority of God, and to cast off all obedience to Him in public matters, or even in private and domestic affairs, is the greatest perversion of liberty and the worst kind of Liberalism; and what We have said must be understood to apply to this alone in its fullest sense.

### Some Adhere Only to Natural Reason

38. Next comes the system of those who admit indeed the duty of submitting to God, the Creator and Ruler of the world, inasmuch as all nature is dependent on His will, but who boldly reject all laws of faith and morals which are above natural reason but are revealed by the authority of God; or who at least impudently assert that there is no reason why regard should be paid to these laws, at any rate publicly, by the State. How mistaken these men also are, and how inconsistent, we have seen above. From this teaching, as from its source and principle, flows that fatal principle of the separation of Church and State; whereas it is, on the contrary, clear that the two powers, though dissimilar in functions and unequal in degree, ought nevertheless to live in concord, by harmony in their action and the faithful discharge of their respective duties.

*Separation of Church and State Is Unacceptable*

39. But this teaching is understood in two ways. Many wish the State to be separated from the Church wholly and entirely, so that with regard to every right of human society, in institutions, customs and laws, the offices of State and the education of youth, they would pay no more regard to the Church than if she did not exist; and, at most, would allow the citizens individually to attend to their religion in private if so minded. Against such as these, all the arguments by which We disprove the principle of separation of Church and State are conclusive, with this super-added, that it is absurd the citizen should respect the Church, while the State may hold her in contempt.

*The Rights of the Church*

40. Others oppose not the existence of the Church, nor indeed could they; yet they despoil her of the nature and rights of a perfect society, and maintain that it does not belong to her to legislate, to judge, or to punish, but only to exhort, to advise and to rule her subjects in accordance with their own consent and will. By such opinion they pervert the nature of this divine society, and attenuate and narrow its authority, its office of teacher and its whole efficiency; and at the same time they aggrandize the power of the civil government to such extent as to subject the Church of God to the empire and sway of the State, like any voluntary association of citizens. To refute completely such teaching, the arguments often used by the defenders of Christianity, and set forth by Us, especially in the encyclical letter *Immortale Dei*, are of great avail; for by those arguments it is proved that, by a divine provision, all the rights which essentially belong to a society that is legitimate, supreme and perfect in all its parts exist in the Church.

*Adaptation to the Times by the Church*

41. Lastly, there remain those who, while they do not approve the separation of Church and State, think nevertheless that the

Church ought to adapt herself to the times and conform to what is required by the modern system of government. Such an opinion is sound, if it is to be understood of some equitable adjustment consistent with truth and justice; in so far, namely, that the Church, in the hope of some great good, may show herself indulgent, and may conform to the times in so far as her sacred office permits. But it is not so in regard to practices and doctrines which a perversion of morals and a warped judgment have unlawfully introduced. Religion, truth and justice must ever be maintained; and, as God has entrusted these great and sacred matters to the care of the Church, she can never be so unfaithful to her office as to dissemble in regard to what is false or unjust, or to connive at what is hurtful to religion.

### Unconditional Freedom Is Unlawful

42. From what has been said it follows that it is quite unlawful to demand, to defend, or to grant unconditional freedom of thought, of speech, of writing, or of worship, as if these were so many rights given by nature to man. For, if nature had really granted them, it would be lawful to refuse obedience to God, and there would be no restraint on human liberty. It likewise follows that freedom in these things may be tolerated wherever there is just cause, but only with such moderation as will prevent its degenerating into license and excess. And, where such liberties are in use, men should employ them in doing good, and should estimate them as the Church does; for liberty is to be regarded as legitimate in so far only as it affords greater facility for doing good, but no farther.

### Suppression of True Liberty May Justify a Change of Government

43. Whenever there exists, or there is reason to fear, an unjust oppression of the people on the one hand, or a deprivation of the liberty of the Church on the other, it is lawful to seek for such a change of government as will bring about due liberty of action. In

such case, an excessive and vicious liberty is not sought, but only some relief, for the common welfare, in order that, while license for evil is allowed by the State, the power of doing good may not be hindered.

## Democratic Form of Government

44. Again, it is not of itself wrong to prefer a democratic form of government, if only the Catholic doctrine be maintained as to the origin and exercise of power. Of the various forms of government, the Church does not reject any that are fitted to procure the welfare of the subject; she wishes only—and this nature itself requires—that they should be constituted without involving wrong to any one, and especially without violating the rights of the Church.

## The Church Encourages Participation in Public Affairs

45. Unless it be otherwise determined, by reason of some exceptional condition of things, it is expedient to take part in the administration of public affairs. And the Church approves of every one devoting his services to the common good and doing all that he can for the defense, preservation and prosperity of his country.

## The Church Fosters Civil Liberty

46. Neither does the Church condemn those who, if it can be done without violation of justice, wish to make their country independent of any foreign or despotic power. Nor does she blame those who wish to assign to the State the power of self-government, and to its citizens the greatest possible measure of prosperity. The Church has always most faithfully fostered civil liberty, and this was seen especially in Italy, in the municipal prosperity and wealth and glory which were obtained at a time when the salutary power of the Church had spread, without opposition, to all parts of the State.

*Supplication to God*

47. These things, Venerable Brethren, which, under the guidance of faith and reason, in the discharge of Our Apostolic office, We have now delivered to you, We hope, especially by your cooperation with Us, will be useful unto very many. In lowliness of heart We raise Our eyes in supplication to God, and earnestly beseech Him to shed mercifully the light of His wisdom and of His counsel upon men, so that, strengthened by these heavenly gifts, they may in matters of such moment discern what is true, and may afterwards, in public and in private, at all times and with unshaken constancy, live in accordance with the truth. As a pledge of these heavenly gifts, and in witness of Our good will to you, Venerable Brethren, and to the clergy and people committed to each of you, We most lovingly grant in the Lord the Apostolic Benediction.

Given at St. Peter's in Rome, the twentieth day of June, 1888, the tenth year of Our Pontificate.

Leo XIII, Pope

### NOTES

1. Thomas Aquinas, *On the Gospel of St. John*, cap. 8, lect. 4, n. 3 (ed. Vives, Vol. 20, p. 95).
2. Augustine, *De libero arbitrio*, lib. 1, cap. 6, n. 15 (PL 32, 1229).
3. *Summa theologiae*, IIa-IIae, q. 81, a. 6, answer.
4. Augustine, *De libero arbitrio*, lib. 1, cap. 6, n. 14 (PL 32, 1228).
5. *Summa theologiae*, Ia, q. 19, a. 9, ad 3m.

Encyclical Letter of Pope Leo XIII

# ON THE CONDITION OF THE WORKING CLASSES
## *(Rerum Novarum)*

May 15, 1891

To Our Venerable Brethren
The Patriarchs, Primates, Archbishops, Bishops
and other Ordinaries of Places
Having Peace and Communion with the Apostolic See

Venerable Brethren,
Health and Apostolic Benediction

1. Once the passion for revolutionary change was aroused—
a passion long disturbing governments—it was bound to follow
sooner or later that eagerness for change would pass from the
political sphere over into the related field of economics. In fact,
new developments in industry, new techniques striking out on
new paths, changed relations of employer and employee, abound-
ing wealth among a very small number and destitution among the
masses, increased self-reliance on the part of workers as well as
a closer bond of union with one another, and, in addition to all
this, a decline in morals have caused conflict to break forth.

### *Problems Are of Universal Interest*

2. The momentous nature of the questions involved in this
conflict is evident from the fact that it keeps men's minds in anx-

ious expectation, occupying the talents of the learned, the discussions of the wise and experienced, the assemblies of the people, the judgment of lawmakers and the deliberations of rulers, so that now no topic more strongly holds men's interests.

### A Thorough Examination

3. Therefore, Venerable Brethren, with the cause of the Church and the common welfare before Us, We have thought it advisable, following Our custom on other occasions when We issued to you the Encyclicals *On Political Power, On Human Liberty, On the Christian Constitution of States*, and others of similar nature, which seemed opportune to refute erroneous opinions, that We ought to do the same now, and for the same reasons, *On the Condition of the Working Classes*. We have on occasion touched more than once upon this subject. In this Encyclical, however, consciousness of Our Apostolic office admonishes Us to treat the entire question thoroughly, in order that the principles may stand out in clear light and the conflict may thereby be brought to an end as required by truth and equity.

### Relations Between Capital and Labor

4. The problem is difficult to resolve and is not free from dangers. It is hard indeed to fix the boundaries of the rights and duties within which the rich and the proletariat—those who furnish material things and those who furnish work—ought to be restricted in relation to each other. The controversy is truly dangerous, for in various places it is being twisted by turbulent and crafty men to pervert judgment as to truth and seditiously to incite the masses.

### The Poor Deserve Relief

5. In any event, We see clearly, and all are agreed that the poor must be speedily and fittingly cared for, since the great majority of them live undeservedly in miserable and wretched conditions.

## Workers No Longer Protected

6. After the old trade guilds had been destroyed in the last century, and no protection was substituted in their place, and when public institutions and legislation had cast off traditional religious teaching, it gradually came about that the present age handed over the workers, each alone and defenseless, to the inhumanity of employers and the unbridled greed of competitors. A devouring usury, although often condemned by the Church, but practiced nevertheless under another form by avaricious and grasping men, has increased the evil; and in addition, the whole process of production as well as trade in every kind of goods has been brought almost entirely under the power of a few, so that a very few rich and exceedingly rich men have laid a yoke almost of slavery on the unnumbered masses of non-owning workers.

## Socialists Abolish Private Property

7. To cure this evil, the Socialists, exciting the envy of the poor toward the rich, contend that it is necessary to do away with private possession of goods and in its place to make the goods of individuals common to all, and that the men who preside over a municipality or who direct the entire State should act as administrators of these goods. They hold that, by such a transfer of private goods from private individuals to the community, they can cure the present evil through dividing wealth and benefits equally among the citizens.

## Socialism Is Highly Unjust

8. But their program is so unsuited for terminating the conflict that it actually injures the workers themselves. Moreover, it is highly unjust, because it violates the rights of lawful owners, perverts the functions of the State and throws governments into utter confusion.

## Private Property Gives Workers Hope

9. Clearly the essential reason why those who engage in any gainful occupation undertake labor, and at the same time the end to which workers immediately look, is to procure property for themselves and to retain it by individual right as theirs and as their very own. When the worker places his energy and his labor at the disposal of another, he does so for the purpose of getting the means necessary for livelihood. He seeks in return for the work done, accordingly, a true and full right not only to demand his wage but to dispose of it as he sees fit. Therefore, if he saves something by restricting expenditures and invests his savings in a piece of land in order to keep the fruit of his thrift more safe, a holding of this kind is certainly nothing else than his wage under a different form; and on this account, land which the worker thus buys is necessarily under his full control as much as the wage which he earned by his labor. But, as is obvious, it is clearly in this that the ownership of movable and immovable goods consists. Therefore, inasmuch as the Socialists seek to transfer the goods of private persons to the community at large, they make the lot of all wage earners worse, because in abolishing the freedom to dispose of wages, they take away from them by this very act the hope and the opportunity of increasing their property and of securing advantages for themselves.

## Private Property: A Natural Right

10. But, what is of more vital concern, they propose a remedy openly in conflict with justice, inasmuch as nature confers on man the right to possess things privately as his own.

## Man Is Made to Possess

11. In this respect also there is the widest difference between man and other living things. For brute beasts are not self-ruling, but are ruled and governed by a twofold innate instinct which not only keeps their faculty of action alert and

develops their powers properly, but also impels and determines their individual movements. By one instinct they are induced to protect themselves and their lives; by the other, to preserve their species. In truth, they attain both ends readily by using what is before them and within immediate range; and they cannot, of course, go further because they are moved to action by the senses alone and by the separate things perceived by the senses. Man's nature is quite different. In man there is likewise the entire and full perfection of animal nature, and consequently on this ground there is given to man, certainly no less than to every kind of living thing, to enjoy the benefits of corporeal goods. Yet animal nature, however perfectly possessed, is far from embracing human nature, but rather is much lower than human nature, having been created to serve and obey it. What stands out and excels in us, what makes man man and distinguishes him generically from the brute, is the mind or reason. And owing to the fact that this animal alone has reason, it is necessary that man have goods not only to be used, which is common to all living things, but also to be possessed by stable and perpetual right; and this applies not merely to those goods which are consumed by use, but to those also which endure after being used.

### Man Must Provide for His Future

12. This is even more clearly evident, if the essential nature of human beings is examined more closely. Since man by his reason understands innumerable things, linking and combining the future with the present, and since he is master of his own actions, therefore, under the eternal law, and under the power of God most wisely ruling all things, he rules himself by the foresight of his own counsel. Wherefore it is in his power to choose the things which he considers best adapted to benefit him not only in the present but also in the future. Whence it follows that dominion not only over the fruits of the earth but also over the earth itself ought to rest in man, since he sees that things necessary for the future are furnished him out of the produce of the earth. The needs of every man are subject, as it were, to constant recurrences, so that,

satisfied today, they make new demands tomorrow. Therefore, nature necessarily gave man something stable and perpetually lasting on which he can count for continuous support. But nothing can give continuous support of this kind save the earth with its great abundance.

### Man Is Prior to the State

13. There is no reason to interpose provision by the State, for man is older than the State. Wherefore he had to possess by nature his own right to protect his life and body before any polity had been formed.

### Private Ownership Serves the Common Good

14. The fact that God gave the whole human race the earth to use and enjoy cannot indeed in any manner serve as an objection against private possessions. For God is said to have given the earth to mankind in common, not because He intended indiscriminate ownership of it by all, but because He assigned no part to anyone in ownership, leaving the limits of private possessions to be fixed by the industry of men and the institutions of peoples. Yet, however the earth may be apportioned among private owners, it does not cease to serve the common interest of all, inasmuch as no living being is sustained except by what the fields bring forth. Those who lack resources supply labor, so that it can be truly affirmed that the entire scheme of securing a livelihood consists in the labor which a person expends either on his own land or in some working occupation, the compensation for which is drawn ultimately from no other source than from the varied products of the earth and is exchanged for them.

### Man Earns His Right to Property

15. For this reason it also follows that private possessions are clearly in accord with nature. The earth indeed produces in great abundance the things to preserve and, especially, to perfect life,

but of itself it could not produce them without human cultivation and care. Moreover, since man expends his mental energy and his bodily strength in procuring the goods of nature, by this very act he appropriates that part of physical nature to himself which he has cultivated. On it he leaves impressed, as it were, a kind of image of his person, so that it must be altogether just that he should possess that part as his very own and that no one in any way should be permitted to violate his right.

### Laborers Deserve the Fruits of Their Toil

16. The force of these arguments is so evident that it seems amazing that certain revivers of obsolete theories dissent from them. These men grant the individual the use of the soil and the varied fruits of the farm, but absolutely deny him the right to hold as owner either the ground on which he has built or the farm he has cultivated. When they deny this right they fail to see that a man will be defrauded of the things his labor has produced. The land, surely, that has been worked by the hand and the art of the tiller greatly changes in aspect. The wilderness is made fruitful; the barren field, fertile. But those things through which the soil has been improved so inhere in the soil and are so thoroughly intermingled with it, that they are for the most part quite inseparable from it. And, after all, would justice permit anyone to own and enjoy that upon which another has toiled? As effects follow the cause producing them, so it is just that the fruit of labor belongs precisely to those who have performed the labor.

### Divine Law Protects Property Rights

17. Rightly therefore, the human race as a whole, moved in no wise by the dissenting opinions of a few, and observing nature carefully, has found in the law of nature itself the basis of the distribution of goods, and, by the practice of all ages, has consecrated private possession as something best adapted to man's nature and to peaceful and tranquil living together. Now civil laws, which, when just, derive their power from the natural law itself, confirm

and, even by the use of force, protect this right of which we speak—and this same right has been sanctioned by the authority of the divine law, which forbids us most strictly even to desire what belongs to another. "Thou shalt not covet thy neighbour's wife: nor his house, nor his field, nor his man-servant, nor his maid-servant, nor his ox, nor his ass, nor any thing that is his." (*Deut.* 5:21)

## Obligations of Family Life

18. Rights of this kind which reside in individuals are seen to have much greater validity when viewed as fitted into and connected with the obligations of human beings in family life.

## Right of Ownership by Head of the Family

19. There is no question that in choosing a state of life it is within the power and discretion of individuals to prefer the one or the other state, either to follow the counsel of Jesus Christ regarding virginity or to bind oneself in marriage. No law of man can abolish the natural and primeval right of marriage, or in any way set aside the chief purpose of matrimony established in the beginning by the authority of God: "Increase and multiply." (*Gen.* 1:28). Behold, therefore, the family, or rather the society of the household, a very small society indeed, but a true one, and older than any polity! For that reason it must have certain rights and duties of its own entirely independent of the State. Thus, right of ownership, which we have shown to be bestowed on individual persons by nature, must be assigned to man in his capacity as head of a family. Nay, rather, this right is all the stronger since the human person in family life embraces much more.

## Authority of the Father

20. It is a most sacred law of nature that the father of a family see that his offspring are provided with all the necessities of life, and nature even prompts him to desire to provide and to fur-

nish his children, who in fact reflect and in a sense continue his person, with the means of decently providing themselves against harsh fortune in the uncertainties of life. He can do this surely in no other way than by owning fruitful goods to transmit by inheritance to his children. As already noted, the family, like the State, is by the same token a society in the strictest sense of the term, and it is governed by its own proper authority, namely, by that of the father. Wherefore, assuming, of course, that those limits be observed which are fixed by its immediate purpose, the family assuredly possesses rights, at least equal with those of civil society, in respect to choosing and employing the things necessary for its protection and its just liberty. We say "at least equal" because, inasmuch as domestic living together is prior both in thought and in fact to uniting into a polity, it follows that its rights and duties are also prior and more in conformity with nature. But if citizens, if families, after becoming participants in common life and society, were to experience injury in a commonwealth instead of help, impairment of their rights instead of protection, society would be something to be repudiated rather than to be sought for.

*Paternal Authority Must Not Be Absorbed by the State*

21. To desire, therefore, that the civil power should enter arbitrarily into the privacy of homes is a great and pernicious error. If a family perchance is in such extreme difficulty and is so completely without plans that it is entirely unable to help itself, it is right that the distress be remedied by public aid, for each individual family is a part of the community. Similarly, if anywhere there is a grave violation of mutual rights within the family walls, public authority shall restore to each his right: for this is not usurping the rights of citizens, but protecting and confirming them with just and due care. Those in charge of public affairs, however, must stop here: nature does not permit them to go beyond these limits. Paternal authority is such that it can be neither abolished nor absorbed by the State, because it has the same origin in common with that of man's own life. "Children are a part of their father" and, as it were, a kind of extension of the father's person; and,

strictly speaking, not through themselves, but through the medium of the family society in which they are begotten, they enter into and participate in civil society. And for the very reason that children "are by nature part of their father . . . before they have the use of free will, they are kept under the care of their parents."[1] Inasmuch as the Socialists, therefore, disregard care by parents and in its place introduce care by the State, they act *against natural justice* and dissolve the structure of the home.

### Socialism Dries Up the Fountains of Wealth

22. And apart from the injustice involved, it is also only too evident what turmoil and disorder would obtain among all classes, and what a harsh and odious enslavement of citizens would result! The door would be open to mutual envy, detraction and dissension. If incentives to ingenuity and skill in individual persons were to be abolished, the very fountains of wealth would necessarily dry up; and the equality conjured up by the Socialist imagination would, in reality, be nothing but uniform wretchedness and meanness for one and all, without distinction.

### Socialism Is Fundamentally Wrong

23. From all these conversations, it is perceived that the fundamental principle of Socialism which would make all possessions public property is to be utterly rejected because it injures the very ones whom it seeks to help, contravenes the natural rights of individual persons, and throws the functions of the State and public peace into confusion. Let it be regarded, therefore, as established that in seeking help for the masses this principle before all is to be considered as basic, namely, that private ownership must be preserved inviolate. With this understood, we shall explain whence the desired remedy is to be sought.

### No Satisfactory Solution without Religion

24. We approach the subject with confidence and surely by

Our right, for the question under consideration is certainly one for which no satisfactory solution will be found unless religion and the Church have been called upon to aid. Moreover, since the safeguarding of religion and of all things within the jurisdiction of the Church is primarily Our stewardship, silence on Our part might be regarded as failure in Our duty.

## The Church Is Our Guide

25. Assuredly, a question as formidable as this requires the attention and effort of others as well, namely, the heads of the State, employers and the rich and, finally, those in whose behalf efforts are being made, the workers themselves. Yet without hesitation We affirm that if the Church is disregarded, human striving will be in vain. Manifestly, it is the Church which draws from the Gospel the teachings through which the struggle can be calmed entirely or, after its bitterness is removed, can certainly become more tempered. It is the Church, again, that strives not only to instruct the mind but to regulate by her precepts the life and morals of individuals, that ameliorates the condition of the workers through her numerous and beneficent institutions, and that wishes and aims to have the thought and energy of all classes of society united to this end, that the interests of the workers be protected as fully as possible. And to accomplish this purpose she holds that the laws and the authority of the State, within reasonable limits, ought to be employed.

## Men Are by Nature Unequal

26. Therefore, let it be laid down in the first place that a condition of human existence must be borne with, namely, that in civil society the lowest cannot be made equal with the highest. Socialists, of course, agitate the contrary, but all struggling against nature is vain. There are truly very great and very many natural differences among men. Neither the talents, nor the skill, nor the health, nor the capacities of all are the same, and unequal fortune follows of itself upon necessary inequality in respect to

these endowments. And clearly this condition of things is adapted
to benefit both individuals and the community; for to carry on its
affairs community life requires varied aptitudes and diverse services, and to perform these diverse services men are impelled
most by differences in individual property holdings.

### Man Is Meant to Labor

27. So far as bodily labor is concerned, man even before the
Fall was not destined to be wholly idle; but certainly what his will
at that time would have freely embraced to his soul's delight,
necessity afterwards forced him to accept, with a feeling of irk-
someness, for the expiation of his guilt. "Cursed is the earth in thy
work; with labour and toil shalt thou eat thereof all the days of thy
life." (*Gen.* 3:17). Likewise there is to be no end on earth of other
hardships, for the evil consequences of sin are hard, trying and
bitter to bear, and will necessarily accompany men even to the end
of life. Therefore, to suffer and endure is human, and although
men may strive in all possible ways, they will never be able by any
power or art wholly to banish such tribulations from human life.
If any claim they can do this, if they promise the poor in their misery a life free from all sorrow and vexation and filled with repose
and perpetual pleasures, they actually impose upon these people
and perpetuate a fraud which will ultimately lead to evils greater
than the present. The best course is to view human affairs as they
are and, as We have stated, at the same time seek appropriate relief
for these troubles elsewhere.

### Classes Can Be in Harmony

28. It is a capital evil with respect to the question We are dis-
cussing to take for granted that the one class of society is of itself
hostile to the other, as if nature had set rich and poor against each
other to fight fiercely in implacable war. This is so abhorrent to
reason and truth that the exact opposite is true; for just as in the
human body the different members harmonize with one another,
whence arises that disposition of parts and proportion in the

human figure rightly called symmetry, so likewise nature has commanded in the case of the State that the two classes mentioned should agree harmoniously and should properly form equally balanced counterparts to each other. Each needs the other completely: neither capital can do without labor, nor labor without capital. Concord begets beauty and order in things. Conversely, from perpetual strife there must arise disorder accompanied by bestial cruelty. But for putting an end to conflict and for cutting away its very roots, there is wondrous and multiple power in Christian institutions.

### Faith Unites Us

29. And first and foremost, the entire body of religious teaching and practice, of which the Church is interpreter and guardian, can pre-eminently bring together and unite the rich and the poor by recalling the two classes of society to their mutual duties, and in particular to those duties which derive from justice.

### Duties of Workers

30. Among these duties the following concern the poor and the workers: To perform entirely and conscientiously whatever work has been voluntarily and equitably agreed upon; not in any way to injure the property or to harm the person of employers; in protecting their own interests, to refrain from violence and never to engage in rioting; not to associate with vicious men who craftily hold out exaggerated hopes and make huge promises, a course usually ending in vain regrets and in the destruction of wealth.

### Duties of Employers

31. The following duties, on the other hand, concern rich men and employers: Workers are not to be treated as slaves; justice demands that the dignity of human personality be respected in them, ennobled as it has been through what we call the Christian

character. If we hearken to natural reason and to Christian philosophy, gainful occupations are not a mark of shame to man, but rather of respect, as they provide him with an honorable means of supporting life. It is shameful and inhuman, however, to use men as things for gain and to put no more value on them than what they are worth in muscle and energy. Likewise it is enjoined that the religious interests and the spiritual well-being of the workers receive proper consideration. Wherefore, it is the duty of employers to see that the worker is free for adequate periods to attend to his religious obligations; not to expose anyone to corrupting influences or the enticements of sin, and in no way to alienate him from care for his family and the practice of thrift. Likewise, more work is not to be imposed than strength can endure, nor that kind of work which is unsuited to a worker's age or sex.

### Workers Deserve a Just Wage

32. Among the most important duties of employers the principal one is to give every worker what is justly due him. Assuredly, to establish a rule of pay in accord with justice, many factors must be taken into account. But, in general, the rich and employers should remember that no laws, either human or divine, permit them for their own profit to oppress the needy and the wretched or to seek gain from another's want. To defraud anyone of the wage due him is a great crime that calls down avenging wrath from Heaven. "Behold the hire of the labourers, who have reaped down your fields, which by fraud has been kept back by you, crieth: and the cry of them hath entered into the ears of the Lord of sabaoth." (*James* 5:4). Finally, the rich must religiously avoid harming in any way the savings of the workers either by coercion, or by fraud, or by the arts of usury; and the more for this reason, that the workers are not sufficiently protected against injustices and violence, and their property, being so meagre, ought to be regarded as all the more sacred. Could not the observance alone of the foregoing laws remove the bitterness and the causes of conflict?

### We Are Made for Heaven

33. But the Church, with Jesus Christ as her teacher and leader, seeks greater things than this; namely, by commanding something more perfect, she aims at joining the two social classes to each other in closest neighborliness and friendship. We cannot understand and evaluate mortal things rightly unless the mind reflects upon the other life, the life which is immortal. If this other life indeed were taken away, the form and true notion of the right would immediately perish; nay, this entire world would become an enigma insoluble to man. Therefore, what we learn from nature itself as our teacher is also a Christian dogma and on it the whole system and structure of religion rests, as it were, on its main foundation; namely, that when we have left this life, only then shall we truly begin to live. God has not created man for the fragile and transitory things of this world, but for Heaven and eternity, and He has ordained the earth as a place of exile, not as our permanent home. Whether you abound in, or whether you lack, riches and all the other things which are called good, is of no importance in relation to eternal happiness. But how you use them, that is truly of utmost importance. Jesus Christ by His "plentiful redemption" has by no means taken away the various tribulations with which mortal life is interwoven, but has so clearly transformed them into incentives to virtue and sources of merit that no mortal can attain eternal reward unless he follows the blood-stained footsteps of Jesus Christ. "If we suffer . . . we shall also reign with Him." (2 Tim. 2:12). By the labors and suffering which He voluntarily accepted, He has wondrously lightened the burden of suffering and labor, and not only by His example but also by His grace and by holding before us the hope of eternal reward. He has made endurance of sorrows easier: "for that which is at present momentary and light of our tribulation, worketh for us above measure exceedingly an eternal weight of glory." (2 Cor. 4:17).

### Wealth a Hindrance to Attaining Eternal Life

34. Therefore, the well-to-do are admonished that wealth does

not give surcease of sorrow, and that wealth is of no avail unto the happiness of eternal life but is rather a hindrance (*Matt.* 19:23, 24); that the threats pronounced by Jesus Christ, so unusual coming from Him, ought to cause the rich to fear (*Luke* 6:24, 25); and that one day the strictest account for the use of wealth must be rendered to God as Judge.

### The Just Use of Wealth

35. On the use of wealth we have the excellent and extremely weighty teaching which, although found in a rudimentary stage in pagan philosophy, the Church has handed down in a completely developed form and causes to be observed not only in theory but in everyday life. The foundation of this teaching rests on this, that the just ownership of money is distinct from the just use of money.

### Charity toward the Poor

36. To own goods privately, as We saw above, is a right natural to man, and to exercise this right, especially in life in society, is not only lawful, but clearly necessary. "It is lawful for man to own his own things. It is even necessary for human life."[2] But if the question be asked: How ought man use his possessions? the Church replies without hesitation: "As to this point, man ought not regard external goods as his own, but as common, so that, in fact, a person should readily share them when he sees others in need. Wherefore the Apostle says: 'Charge the rich of this world . . . to give easily, to communicate to others.'"[3] No one, certainly, is obliged to assist others out of what is required for his own necessary use or for that of his family, or even to give to others what he himself needs to maintain his station in life becomingly and decently: "No one is obliged to live unbecomingly."[4] But when the demands of necessity and propriety have been sufficiently met, it is a duty to give to the poor out of that which remains. "But yet that which remaineth, give alms." (*Luke* 11:41). These are duties not of justice, except in cases of extreme need, but of Christian charity, which obviously cannot be enforced by legal action. But

the laws and judgments of men yield precedence to the law and judgment of Christ the Lord, who in many ways urges the practice of almsgiving: "It is a more blessed thing to give, rather than to receive" (*Acts* 20:35), and who will judge a kindness done or denied to the poor as done or denied to Himself. "As long as you did it to one of these my least brethren, you did it to me." (*Matt.* 25:40). The substance of all this is the following: Whoever has received from the bounty of God a greater share of goods, whether corporeal and external, or of the soul, has received them for this purpose, namely, that he employ them for his own perfection and, likewise, as a servant of Divine Providence, for the benefit of others. "Therefore, he that hath talent, let him constantly see to it that he be not silent; he that hath an abundance of goods, let him be on the watch that he grow not slothful in the generosity of mercy; he that hath a trade whereby he supports himself, let him be especially eager to share with his neighbor the use and benefit thereof."[5]

## *True Dignity Attainable by All*

37. Those who lack fortune's goods are taught by the Church that, before God as Judge, poverty is no disgrace, and that no one should be ashamed because he makes his living by toil. And Jesus Christ has confirmed this by fact and by deed, who for the salvation of men, "being rich he became poor" (*2 Cor.* 8:9); and although He was the Son of God and God Himself, yet He willed to seem and to be thought the son of a carpenter; nay, He even did not disdain to spend a great part of His life at the work of a carpenter. "Is not this the carpenter, the son of Mary?" (*Mark* 6:3). Those who contemplate this Divine example will more easily understand these truths: True dignity and excellence in men resides in moral living, that is, in virtue; virtue is the common inheritance of man, attainable equally by the humblest and the mightiest, by the rich and the poor; and the reward of eternal happiness will follow upon virtue and merit alone, regardless of the person in whom they may be found. Nay, rather the favor of God Himself seems to incline more toward the unfortunate as a class;

for Jesus Christ calls the poor blessed (*Matt.* 5:3), and He invites most lovingly all who are in labor or sorrow to come to Him for solace (*Matt.* 11:28), embracing with special love the lowly and those harassed by injustice. At the realization of these things the proud spirit of the rich is easily brought down, and the downcast heart of the afflicted is lifted up; the former are moved toward kindness, the latter toward reasonableness in their demands. Thus the distance between the classes which pride seeks is reduced, and it will easily be brought to pass that the two classes, with hands clasped in friendship, will be united in heart.

### The Bonds of Christian Brotherhood

38. Yet, if they obey Christian teachings, not merely friendship but brotherly love also will bind them to each other. They will feel and understand that all men indeed have been created by God, their common Father; that all strive for the same object of good, which is God Himself, who alone can communicate to both men and Angels perfect and absolute happiness; that all equally have been redeemed by the grace of Jesus Christ and restored to the dignity of the sons of God, so that they are clearly united by the bonds of brotherhood not only with one another but also with Christ the Lord, "the firstborn amongst many brethren" (*Rom.* 8:29), and further, that the goods of nature and the gifts of divine grace belong in common and without distinction to all human kind, and that no one, unless he is unworthy, will be deprived of the inheritance of Heaven. "And if sons, heirs also; heirs indeed of God, and joint heirs with Christ." (*Rom.* 8:17).

### Christian Philosophy Resolves Conflicts

39. Such is the economy of duties and rights according to Christian philosophy. Would it not seem that all conflict would soon cease wherever this economy were to prevail in civil society?

*The Church Has Divine Power to Penetrate Hearts*

40. Finally, the Church does not consider it enough to point out the way of finding the cure, but she administers the remedy herself. For she occupies herself fully in training and forming men according to discipline and doctrine; and through the agency of bishops and clergy, she causes the health-giving streams of this doctrine to be diffused as widely as possible. Furthermore, she strives to enter into men's minds and to bend their wills so that they may suffer themselves to be ruled and governed by the discipline of the divine precepts. And in this field, which is of first and greatest importance because in it the whole substance and matter of benefits consists, the Church indeed has a power that is especially unique. For the instruments which she uses to move souls were given her for this very purpose by Jesus Christ, and they have an efficacy implanted in them by God. Such instruments alone can properly penetrate the inner recesses of the heart and lead man to obedience to duty, to govern the activities of his self-seeking mind, to love God and his neighbors with a special and sovereign love and to overcome courageously all things that impede the path of virtue.

*Only Christian Life and Institutions Will Heal Society*

41. In this connection it is sufficient briefly to recall to mind examples from history. We shall mention events and facts that admit of no doubt, namely, that human society in its civil aspects was renewed fundamentally by Christian institutions; that, by virtue of this renewal, mankind was raised to a higher level, nay, was called back from death to life, and enriched with such a degree of perfection as has never existed before and was not destined to be greater in any succeeding age; and that, finally, the same Jesus Christ is the beginning and the end of these benefits; for as all things have proceeded from Him, so they must be referred back to Him. When, with the acceptance of the light of the Gospel, the world had learned the great mystery of the Incarnation of the Word and the redemption of man, the life of Jesus Christ, God and man, spread through the nations and imbued

them wholly with His doctrine, with His precepts and with His laws. Wherefore, if human society is to be healed, only a return to Christian life and institutions will heal it. In the case of decaying societies it is most correctly prescribed that, if they wish to be regenerated, they must be recalled to their origins. For the perfection of all associations is this, namely, to work for and to attain the purpose for which they were formed, so that all social actions should be inspired by the same principle which brought the society itself into being. Wherefore, turning away from the original purpose is corruption, while going back to this purpose is recovery. And just as we affirm this as unquestionably true of the entire body of the commonwealth, in like manner we affirm it of that order of citizens who sustain life by labor and who constitute the vast majority of society.

### Christian Morals Yield Prosperity

42. But it must not be supposed that the Church so concentrates her energies on caring for souls as to overlook things which pertain to mortal and earthly life. As regards the non-owning workers specifically, she desires and strives that they rise from their most wretched state and enjoy better conditions. And to achieve this result she makes no small contribution by the very fact that she calls men to and trains them in virtue. For when Christian morals are completely observed, they yield of themselves a certain measure of prosperity to material existence, because they win the favor of God, the source and fountain of all goods; because they restrain the twin plagues of life—excessive desire for wealth (*1 Tim.* 6:10) and thirst for pleasure—which too often make man wretched amidst the very abundance of riches; and because, finally, Christian morals make men content with a moderate livelihood and make them supplement income by thrift, removing them far from the vices which swallow up both modest sums and huge fortunes, and dissipate splendid inheritances.

*Works of Mercy*

43. But, in addition, the Church provides directly for the well-being of the non-owning workers by instituting and promoting activities which she knows to be suitable to relieve their distress. Nay, even in the field of works of mercy, she has always so excelled that she is highly praised by her very enemies. The force of mutual charity among the first Christians was such that the wealthier very often divested themselves of their riches to aid others; wherefore: "For neither was there any one needy among them." (*Acts* 4:34). To the deacons, an order founded expressly for this purpose, the Apostles assigned the duty of dispensing alms daily; and the Apostle Paul, although burdened with the care of all the churches, did not hesitate to spend himself on toilsome journeys in order to bring alms personally to the poorer Christians. Monies of this kind, contributed voluntarily by the Christians in every assembly, Tertullian calls "piety's deposit fund," because they were expended to "support and bury poor people, to supply the wants of orphan boys and girls without means of support, of aged household servants and of such, too, as had suffered shipwreck."[6]

### The Church Protects the Poor

44. Thence, gradually there came into existence that patrimony which the Church has guarded with religious care as the property of the poor. Nay, even disregarding the feeling of shame associated with begging, she provided aid for the wretched poor. For, as the common parent of rich and poor, with charity everywhere stimulated to the highest degree, she founded religious societies and numerous other useful bodies, so that, with the aid which these furnished, there was scarcely any form of human misery that went uncared for.

### Only Christ Inspires True Charity

45. And yet many today go so far as to condemn the Church,

as the ancient pagans once did, for such outstanding charity, and would substitute in lieu thereof a system of benevolence established by the laws of the State. But no human devices can ever be found to supplant Christian charity, which gives itself entirely for the benefit of others. This virtue belongs to the Church alone, for, unless it is derived from the Most Sacred Heart of Jesus, it is in no wise a virtue; and whosoever departs from the Church wanders far from Christ.

## Men Must Cooperate

46. But there can be no question that, to attain Our purpose, those helps also which are within the power of men are necessary. Absolutely all who are concerned with the matter must, according to their capacity, bend their efforts to this same end and work for it. And this activity has a certain likeness to Divine Providence governing the world; for generally we see effects flow from the concert of all the elements upon which as causes these effects depend.

## Duty of the State

47. But it is now in order to inquire what portion of the remedy should be expected from the State. By State here We understand not the form of government which this or that people has, but rather that form which right reason in accordance with nature requires and the teachings of Divine wisdom approve, matters that We have explained specifically in Our Encyclical *On the Christian Constitution of States*.

## Protecting the Common Good

48. Therefore, those governing the State ought primarily to devote themselves to the service of individual groups and of the whole commonwealth, and through the entire scheme of laws and institutions to cause both public and individual well-being to develop spontaneously out of the very structure and administra-

tion of the State. For this is the duty of wise statesmanship and the essential office of those in charge of the State. Now, States are made prosperous especially by wholesome morality, properly ordered family life, protection of religion and justice, moderate imposition and equitable distribution of public burdens, progressive development of industry and trade, thriving agriculture and by all other things of this nature, which the more actively they are promoted, the better and happier the life of the citizens is destined to be. Therefore, by virtue of these things, it is within the competence of the rulers of the State that, as they benefit other groups, they also improve in particular the condition of the workers. Furthermore, they do this with full right and without laying themselves open to any charge of unwarranted interference. For the State is bound by the very law of its office to serve the common interest. And the richer the benefits which come from this general providence on the part of the State, the less necessary it will be to experiment with other measures for the well-being of workers.

### Purpose of the State

49. This ought to be considered, as it touches the question more deeply, namely, that the State has one basic purpose for existence, which embraces in common the highest and the lowest of its members. Non-owning workers are unquestionably citizens by nature in virtue of the same right as the rich, that is, true and vital parts whence, through the medium of families, the body of the State is constituted; and it hardly need be added that they are by far the greatest number in every urban area. Since it would be quite absurd to look out for one portion of the citizens and to neglect another, it follows that public authority ought to exercise due care in safeguarding the well-being and the interests of non-owning workers. Unless this is done, justice, which commands that everyone be given his own, will be violated. Wherefore St. Thomas says wisely: "Even as part and whole are in a certain way the same, so too that which pertains to the whole pertains in a certain way to the part also."[7] Consequently, among the numerous and weighty duties of rulers who would serve their people well,

this is first and foremost, namely, that they protect equitably each and every class of citizen, maintaining inviolate that justice especially which is called *distributive*.

## All Should Contribute to the Common Good

50. Although all citizens, without exception, are obliged to contribute something to the sum-total common goods, some share of which naturally goes back to each individual, yet all can by no means contribute the same amount and in equal degree. Whatever the vicissitudes that occur in the forms of government, there will always be those differences in the condition of citizens without which society could neither exist nor be conceived. It is altogether necessary that there be some who dedicate themselves to the service of the State, who make laws, who dispense justice and finally, by whose counsel and authority civil and military affairs are administered. These men, as is clear, play the chief role in the State, and among every people are to be regarded as occupying first place, because they work for the common good most directly and pre-eminently. On the other hand, those engaged in some calling benefit the State, but not in the same way as the men just mentioned, nor by performing the same duties; yet they, too, in a high degree, although less directly, serve the public weal. Assuredly, since social good must be of such a character that men through its acquisition are made better, it must necessarily be founded chiefly on virtue.

## Wealth Originates from Labor

51. Nevertheless, an abundance of corporeal and external goods is likewise a characteristic of a well constituted State, "the use of which goods is necessary for the practice of virtue."[8] To produce these goods the labor of the workers, whether they expend their skill and strength on farms or in factories, is most efficacious and necessary. Nay, in this respect, their energy and effectiveness are so important that it is incontestable that the wealth of nations originates from no other source than from the

labor of workers. Equity therefore commands that public authority show proper concern for the worker so that from what he contributes to the common good he may receive what will enable him, housed, clothed and secure, to live his life without hardship. Whence it follows that all those measures ought to be favored which seem in any way capable of benefiting the condition of workers. Such solicitude is so far from injuring anyone that it is destined rather to benefit all, because it is of absolute interest to the State that those citizens should not be miserable in every respect from whom such necessary goods proceed.

### Duties of Those Who Govern

52. It is not right, as We have said, for either the citizen or the family to be absorbed by the State; it is proper that the individual and the family should be permitted to retain their freedom of action, so far as this is possible without jeopardizing the common good and without injuring anyone. Nevertheless, those who govern must see to it that they protect the community and its constituent parts: the community, because nature has entrusted its safeguarding to the sovereign power in the State to such an extent that the protection of the public welfare is not only the supreme law, but is the entire cause and reason for sovereignty; and the constituent parts, because philosophy and Christian faith agree that the administration of the State has from nature as its purpose, not the benefit of those to whom it has been entrusted, but the benefit of those who have been entrusted to it. And since the power of governing comes from God and is a participation, as it were, in His supreme sovereignty, it ought to be administered according to the example of the Divine power, which looks with paternal care to the welfare of individual creatures as well as to that of all creation. If, therefore, any injury has been done to or threatens either the common good or the interests of individual groups, which injury cannot in any other way be repaired or prevented, it is necessary for public authority to intervene.

### When the Law Should Intervene

53. It is vitally important to public as well as to private welfare that there be peace and good order; likewise, that the whole regime of family life be directed according to the ordinances of God and the principles of nature, that religion be observed and cultivated, that sound morals flourish in private and public life, that justice be kept sacred and that no one be wronged with impunity by another and that strong citizens grow up, capable of supporting, and, if necessary, of protecting the State. Wherefore, if at any time disorder should threaten because of strikes or concerted stoppages of work, if the natural bonds of family life should be relaxed among the poor, if religion among the workers should be outraged by failure to provide sufficient opportunity for performing religious duties, if in factories danger should assail the integrity of morals through the mixing of the sexes or other pernicious incitements to sin, or if the employer class should oppress the working class with unjust burdens or should degrade them with conditions inimical to human personality or to human dignity, if health should be injured by immoderate work and such as is not suited to sex or age—in all these cases, the power and authority of the law, but of course within certain limits, manifestly ought to be employed. And these limits are determined by the same reason which demands the aid of the law, that is, the law ought not undertake more, nor go further, than the remedy of evils or the removal of danger requires.

### Special Care to Protect Workers

54. Rights indeed, by whomsoever possessed, must be religiously protected; and public authority, in warding off injuries and punishing wrongs, ought to see to it that individuals may have and hold what belongs to them. In protecting the rights of private individuals, however, special consideration must be given to the weak and the poor. For the nation, as it were, of the rich, is guarded by its own defenses and is in less need of governmental protection, whereas the suffering multitude, without the means to protect

itself, relies especially on the protection of the State. Wherefore, since wage workers are numbered among the great mass of the needy, the State must include them under its special care and foresight.

### Laws Must Protect Private Property

55. But it will be well to touch here expressly on certain matters of special importance. The capital point is this, that private property ought to be safeguarded by the sovereign power of the State and through the bulwark of its laws. And especially, in view of such a great flaming up of passion at the present time, the masses ought to be kept within the bounds of their moral obligations. For while justice does not oppose our striving for better things, on the other hand, it does forbid anyone to take from another what is his and, in the name of a certain absurd equality, to seize forcibly the property of others; nor does the interest of the common good itself permit this. Certainly, the great majority of working people prefer to secure better conditions by honest toil, without doing wrong to anyone. Nevertheless, not a few individuals are found who, imbued with evil ideas and eager for revolution, use every means to stir up disorder and incite to violence. The authority of the State, therefore, should intervene and, by putting restraint upon such disturbers, protect the morals of workers from their corrupting arts and lawful owners from the danger of spoliation.

### Public Authority and Labor Strikes

56. Labor which is too long and too hard and the belief that pay is inadequate not infrequently give workers cause to strike and become voluntarily idle. This evil, which is frequent and serious, ought to be remedied by public authority, because such interruption of work inflicts damage not only upon employers and upon the workers themselves, but also injures trade and commerce and the general interests of the State; and, since it is usually not far removed from violence and rioting, it very frequently jeopardizes

public peace. In this matter it is more effective and salutary that the authority of the law anticipate and completely prevent the evil from breaking out by removing early the causes from which it would seem that conflict between employers and workers is bound to arise.

### The State Must Protect the Soul

57. And in like manner, in the case of the worker, there are many things which the power of the State should protect; and, first of all, the goods of his soul. For however good and desirable mortal life be, yet it is not the ultimate goal for which we are born, but a road only and a means for perfecting, through knowledge of truth and love of good, the life of the soul. The soul bears the express image and likeness of God, and there resides in it that sovereignty through the medium of which man has been bidden to rule all created nature below him and to make all lands and all seas serve his interests. "Fill the earth, and subdue it, and rule over the fishes of the sea, and the fowls of the air and all living creatures that move upon the earth." (*Gen.* 1:28). In this respect all men are equal, and there is no difference between rich and poor, between masters and servants, between rulers and subjects: "For the same is Lord over all." (*Rom.* 10:12). No one may with impunity outrage the dignity of man, which God Himself treats with great reverence, nor impede his course to that level of perfection which accords with eternal life in Heaven. Nay, more, in this connection a man cannot even by his own free choice allow himself to be treated in a way inconsistent with his nature, and suffer his soul to be enslaved; for there is no question here of rights belonging to man, but of duties owed to God, which are to be religiously observed.

### Sundays and Holy Days of Obligation

58. Hence follows necessary cessation from toil and work on Sundays and Holy Days of Obligation. Let no one, however, understand this in the sense of greater indulgence of idle leisure,

and much less in the sense of that kind of cessation from work, such as many desire, which encourages vice and promotes wasteful spending of money, but solely in the sense of a repose from labor made sacred by religion. Rest combined with religion calls man away from toil and the business of daily life to admonish him to ponder on heavenly goods and to pay his just and due homage to the Eternal Deity. This is especially the nature, and this the cause, of the rest to be taken on Sundays and Holy Days of Obligation, and God has sanctioned the same in the Old Testament by a special law: "Remember thou keep holy the sabbath day" (*Exod.* 20:8), and He Himself taught it by His own action: namely the mystical rest taken immediately after He had created man: "He rested on the seventh day from all His work which He had done." (*Gen.* 2:2).

## Protection of Physical Health

59. Now as concerns the protection of corporeal and physical goods, the oppressed workers, above all, ought to be liberated from the savagery of greedy men, who inordinately use human beings as things for gain. Assuredly, neither justice nor humanity can countenance the exaction of so much work that the spirit is dulled from excessive toil and that along with it the body sinks crushed from exhaustion. The working energy of a man, like his entire nature, is circumscribed by definite limits beyond which it cannot go. It is developed indeed by exercise and use, but only on condition that a man cease from work at regular intervals and rest. With respect to daily work, therefore, care ought to be taken not to extend it beyond the hours that human strength warrants. The length of rest intervals ought to be decided on the basis of the varying nature of the work, of the circumstances of time and place and of the physical condition of the workers themselves. Since the labor of those who quarry stone from the earth, or who mine iron, copper and other underground materials, is much more severe and harmful to health, the working period for such men ought to be correspondingly shortened. The seasons of the year also must be taken into account; for often a given kind of work is easy to

endure in one season but cannot be endured at all in another, or not without the greatest difficulty.

### Protection of Women and Children

60. Finally, it is not right to demand of a woman or a child what a strong adult man is capable of doing or would be willing to do. Nay, as regards children, special care ought to be taken that the factory does not get hold of them before age has sufficiently matured their physical, intellectual and moral powers. For budding strength in childhood, like greening verdure in spring, is crushed by premature harsh treatment; and under such circumstances all education of the child must needs be foregone. Certain occupations likewise are less fitted for women, who are intended by nature for work of the home—work indeed which especially protects modesty in women and accords by nature with the education of children and the well-being of the family. Let it be the rule everywhere that workers be given as much leisure as will compensate for the energy consumed by toil, for rest from work is necessary to restore strength consumed by use. In every obligation which is mutually contracted between employers and workers, this condition, either written or tacit, is always present, that both kinds of rest be provided for; nor would it be equitable to make an agreement otherwise, because no one has the right to demand of, or to make an agreement with anyone to neglect those duties which bind a man to God or to himself.

### Fixing Wages

61. We shall now touch upon a matter of very great importance, and one which must be correctly understood in order to avoid falling into error on one side or the other. We are told that free consent fixes the amount of a wage; that therefore the employer, after paying the wage agreed to, would seem to have discharged his obligation and not to owe anything more; that only then would injustice be done if either the employer should refuse to pay the whole amount of the wage, or the worker

should refuse to perform all the work to which he had committed himself; and that in these cases, but in no others, is it proper for the public authority to intervene to safeguard the rights of each party.

### Necessity of a Just Wage

62. An impartial judge would not assent readily or without reservation to this reasoning, because it is not complete in all respects; one factor to be considered, and one of the greatest importance, is missing. To work is to expend one's energy for the purpose of securing the things necessary for the various needs of life, and especially for its preservation. "In the sweat of thy face shalt thou eat bread." (*Gen.* 3:19). Accordingly, in man labor has two marks, as it were, implanted by nature, so that it is truly *personal*, because work energy inheres in the person and belongs completely to him by whom it is expended and for whose use it is destined by nature; and, secondly, that it is *necessary*, because man has need of the fruit of his labors to preserve his life, and nature itself, which must be most strictly obeyed, commands him to preserve it. If labor should be considered only under the aspect that it is personal, there is no doubt that it would be entirely in the worker's power to set the amount of the agreed wage at too low a figure. For inasmuch as he performs work by his own free will, he can also by his own free will be satisfied with either a paltry wage for his work or even with none at all. But this matter must be judged far differently, if with the factor of *personality* we combine the factor of *necessity*, from which indeed the former is separable in thought but not in reality. In fact, to preserve one's life is a duty common to all individuals, and to neglect this duty is a crime. Hence arises necessarily the right of securing things to sustain life, and only a wage earned by his labor gives a poor man the means to acquire these things.

### Wages and Natural Justice

63. Let it be granted then that worker and employer may enter

freely into agreements and, in particular, concerning the amount of the wage; yet there is always underlying such agreements an element of natural justice, and one greater and more ancient than the free consent of contracting parties, namely, that the wage shall not be less than enough to support a worker who is thrifty and upright. If, compelled by necessity or moved by fear of a worse evil, a worker accepts a harder condition, which although against his will he must accept because the employer or contractor imposes it, he certainly submits to force, against which justice cries out in protest.

### Safe Working Conditions

64. But in these and similar questions, such as the number of hours of work in each kind of occupation and the health safeguards to be provided, particularly in factories, it will be better, in order to avoid unwarranted governmental intervention, especially since circumstances of business, season and place are so varied, that decision be reserved to the organizations of which We are about to speak below, or else to pursue another course whereby the interests of the workers may be adequately safeguarded—the State, if the occasion demands, to furnish help and protection.

### The Law Should Favor Ownership of Property

65. If a worker receives a wage sufficiently large to enable him to provide comfortably for himself, his wife and his children, he will, if prudent, gladly strive to practice thrift; and the result will be, as nature itself seems to counsel, that after expenditures are deducted there will remain something over and above through which he can come into the possession of a little wealth. We have seen, in fact, that the whole question under consideration cannot be settled effectually unless it is assumed and established as a principle that the right of private property must be regarded as sacred. Wherefore, the law ought to favor this right and, so far as it can, see that the largest possible number among the masses of the population prefer to own property.

*Benefits of Private Ownership of Land*

66. If this is done, excellent benefits will follow, foremost among which will surely be a more equitable division of goods. For the violence of public disorder has divided cities into two classes of citizens, with an immense gulf lying between them. On the one side is a faction exceedingly powerful because exceedingly rich. Since it alone has under its control every kind of work and business, it diverts to its own advantage and interest all production sources of wealth and exerts no little power in the administration itself of the State. On the other side are the needy and helpless masses, with minds inflamed and always ready for disorder. But if the productive activity of the multitude can be stimulated by the hope of acquiring some property in land, it will gradually come to pass that, with the difference between extreme wealth and extreme penury removed, one class will become neighbor to the other. Moreover, there will surely be a greater abundance of the things which the earth produces. For when men know they are working on what belongs to them, they work with far greater eagerness and diligence. Nay, in a word, they learn to love the land cultivated by their own hands, whence they look not only for food but for some measure of abundance for themselves and their dependents. All can see how much this willing eagerness contributes to an abundance of produce and the wealth of a nation. Hence, in the third place, will flow the benefit that men can easily be kept from leaving the country in which they have been born and bred; for they would not exchange their native country for a foreign land if their native country furnished them sufficient means of living.

*Unjust Taxes Crush Prosperity*

67. But these advantages can be attained only if private wealth is not drained away by crushing taxes of every kind. For since the right of possessing goods privately has been conferred not by man's law, but by nature, public authority cannot abolish it, but can only control its exercise and bring it into conformity with the

commonweal. Public authority therefore would act unjustly and inhumanly if in the name of taxes it should appropriate from the property of private individuals more than is equitable.

## Caring for the Needy

68. Finally, employers and workers themselves can accomplish much in this matter, manifestly through those institutions by the help of which the poor are opportunely assisted and the two classes of society are brought closer to each other. Under this category come associations for giving mutual aid; various agencies established by the foresight of private persons to care for the worker and likewise for his dependent wife and children in the event that an accident, sickness or death befalls him; and foundations to care for boys and girls, for adolescents and for the aged.

## Benefits of Associations of Workers

69. But associations of workers occupy first place, and they include within their circle nearly all the rest. The beneficent achievements of the guilds of artisans among our ancestors have long been well known. Truly, they yielded noteworthy advantages not only to artisans, but, as many monuments bear witness, brought glory and progress to the arts themselves. In our present age of greater culture, with its new customs and ways of living, and with the increased number of things required by daily life, it is most clearly necessary that workers' associations be adapted to meet the present need. It is gratifying that societies of this kind composed either of workers alone or of workers and employers together are being formed everywhere, and it is truly to be desired that they grow in number and in active vigor. Although We have spoken of them more than once, it seems well to show in this place that they are highly opportune and are formed by their own right, and likewise to show how they should be organized and what they should do.

### Enlisting the Help of Others

70. Inadequacy of his own strength, learned from experience, impels and urges a man to enlist the help of others. Such is the teaching of Holy Scripture: "It is better therefore that two should be together, than one: for they have the advantage of their society: If one fall he shall be supported by the other: woe to him that is alone, for when he falleth, he hath none to lift him up." (Eccles. 4:9-10). And this also: "A brother that is helped by his brother, is like a strong city." (Prov. 18:19). Just as man is drawn by this natural propensity into civil union and association, so also he seeks with his fellow citizens to form other societies, admittedly small and not perfect, but societies none the less.

### Public and Private Societies

71. Between these latter and the large society of the State there is, because of their different immediate purposes, a very great distinction. The end of civil society concerns absolutely all members of this society, since the end of civil society is centered in the common good, in which latter one and all in due proportion have a right to participate. Wherefore this society is called *public*, because through it "men share with one another in establishing a commonwealth."[9] On the other hand, societies which are formed, so to speak, within its bosom are considered *private* and are such because their immediate object is private advantage, appertaining to those alone who are thus associated together. "Now a private society is one which is formed to carry out some private business, as when two or three enter into association for the purpose of engaging together in trade."[10]

### Private Societies and the State

72. Although private societies exist within the State and are, as it were, so many parts of it, still it is not within the authority of the State universally and *per se* to forbid them to exist as such. For man is permitted by a right of nature to form private societies; the

State, on the other hand, has been instituted to protect and not to destroy natural right, and if it should forbid its citizens to enter into associations, it would clearly do something contradictory to itself because both the State itself and private associations are begotten of one and the same principle, namely, that men are by nature inclined to associate. Occasionally there are times when it is proper for the laws to oppose associations of this kind, that is, if they professedly seek after any objective which is clearly at variance with good morals, with justice or with the welfare of the State. Indeed, in these cases the public power shall justly prevent such associations from forming and shall also justly dissolve those already formed. Nevertheless, it must use the greatest precaution lest it appear to infringe on the rights of its citizens, and lest under the pretext of public benefit it enact any measure that sound reason would not support. For laws are to be obeyed only in so far as they conform with right reason and thus with the eternal law of God.[11]

### Rights of Catholic Associations Violated

73. Here come to Our mind for consideration the various confraternities, societies and religious orders which the authority of the Church and the piety of Christians have brought into being; and history down to our own times speaks of the wonderful benefit they have been to the human race. Since societies of this character, even if judged in the light of reason alone, have been formed for an honest purpose, it is clear that they have been formed in accordance with natural right. But in whatever respect they concern religion, they are properly subject to the Church alone. Therefore those in charge of the State cannot in justice arrogate to themselves any right over them or assume their administration to themselves. Rather it is the office of the State to respect, to conserve and, as occasion may require, to protect them from injustice. Yet we have seen something entirely different being done, especially at the present time. In many places the State has violated associations of this kind, and, in fact, with manifold injury, since it has put them in the bonds of the civil law, has

divested them of their lawful right to be considered legal persons and has robbed them of their property. In this property the Church possessed her rights, and individual association members possessed theirs, as did also the persons who donated this property for a designated purpose, as well as those for whose benefit and relief it had been donated. Consequently, We cannot refrain from deploring such vicious and unjust acts of robbery, and so much the more because We see the road being closed to Catholic associations, which are law-abiding and in every respect useful, at the very time when it is being decreed that most assuredly men are permitted by law to form associations, and at the very time when this freedom is being lavishly granted in actual fact to men urging courses of conduct pernicious at once to religion and to the State.

### Associations that Endanger Religion

74. Certainly, the number of associations of almost every possible kind, especially of associations of workers, is now far greater than ever before. This is not the place to inquire whence many of them originate, what object they have or how they proceed. But the opinion is, and it is one confirmed by a good deal of evidence, that they are largely under the control of secret leaders and that these leaders apply principles which are in harmony with neither Christianity nor the welfare of States, and that, after having possession of all available work, they contrive that those who refuse to join with them will be forced by want to pay the penalty. Under these circumstances, workers who are Christians must choose one of two things; either to join associations in which it is greatly to be feared that there is danger to religion, or to form their own associations and unite their forces in such a way that they may be able manfully to free themselves from such unjust and intolerable oppression. Can they who refuse to place man's highest good in imminent jeopardy hesitate to affirm that the second course is by all means to be followed?

*Catholics Uniting to Help the Working Class*

75. Many of our Faith are indeed to be highly commended, who, having rightly perceived what the times require of them, are experimenting and striving to discover how by honest means they can raise the non-owning working class to higher living levels. They have championed their cause and are endeavoring to increase the prosperity of both families and individuals, and at the same time to regulate justly the mutual obligations which rest upon workers and employers and to foster and strengthen in both consciousness of duty and observance of the precepts of the Gospel—precepts, in truth, which hold man back from excess and prevent him from overstepping the bounds of moderation and, in the midst of the widest divergences among persons and things, maintain harmony in the State. For this reason, we see eminent men meeting together frequently to exchange ideas, to combine their forces and to deliberate on the most expedient programs of action. Others are endeavoring to unite the various kinds of workers in suitable associations, are assisting them with advice and money, and making plans to prevent a lack of honest and profitable work. The bishops are giving encouragement and bestowing support; and under their authority and auspices many from the ranks of the clergy, both regular and diocesan, are showing zealous care for all that pertains to the spiritual improvement of the members of these associations. Finally, there are not wanting Catholics of great wealth, yet voluntary sharers, as it were, in the lot of the wage workers, who by their own generous contributions are striving to found and extend associations through which the worker is readily enabled to obtain from his toil not only immediate benefits, but also assurance of honorable retirement in the future. How much good such manifold and enthusiastic activity has contributed to the benefit of all is too well known to make discussion necessary. From all this, We have taken auguries of good hope for the future, provided that societies of this kind continually grow and that they are founded with wise organization. Let the State protect these lawfully associated bodies of citizens; let it not, however, interfere with their private concerns and order of

life; for vital activity is set in motion by an inner principle, and it is very easily destroyed, as We know, by intrusion from without.

## The Proper Object of Workers' Associations

76. Unquestionably, wise direction and organization are essential to these associations in order that in their activities there be unity of purpose and concord of wills. Furthermore, if citizens have free right to associate, as in fact they do, they also must have the right freely to adopt the organization and the rules which they judge most appropriate to achieve their purpose. We do not feel that the precise character in all details which the aforementioned direction and organization of associations ought to have can be determined by fast and fixed rules, since this is a matter to be decided rather in the light of the temperament of each people, of experiment and practice, of the nature and character of the work, of the extent of trade and commerce and of other circumstances of a material and temporal kind, all of which must be carefully considered. In summary, let this be laid down as a general and constant law: Workers' associations ought to be so constituted and so governed as to furnish the most suitable and most convenient means to attain the object proposed, which consists in this, that the individual members of the association secure, so far as possible, an increase in the goods of body, of soul and of prosperity.

## Moral and Religious Perfection Their Principal Goal

77. It is clear, however, that moral and religious perfection ought to be regarded as their principal goal, and that their social organization as such ought above all to be directed completely by this goal. For otherwise they would degenerate in nature and would be little better than those associations in which no account is ordinarily taken of religion. Besides, what would it profit a worker to secure through an association an abundance of goods if his soul, through lack of its proper food, should run the risk of perishing? "What doth it profit a man, if he gain the whole world, but suffer the loss of his own soul?" (*Matt.* 16:26). Christ Our

Lord teaches that this in fact must be considered the mark whereby a Christian is distinguished from a pagan: "For after all these things do the heathens seek . . . seek ye therefore first the kingdom of God, and his justice, and all these things shall be added unto you." (*Matt.* 6:32, 33). Therefore, having taken their principles from God, let those associations provide ample opportunity for religious instruction so that individual members may understand their duties to God, that they may well know what to believe, what to hope for and what to do for eternal salvation, and that with special care they may be fortified against erroneous opinions and various forms of corruption. Let the worker be exhorted to the worship of God and the pursuit of piety, especially to religious observance of Sundays and Holy Days. Let him learn to reverence and love the Church, the common Mother of all, and likewise to observe her precepts and to frequent her Sacraments, which are the divine means for purifying the soul from the stains of sin and for attaining sanctity.

## Associations Founded upon Religion

78. When the regulations of associations are founded upon religion, the way is easy toward establishing the mutual relations of the members so that peaceful living together and prosperity will result. Offices in the associations are to be distributed properly in accordance with the common interest, and in such a way, moreover, that wide difference in these offices may not create discord. It is of special importance that obligations be apportioned wisely and be clearly defined, to the end that no one is done an injustice. Let the funds be disbursed equitably in such way that the amount of benefit to be paid out to members is fixed beforehand in accordance with individual needs, and let the rights and duties of employers be properly adjusted to the rights and duties of workers. If any one in these two groups feels that he has been injured in any way, nothing is more to be desired than that prudent and upright men of the same body be available and that the association regulations themselves prescribe that the dispute be settled according to the decision of these men.

### Associations Protect the Unfortunate

79. It must also be specifically provided that the worker at no time be without sufficient work, and that the monies paid into the treasury of the association furnish the means of assisting individual members in need, not only during sudden and unforeseen changes in industry, but also whenever anyone is stricken by sickness, by old age or by misfortune.

### Associations of Catholics Promote Prosperity in the State

80. Through these regulations, provided they are readily accepted, the interests and welfare of the poor will be adequately cared for. Associations of Catholics, moreover, will undoubtedly be of great importance in promoting prosperity in the State. Through past events we can, without temerity, foresee the future. Age presses hard upon age, but there are wondrous similarities in history, governed as it is by the Providence of God, who guides and directs the continuity and the chain of events in accordance with that purpose which He set before Himself in creating the human race. In the early ages, when the Church was in her youth, We know that the reproach was hurled at the Christians that the great majority of them lived by precarious alms or by toil. Yet, although destitute of wealth and power, they succeeded in winning the good will of the rich and the protection of the mighty. All could see that they were energetic, industrious, peace-loving and exemplarily devoted to the practice of justice and especially of charity. In the presence of life and conduct such as this, all prejudice vanished, the taunting voices of the malevolent were silenced and the falsehoods of inveterate superstition yielded little by little to Christian truth.

### Outreach to the Fallen-Away

81. The condition of workers is a subject of bitter controversy at the present time; and whether this controversy is resolved in accordance with reason or otherwise is in either event of utmost

importance to the State. But Christian workers will readily resolve it in accordance with reason if, united in associations and under wise leaders, they enter upon the path which their fathers and their ancestors followed to their own best welfare as well as to that of the State. For, no matter how strong the power of prejudice and passion in man, yet, unless perversity of will has deadened the sense of the right and just, the good will of citizens is certain to be more freely inclined toward those whom they learn to know as industrious and temperate, and who clearly place justice before profit and conscientious observance of duty before all else. Under these circumstances there will follow also this great advantage, that no little hope and opportunity for developing a sound attitude will be afforded those workers who live in complete disdain of the Christian Faith or in a manner foreign to its profession. These men indeed, for the most part, know that they have been deceived by illusory hopes and by false appearances. They are conscious of being most inhumanly treated by greedy employers, that almost no greater value is being placed on them than the amount of gain they yield by their toil, and that in the associations, moreover, in whose meshes they are caught, there exist, in place of charity and love, internal dissensions which are the inseparable companions of aggravating and irreligious poverty. Broken in spirit, and worn out in body, how gladly many would free themselves from a servitude so degrading! Yet they dare not because either human shame or the fear of want prevents them. It is remarkable how much associations of Catholics can contribute to the welfare of all such men if they invite those wavering in uncertainty to their bosom in order to remedy their difficulties, and if they receive the penitents into their trust and protection.

### No Well-Being Without Christian Morals

82. These, Venerable Brethren, are the persons, and this is the procedure to be employed in dealing with this most difficult question. Everyone according to his position ought to gird himself for the task, and indeed as speedily as possible, lest, by delaying the remedy, the evil, which is already of vast dimensions, become

incurable. Let those in charge of States make use of the provision afforded by laws and institutions; let the rich and employers be mindful of their duties; let the workers, whose cause is at stake, press their claims with reason. And since religion alone, as We said in the beginning, can remove the evil, root and branch, let all reflect upon this: First and foremost, Christian morals must be re-established, without which even the weapons of prudence, which are considered especially effective, will be of no avail to secure well-being.

### The Efforts of the Church

83. So far as the Church is concerned, at no time and in no manner will she permit her efforts to be wanting, and she will contribute all the more help in proportion as she has more free-dom of action. Let this be understood in particular by those whose duty it is to promote the public welfare. Let the members of the Sacred Ministry exert all their strength of mind and all their dili-gence, and Venerable Brethren, under the guidance of your authority and example, let them not cease to impress upon men of all ranks the principles of Christian living as found in the Gospel; by all means in their power let them strive for the well-being of people; and especially let them aim both to preserve in themselves and to arouse in others, in the highest equally as well as in the lowest, the mistress and queen of the virtues, Charity. Certainly, the well-being which is so longed for is chiefly to be expected from an abundant outpouring of charity; of Christian charity, We mean, which is in epitome the law of the Gospel, and which, always ready to sacrifice itself for the benefit of others, is man's surest antidote against the insolence of the world and immoderate love of self, the divine office and features of this virtue being described by the Apostle Paul in these words: "Charity is patient, is kind . . . seeketh not her own . . . beareth with all things . . . endureth all things." (*1 Cor.* 13:4-7).

### The Apostolic Blessing

84. As a pledge of Divine favor and as a token of Our affection, most lovingly in the Lord We bestow on each of you, Venerable Brethren, on your clergy and on your people, the Apostolic Blessing.

85. Given in Rome, at St. Peter's, the 15th day of May, in the year 1891, the fourteenth of Our Pontificate.

Leo XIII, Pope


### NOTES

1. St. Thomas, *Summa Theologica*, II-II, Q.10, art. 12.
2. *Ibid.*, Q.66, art. 2.
3. *Ibid.*, Q.65, art. 2.
4. *Ibid.*, Q.32, art. 6.
5. St. Gregory the Great, *In Evang. Hom.* 9, 7.
6. *Apol.* II, 39.
7. *Summa Theologica*, II-II, Q.61, art. 1 and 2.
8. St. Thomas, *De regimine principum*, I, 15.
9. St. Thomas, *Contra impugnantes Dei cultum et religionem*, 2, 8.
10. *Ibid.*
11. "Human law is law only in virtue of its accordance with right reason: and thus it is manifest that it flows from the eternal law. And in so far as it deviates from right reason it is called an unjust law; in such case it is not law at all, but rather a species of violence."—St. Thomas, *Summa Theologica*, I-II, Q.93, art. 3, ad 2.

Encyclical Letter of Pope Leo XIII

# ON CHRISTIAN DEMOCRACY
## (Graves de Communi Re)

January 18, 1901

To Our Venerable Brethren, the Patriarchs, Primates,
Archbishops, Bishops, and other Ordinaries
in Peace and Communion with the Apostolic See

Venerable Brethren,

1. The grave discussions on economic questions which for some time past have disturbed the peace of several countries of the world are growing in frequency and intensity to such a degree that the minds of thoughtful men are filled, and rightly so, with worry and alarm. These discussions take their rise in the bad philosophical and ethical teaching which is now widespread among the people. The changes, also, which the mechanical inventions of the age have introduced, the rapidity of communication between places, and the devices of every kind for diminishing labor and increasing gain, all add bitterness to the strife; and, lastly, matters have been brought to such a pass by the struggle between capital and labor, fomented as it is by professional agitators, that the countries where these disturbances most frequently occur find themselves confronted with ruin and disaster.

## Issue of Socialism Already Addressed

2. At the very beginning of Our pontificate We clearly pointed

out what the peril was which confronted society on this head, and We deemed it Our duty to warn Catholics, in unmistakable language,[1] how great the error was which was lurking in the utterances of Socialism, and how great the danger was that threatened not only their temporal possessions, but also their morality and religion. That was the purpose of Our encyclical letter *Quod Apostolici Muneris* which We published on the 28th of December in the year 1878; but, as these dangers day by day threatened still greater disaster, both to individuals and the commonwealth, We strove with all the more energy to avert them. This was the object of Our encyclical *Rerum Novarum* of the 15th of May, 1891, in which we dwelt at length on the rights and duties which both classes of society—those namely, who control capital, and those who contribute labor—are bound in relation to each other; and at the same time, We made it evident that the remedies which are most useful to protect the cause of religion, and to terminate the contest between the different classes of society, were to be found in the precepts of the Gospel.

### Catholic Response Has Been Positive

3. Nor, with God's grace, were Our hopes entirely frustrated. Even those who are not Catholics, moved by the power of truth, avowed that the Church must be credited with a watchful care over all classes of society, and especially those whom fortune had least favored. Catholics, of course, profited abundantly by these letters, for they not only received encouragement and strength for the excellent undertakings in which they were engaged, but also obtained the light which they needed in order to study this order of problems with greater sureness and success. Hence it happened that the differences of opinion which prevailed among them were either removed or lessened. In the order of action, much has been done in favor of the proletariat, especially in those places where poverty was at its worst. Many new institutions were set on foot, those which were already established were increased and all reaped the benefit of a greater stability. Such are, for instance, the popular bureaus which supply information to the uneducated; the

rural banks which make loans to small farmers; the societies for mutual help or relief; the unions of working men and other associations or institutions of the same kind. Thus, under the auspices of the Church, a measure of united action among Catholics was secured, as well as some planning in the setting up of agencies for the protection of the masses which, in fact, are as often oppressed by guile and exploitation of their necessities as by their own indigence and toil.

### Controversies over the Names of Catholic Movements

4. This work of popular aid had, at first, no name of its own. The name of Christian Socialism, with its derivatives, which was adopted by some was very properly allowed to fall into disuse. Afterward, some asked to have it called the Popular Christian Movement. In the countries most concerned with this matter, there are some who are known as Social Christians. Elsewhere, the movement is described as Christian Democracy and its partisans as Christian Democrats, in opposition to what the Socialists call Social Democracy. Not much exception is taken to the first of these two names, i.e., Social Christians, but many excellent men find the term Christian Democracy objectionable. They hold it to be very ambiguous and for this reason open to two objections. It seems by implication covertly to favor popular government and to disparage other methods of political administration. Secondly, it appears to belittle religion by restricting its scope to the care of the poor, as if the other sections of society were not of its concern. More than that, under the shadow of its name there might easily lurk a design to attack all legitimate power, either civil or sacred. Wherefore, since this discussion is now so widespread, and so bitter, the consciousness of duty warns Us to put a check on this controversy and to define what Catholics are to think on this matter. We also propose to describe how the movement may extend its scope and be made more useful to the commonwealth.

## Social Democracy Defined

5. What Social Democracy is and what Christian Democracy ought to be, assuredly no one can doubt. The first, with due consideration to the greater or less intemperance of its utterance, is carried to such an excess by many as to maintain that there is really nothing existing above the natural order of things, and that the acquisition and enjoyment of corporal and external goods constitute man's happiness. It aims at putting all government in the hands of the masses, reducing all ranks to the same level, abolishing all distinction of class and finally introducing community of goods. Hence, the right to own private property is to be abrogated, and whatever property a man possesses, or whatever means of livelihood he has, is to be common to all.

## Christian Democracy Examined

6. As against this, Christian Democracy, by the fact that it is Christian, is built, and necessarily so, on the basic principles of divine faith, and it must provide better conditions for the masses, with the ulterior object of promoting the perfection of souls made for things eternal. Hence, for Christian Democracy, justice is sacred; it must maintain that the right of acquiring and possessing property cannot be impugned, and it must safeguard the various distinctions and degrees which are indispensable in every well-ordered commonwealth. Finally, it must endeavor to preserve in every human society the form and the character which God ever impresses on it. It is clear, therefore, that there is nothing in common between Social and Christian Democracy. They differ from each other as much as the sect of Socialism differs from the profession of Christianity.

## Democracy in the Context of Catholic Action

7. Moreover, it would be a crime to distort this name of Christian Democracy to politics, for, although democracy, both in its philological and philosophical signification, implies popular gov-

ernment, yet in its present application it must be employed without any political significance, so as to mean nothing else than this beneficent Christian action on behalf of the people. For the laws of nature and of the Gospel, which by right are superior to all human contingencies, are necessarily independent of all particular forms of civil government, while at the same time they are in harmony with everything that is not repugnant to morality and justice. They are, therefore, and they must remain absolutely free from the passions and the vicissitudes of parties, so that, under whatever political constitution, the citizens may and ought to abide by those laws which command them to love God above all things, and their neighbors as themselves. This has always been the policy of the Church. The Roman Pontiffs acted upon this principle, whenever they dealt with different countries, no matter what might be the character of their governments. Hence, the mind and the action of Catholics devoted to promoting the welfare of the working classes can never be actuated with the purpose of favoring and introducing one government in place of another.

### Christian Democracy Seeks Peace among All Classes

8. In the same manner, we must remove from Christian Democracy another possible subject of reproach, namely, that while looking after the advantage of the working people it should seem to overlook the upper classes of society, for they also are of the greatest use in preserving and perfecting the commonwealth. The Christian law of charity, which has just been mentioned, will prevent us from so doing. For it embraces all men, irrespective of ranks, as members of one and the same family, children of the same most beneficent Father, redeemed by the same Saviour and called to the same eternal heritage. Hence the doctrine of the Apostle, who warns us that we are "One body and one Spirit; as you are called in one hope of your calling; one Lord, one faith, one baptism. One God and Father of all, who is above all, and through all, and in us all." (*Eph.* 4:4-6). Wherefore, on account of the union established by nature between the common people and the other classes of society, and which Christian brotherhood

makes still closer, whatever diligence we devote to assisting the people will certainly profit also the other classes, the more so since, as will be thereafter shown, their co-operation is proper and necessary for the success of this undertaking.

## The Spirit of Obedience

9. Let there be no question of fostering under this name of Christian Democracy any intention of diminishing the spirit of obedience, or of withdrawing people from their lawful rulers. Both the natural and the Christian law command us to revere those who in their various grades are shown above us in the State, and to submit ourselves to their just commands. It is quite in keeping with our dignity as men and Christians to obey, not only exteriorly, but from the heart, as the Apostle expresses it, "for conscience' sake," when he commands us to keep our soul subject to the higher powers. (*Rom.* 13:1,5). It is abhorrent to the profession of Christianity that any one should feel unwilling to be subject and obedient to those who rule in the Church, and first of all to the bishops whom (without prejudice to the universal power of the Roman Pontiff) "the Holy Ghost hath placed . . . to rule the Church of God, which he hath purchased with his own blood." (*Acts* 20:28). He who thinks or acts otherwise is guilty of ignoring the grave precept of the Apostle who bids us to obey our rulers and to be subject to them, "For they watch as being to render an account of your souls." (*Heb.* 13:17). Let the faithful everywhere implant these principles deep in their souls, and put them in practice in their daily life, and let the ministers of the Gospel meditate them profoundly, and incessantly labor, not merely by exhortation but especially by example, to teach them to others.

## Protect Christian Democracy from Socialism

10. We have recalled these principles, which on other occasions We had already elucidated, in the hope that all dispute about the name of Christian Democracy will cease and that all suspicion of any danger coming from what the name signifies will be put at

rest. And with reason do We hope so; for, neglecting the opinions of certain men whose views on the nature and efficacy of this kind of Christian Democracy are not free from exaggeration and from error, let no one condemn that zeal which, in accordance with the natural and divine law, aims to make the condition of those who toil more tolerable; to enable them to obtain, little by little, those means by which they may provide for the future; to help them to practice in public and in private the duties which morality and religion inculcate; to aid them to feel that they are not animals but men, not heathens but Christians, and so to enable them to strive more zealously and more eagerly for the one thing which is necessary; *viz.*, that ultimate good for which we are all born into this world. This is the intention; this is the work of those who wish that the people should be animated by Christian sentiments and should be protected from the contamination of Socialism which threatens them.

### Not Only an Economic But a Moral and Religious Issue

11. We have designedly made mention here of virtue and religion. For, it is the opinion of some, and the error is already very common, that the *social* question is merely an *economic* one, whereas in point of fact it is, above all, a moral and religious matter, and for that reason must be settled by the principles of morality and according to the dictates of religion. For, even though wages are doubled and the hours of labor are shortened and food is cheapened, yet, if the working man hearkens to the doctrines that are taught on this subject, as he is prone to do, and is prompted by the examples set before him to throw off respect for God and to enter upon a life of immorality, his labors and his gain will avail him naught.

### Christian Virtue a Necessity

12. Trial and experience have made it abundantly clear that many a workman lives in cramped and miserable quarters, in spite of his shorter hours and larger wages, simply because he has cast

aside the restraints of morality and religion. Take away the instinct which Christian wisdom has planted and nurtured in men's hearts, take away foresight, temperance, frugality, patience and other rightful, natural habits and no matter how much he may strive, he will never achieve prosperity. That is the reason why We have incessantly exhorted Catholics to enter these associations for bettering the condition of the laboring classes, and to organize other undertakings with the same object in view; but We have likewise warned them that all this should be done under the auspices of religion, with its help and under its guidance.

### *Zeal for the Welfare of Souls Praiseworthy*

13. The zeal of Catholics on behalf of the masses is especially praiseworthy because it is engaged in the very same field in which, under the benign inspiration of the Church, the active industry of charity has always labored, adapting itself in all cases to the varying exigencies of the times. For the law of mutual charity perfects, as it were, the law of justice, not merely by giving each man his due and in not impeding him in the exercise of his rights, but also by befriending him, "not in word, nor in tongue, but in deed, and in truth" (*1 John* 3:18); being mindful of what Christ so lovingly said to His own: "A new commandment I give unto you: That you love one another, as I have loved you, that you also love one another. By this shall all men know that you are My disciples, if you have love one for another." (*John* 13:34-35). This zeal in coming to the rescue of our fellow men should, of course, be solicitous, first for the eternal good of souls, but it must not neglect what is good and helpful for this life.

### *Charity Has a Divine Reward*

14. We should remember what Christ said to the disciple of the Baptist who asked him: "Art thou he that art to come, or look we for another?" (*Matt.* 11:3). He invoked, as proof of the mission given to Him among men, His exercise of charity, quoting for them the text of Isaias: "The blind see, the lame walk, the lepers

are cleansed, the deaf hear, the dead rise again, the poor have the Gospel preached to them." (*Matt.* 11:4-5). And speaking also of the last judgment and of the rewards and punishments He will assign, He declared that He would take special account of the charity men exercised toward each other. And in that discourse there is one thing that especially excites our surprise, *viz.*, that Christ omits those works of mercy which comfort the soul and, referring only to those which comfort the body, He regards them as being done to Himself: "For I was hungry, and you gave me to eat; I was thirsty, and you gave me to drink; I was a stranger and you took me in; naked, and you covered me; sick, and you visited me; I was in prison, and you came to me." (*Matt.* 25:35-36).

### Christ's Example Is Our Model

15. To the teachings which enjoin the twofold charity of spiritual and corporal works Christ adds His own example, so that no one may fail to recognize the importance which He attaches to it. In the present instance we recall the sweet words that came from His paternal heart: "I have compassion on the multitude" (*Mark* 8:2), as well as the desire He had to assist them even if it were necessary to invoke His miraculous power. Of His tender compassion we have the proclamation made in Holy Writ, *viz.*, that He "went about doing good and healing all that were oppressed by the devil . . ." (*Acts* 10:38). This law of charity which He imposed upon His Apostles, they, in the most holy and zealous way, put into practice; and after them those who embraced Christianity originated that wonderful variety of institutions for alleviating all the miseries by which mankind is afflicted. And these institutions carried on and continually increased their powers of relief and were the especial glories of Christianity and of the civilization of which it was the source, so that right-minded men never fail to admire those foundations, aware as they are of the proneness of men to concern themselves about their own and neglect the needs of others.

### Justice and Charity Seek the Common Good

16.  Nor are we to eliminate from the list of good works the giving of money for charity, in pursuance of what Christ has said: "But yet that which remaineth, give alms." (*Luke* 11:41). Against this, the Socialist cries out and demands its abolition as injurious to the native dignity of man. But, if it is done in the manner which the Scripture enjoins (*Matt.* 6:2-4), and in conformity with the true Christian spirit, it neither connotes pride in the giver nor inflicts shame upon the one who receives. Far from being dishonorable for man, it draws closer the bonds of human society by augmenting the force of the obligation of the duties which men are under with regard to each other. No one is so rich that he does not need another's help; no one so poor as not to be useful in some way to his fellow man; and the disposition to ask assistance from others with confidence and to grant it with kindness is part of our very nature. Thus, justice and charity are so linked with each other, under the equable and sweet law of Christ, as to form an admirable cohesive power in human society and to lead all of its members to exercise a sort of providence in looking after their own and in seeking the common good as well.

### Permanent Charitable Institutions

17.  As regards not merely the temporary aid given to the laboring classes, but the establishment of permanent institutions on their behalf, it is most commendable for charity to undertake them. It will thus see that more certain and more reliable means of assistance will be afforded to the necessitous. That kind of help is especially worthy of recognition which forms the minds of mechanics and laborers to thrift and foresight, so that in course of time they may be able, in part at least, to look out for themselves. To aim at that is not only to dignify the duty of the rich toward the poor, but to elevate the poor themselves. For, while it urges them to work in order to improve their condition, it preserves them meantime from danger, it refrains immoderation in their desires, and acts as a spur in the practice of virtue. Since, therefore, this is

of such great avail and so much in keeping with the spirit of the times, it is a worthy object for the charity of righteous men to undertake with prudence and zeal.

### Catholics Should Be United

18. Let it be understood, therefore, that this devotion of Catholics to comfort and elevate the mass of the people is in keeping with the spirit of the Church and is most conformable to the examples which the Church has always held up for imitation. It matters very little whether it goes under the name of the Popular Christian Movement or Christian Democracy, if the instructions that have been given by Us be fully carried out with fitting obedience. But it is of the greatest importance that Catholics should be one in mind, will and action in a matter of such great moment. And it is also of importance that the influence of these undertakings should be extended by the multiplication of men and means devoted to the same object.

### The Wealthy Must Remember the Common Good

19. Especially must there be appeals to the kindly assistance of those whose rank, wealth and intellectual as well as spiritual culture give them a certain standing in the community. If their help is not extended, scarcely anything can be done which will help in promoting the well-being of the people. Assuredly, the more earnestly many of those who are prominent citizens conspire effectively to attain that object, the quicker and surer will the end be reached. We would, however, have them understand that they are not at all free to look after or neglect those who happen to be beneath them, but that it is a strict duty which binds them. For, no one lives only for his personal advantage in a community; he lives for the common good as well, so that, when others cannot contribute their share for the general good, those who can do so are obliged to make up the deficiency. The very extent of the benefits they have received increases the burden of their responsibility, and a stricter account will have to be rendered to God who

bestowed those blessings upon them. What should also urge all to the fulfillment of their duty in this regard is the widespread disaster which will eventually fall upon all classes of society if this assistance does not arrive in time; and therefore it is that he who neglects the cause of the distressed masses is disregarding his own interest as well as that of the community.

### *Older Institutions Should Work with the New*

20. If this action, which is social in the Christian sense of the term, develops and grows in accordance with its own nature, there will be no danger, as is feared, that those other institutions, which the piety of our ancestors have established and which are now flourishing, will decline or be absorbed by new foundations. Both of them spring from the same root of charity and religion, and not only do not conflict with each other, but can easily be made to coalesce and combine so perfectly as to provide, all the better by the pooling of their beneficent efforts, for the needs of the masses and for the daily increasing perils to which they are exposed.

### *There Is a Need for Immediate Action*

21. The condition of things at present proclaims, and proclaims vehemently, that there is need for a union of brave minds with all the resources they can command. The harvest of misery is before our eyes, and the dreadful projects of the most disastrous national upheavals are threatening us from the growing power of the Socialistic movement. They have insidiously worked their way into the very heart of the community, and in the darkness of their secret gatherings, and in the open light of day, in their writings and their harangues, they are urging the masses onward to sedition. They fling aside religious discipline; they scorn duties; they clamor only for rights; they are working incessantly on the multitudes of the needy which daily grow greater, and which, because of their poverty are easily deluded and led into error. It is equally the concern of the State and of religion, and all good men should deem it a sacred duty to pre-

serve and guard both in the honor which is their due.

### Avoid Useless Controversy and Dissension

22. That this most desirable agreement of wills should be maintained, it is essential that all refrain from giving any cause of dissension which hurts and divides minds. Hence, in newspapers and in speeches to the people, let them avoid subtle and practically useless questions which are neither easy to solve nor easy to understand except by minds of unusual ability and after the most serious study. It is quite natural for people to hesitate on doubtful subjects, and that different men should hold different opinions, but those who sincerely seek after truth will preserve equanimity, modesty and courtesy in matters of dispute. They will not let differences of opinion deteriorate into conflicts of wills. Besides, to whatever opinion a man's judgment may incline, if the matter is yet open to discussion, let him keep it, provided he be always disposed to listen with religious obedience to what the Holy See may decide on the question.

### Established Organizations Should Lead the Cause

23. The action of Catholics, of whatever description it may be, will work with greater effect if all of the various associations, while preserving their individual rights, move together under one primary and directive force.

In Italy, We desire that this directive force should emanate from the Institute of Catholic Congresses and Reunions so often praised by Us, to which Our Predecessor and We Ourselves have committed the charge of controlling the common action of Catholics under the authority and direction of the bishops of the country. So let it be for other nations, in case there be any leading organization of this description to which this matter has been legitimately entrusted.

## *Virtue Must Be Cultivated by All*

24. Now, in all questions of this sort where the interests of the Church and the Christian people are so closely allied, it is evident what they who are in the sacred ministry should do, and it is clear how industrious they should be in inculcating right doctrine and in teaching the duties of prudence and charity. To go out and move among the people, to exert a healthy influence on them by adapting themselves to the present condition of things, is what more than once in addressing the clergy We have advised. More frequently, also, in writing to the bishops and other dignitaries of the Church, and especially of late,[2] We have lauded this affectionate solicitude for the people and declared it to be the special duty of both the secular and regular clergy. But in the fulfillment of this obligation let there be the greatest caution and prudence exerted, and let it be done after the fashion of the Saints. Francis, who was poor and humble; Vincent de Paul, the father of the afflicted classes; and very many others whom the Church keeps ever in her memory were wont to lavish their care upon the people, but in such wise as not to be engrossed overmuch or to be unmindful of themselves or to let it prevent them from laboring with the same assiduity in the perfection of their own soul and the cultivation of virtue.

## *Accepting the Duties of Our State in Life*

25. There remains one thing upon which We desire to insist very strongly, in which not only the ministers of the Gospel, but also all those who are devoting themselves to the cause of the people, can with very little difficulty bring about a most commendable result. That is to inculcate in the minds of the people, in a brotherly way and whenever the opportunity presents itself, the following principles, *viz.*: to keep aloof on all occasions from seditious acts and seditious men; to hold inviolate the rights of others; to show a proper respect to superiors; to willingly perform the work in which they are employed; not to grow weary of the restraint of family life which in many ways is so advantageous; to

keep to their religious practices above all and in their hardships and trials to have recourse to the Church for consolation. In the furtherance of all this, it is of great help to propose the splendid example of the Holy Family of Nazareth, and to advise the invocation of its protection, and it also helps to remind the people of the examples of sanctity which have shone in the midst of poverty, and to hold up before them the reward that awaits them in the better life to come.

### Associations Should Form under Episcopal Authority

26. Finally, We recur again to what We have already declared and We insist upon it most solemnly, *viz.*, that whatever projects individuals or associations form in this matter should be formed under episcopal authority. Let them not be led astray by an excessive zeal in the cause of charity. If it leads them to be wanting in proper submission, it is not a sincere zeal; it will not have any useful result and cannot be acceptable to God. God delights in the souls of those who put aside their own designs and obey the rulers of His Church as if they were obeying Him. He assists them even when they attempt difficult things and benignly leads them to their desired end. Let them show, also, examples of virtue, so as to prove that a Christian is a hater of idleness and self-indulgence, that he gives willingly from his goods for the help of others and that he stands firm and unconquered in the midst of adversity. Examples of that kind have a power of moving people to dispositions of soul that make for salvation, and have all the greater force as the condition of those who give them is higher on the social scale.

### Tranquility and True Prosperity

27. We exhort you, Venerable Brethren, to provide for all this, as the necessities of men and of places may require, according to your prudence and your zeal, meeting as usual in council to combine with each other in your plans for the furtherance of these projects. Let your solicitude watch and let your authority be effective

in controlling, compelling and also in preventing, lest any one under the pretext of good should cause the vigor of sacred discipline to be relaxed or the order which Christ has established in His Church to be disturbed. Thus, by the rightful, harmonious and ever-increasing labor of all Catholics, let it become more and more evident that the tranquility of order and the true prosperity flourish especially among those peoples whom the Church controls and influences; and that she holds it as her sacred duty to admonish every one of what the law of God enjoins, to unite the rich and the poor in the bonds of fraternal charity and to lift up and strengthen men's souls in the times when adversity presses heavily upon them.

### Admonition to Be Charitable

28. Let Our commands and Our wishes be confirmed by the words so full of apostolic charity which the blessed Paul addressed to the Romans: "I beseech you therefore, brethren, . . . be reformed in the newness of your mind . . . he that giveth, with simplicity; he that ruleth, with carefulness; he that sheweth mercy, with cheerfulness. Let love be without dissimulation. Hating that which is evil; cleaving to that which is good. Loving one another with the charity of brotherhood, with honour preventing one another. In carefulness not slothful . . . Rejoicing in hope. Patient in tribulation. Instant in prayer. Communicating to the necessities of the saints. Pursuing hospitality . . . Rejoice with them that rejoice; weep with them that weep. Being of one mind one towards another . . . To no man rendering evil for evil. Providing good things, not only in the sight of God, but also in the sight of all men." (*Rom.* 12:1-2,8-13,15-17).

### Apostolic Blessing

29. As a pledge of these benefits receive the Apostolic Benediction which, Venerable Brethren, We grant most lovingly in the Lord to you and your clergy and people.

Given at St. Peter's in Rome, the eighteenth day of January, 1901, the thirteenth year of Our pontificate.

Leo XIII, Pope

## NOTES

1. See *Rerum Novarum.*
2. Letter to the Minister General of the Minorites, November 25, 1898. In this letter, the Pope recalled the instructions given in *Aeterni Patris* concerning the way to be followed in higher studies; the doctrine of Thomas Aquinas should be followed by all the religious who wish truly to philosophize (*qui vere philosophari volunt*); paramount importance of the study of holy Scripture; how to preach the word of God; forceful exhortation addressed to the Franciscans to go out of their monasteries and, following the example of St. Francis, devote themselves to the salvation of the masses; importance of the Third Order of St. Francis with regard to this work.

Decree issued by Pope St. Pius X

# Syllabus Condemning The Errors of the Modernists
## *(Lamentabili Sane)*

July 3, 1907

With truly lamentable results, our age, casting aside all restraint in its search for the ultimate causes of things, frequently pursues novelties so ardently that it rejects the legacy of the human race. Thus it falls into very serious errors, which are even more serious when they concern sacred authority, the interpretation of Sacred Scripture and the principal mysteries of Faith. The fact that many Catholic writers also go beyond the limits determined by the Fathers and the Church herself is extremely regrettable. In the name of higher knowledge and historical research (they say), they are looking for that progress of dogmas which is, in reality, nothing but the corruption of dogmas.

These errors are being daily spread among the faithful. Lest they captivate the faithful's minds and corrupt the purity of their faith, His Holiness Pius X, by Divine Providence, Pope, has decided that the chief errors should be noted and condemned by the Office of this Holy Roman and Universal Inquisition.

Therefore, after a very diligent investigation and consultation with the Reverend Consultors, the Most Eminent and Reverend Lord Cardinals, the General Inquisitors in matters of faith and morals have judged the following propositions to be condemned and proscribed. In fact, by this general decree, they are condemned and proscribed.

[The following propositions are hereby
condemned and proscribed:]

1. The ecclesiastical law which prescribes that books concerning
the Divine Scriptures are subject to previous examination does not
apply to critical scholars and students of scientific exegesis of the
Old Testament and New Testament.

2. The Church's interpretation of the Sacred Books is by no
means to be rejected; nevertheless, it is subject to the more accurate judgment and correction of the exegetes.

3. From the ecclesiastical judgments and censures passed against
free and more scientific exegesis, one can conclude that the Faith
the Church proposes contradicts history and that Catholic teaching cannot really be reconciled with the true origins of the Christian religion.

4. Even by dogmatic definitions the Church's Magisterium cannot determine the genuine sense of the Sacred Scriptures.

5. Since the Deposit of Faith contains only revealed truths, the
Church has no right to pass judgment on the assertions of the
human sciences.

6. The "Church learning" and the "Church teaching" collaborate
in such a way in defining truths that it only remains for the
"Church teaching" to sanction the opinions of the "Church learning."

7. In proscribing errors, the Church cannot demand any internal
assent from the faithful by which the judgments she issues are to
be embraced.

8. They are free from all blame who treat lightly the condemnations passed by the Sacred Congregation of the Index or by the
Roman Congregations.

9. They display excessive simplicity or ignorance who believe that God is really the author of the Sacred Scriptures.

10. The inspiration of the books of the Old Testament consists in this: The Israelite writers handed down religious doctrines under a peculiar aspect which was either little or not at all known to the Gentiles.

11. Divine inspiration does not extend to all of Sacred Scripture so that it renders its parts, each and every one, free from every error.

12. If he wishes to apply himself usefully to Biblical studies, the exegete must first put aside all preconceived opinions about the supernatural origin of Sacred Scripture and interpret it the same as any other merely human document.

13. The Evangelists themselves, as well as the Christians of the second and third generation, artificially arranged the evangelical parables. In such a way they explained the scanty fruit of the preaching of Christ among the Jews.

14. In many narrations the Evangelists recorded, not so much things that are true, as things which, even though false, they judged to be more profitable for their readers.

15. Until the time the canon was defined and constituted, the Gospels were increased by additions and corrections. Therefore there remained in them only a faint and uncertain trace of the doctrine of Christ.

16. The narrations of John are not properly history, but a mystical contemplation of the Gospel. The discourses contained in his Gospel are theological meditations, lacking historical truth concerning the mystery of salvation.

17. The fourth Gospel exaggerated miracles not only in order that the extraordinary might stand out but also in order that it might

become more suitable for showing forth the work and glory of the Word Incarnate.

18. John claims for himself the quality of witness concerning Christ. In reality, however, he is only a distinguished witness of the Christian life, or of the life of Christ in the Church at the close of the first century.

19. Heterodox exegetes have expressed the true sense of the Scriptures more faithfully than Catholic exegetes.

20. Revelation could be nothing else than the consciousness man acquired of his relation to God.

21. Revelation, constituting the object of the Catholic Faith, was not completed with the Apostles.

22. The dogmas the Church holds out as revealed are not truths which have fallen from Heaven. They are an interpretation of religious facts which the human mind has acquired by laborious effort.

23. Opposition may, and actually does, exist between the facts narrated in Sacred Scripture and the Church's dogmas which rest on them. Thus the critic may reject as false facts the Church holds as most certain.

24. The exegete who constructs premises from which it follows that dogmas are historically false or doubtful is not to be reproved as long as he does not directly deny the dogmas themselves.

25. The assent of faith ultimately rests on a mass of probabilities.

26. The dogmas of the Faith are to be held only according to their practical sense; that is to say, as preceptive norms of conduct and not as norms of believing.

27. The Divinity of Jesus Christ is not proved from the Gospels. It is a dogma which the Christian conscience has derived from the notion of the Messias.

28. While He was exercising His ministry, Jesus did not speak with the object of teaching He was the Messias, nor did His miracles tend to prove it.

29. It is permissible to grant that the Christ of history is far inferior to the Christ who is the object of faith.

30. In all the evangelical texts the name "Son of God" is equivalent only to that of "Messias." It does not in the least way signify that Christ is the true and natural Son of God.

31. The doctrine concerning Christ taught by Paul, John and the Councils of Nicea, Ephesus and Chalcedon is not that which Jesus taught but that which the Christian conscience conceived concerning Jesus.

32. It is impossible to reconcile the natural sense of the Gospel texts with the sense taught by our theologians concerning the conscience and the infallible knowledge of Jesus Christ.

33. Everyone who is not led by preconceived opinions can readily see that either Jesus professed an error concerning the immediate Messianic coming or the greater part of His doctrine as contained in the Gospels is destitute of authenticity.

34. The critics can ascribe to Christ a knowledge without limits only on a hypothesis which cannot be historically conceived and which is repugnant to the moral sense. That hypothesis is that Christ as man possessed the knowledge of God and yet was unwilling to communicate the knowledge of a great many things to His disciples and posterity.

35. Christ did not always possess the consciousness of His Messianic dignity.

36. The Resurrection of the Saviour is not properly a fact of the historical order. It is a fact of merely the supernatural order (neither demonstrated nor demonstrable) which the Christian conscience gradually derived from other facts.

37. In the beginning, faith in the Resurrection of Christ was not so much in the fact itself of the Resurrection as in the immortal life of Christ with God.

38. The doctrine of the expiatory death of Christ is Pauline and not evangelical.

39. The opinions concerning the origin of the Sacraments which the Fathers of Trent held and which certainly influenced their dogmatic canons are very different from those which now rightly exist among historians who examine Christianity.

40. The Sacraments had their origin in the fact that the Apostles and their successors, swayed and moved by circumstances and events, interpreted some idea and intention of Christ.

41. The Sacraments are intended merely to recall to man's mind the ever-beneficent presence of the Creator.

42. The Christian community imposed the necessity of Baptism, adopted it as a necessary rite and added to it the obligation of the Christian profession.

43. The practice of administering Baptism to infants was a disciplinary evolution, which became one of the causes why the Sacrament was divided into two, namely, Baptism and Penance.

44. There is nothing to prove that the rite of the Sacrament of Confirmation was employed by the Apostles. The formal distinc-

tion of the two Sacraments of Baptism and Confirmation does not pertain to the history of primitive Christianity.

45. Not everything which Paul narrates concerning the institution of the Eucharist (*1 Cor.* 11:23-25) is to be taken historically.

46. In the primitive Church the concept of the Christian sinner reconciled by the authority of the Church did not exist. Only very slowly did the Church accustom herself to this concept. As a matter of fact, even after Penance was recognized as an institution of the Church, it was not called a Sacrament since it would be held as a disgraceful Sacrament.

47. The words of the Lord, "Receive ye the Holy Ghost; whose sins you shall forgive, they are forgiven them; and whose *sins* you shall retain, they are retained" (*John* 20:22-23) in no way refer to the Sacrament of Penance, in spite of what it pleased the Fathers of Trent to say.

48. In his Epistle (ch. 5:14-15) James did not intend to promulgate a Sacrament of Christ but only commend a pious custom. If in this custom he happens to distinguish a means of grace, it is not in that rigorous manner in which it was taken by the theologians who laid down the notion and number of the Sacraments.

49. When the Christian supper gradually assumed the nature of a liturgical action, those who customarily presided over the supper acquired the sacerdotal character.

50. The elders who fulfilled the office of watching over the gatherings of the faithful were instituted by the Apostles as priests or bishops to provide for the necessary ordering of the increasing communities and not properly for the perpetuation of the Apostolic mission and power.

51. It is impossible that Matrimony could have become a Sacrament of the New Law until later in the Church since it was neces-

sary that a full theological explication of the doctrine of grace and the Sacraments should first take place before Matrimony should be held as a Sacrament.

52. It was far from the mind of Christ to found a Church as a society which would continue on earth for a long course of centuries. On the contrary, in the mind of Christ the kingdom of Heaven together with the end of the world was about to come immediately.

53. The organic constitution of the Church is not immutable. Like human society, Christian society is subject to a perpetual evolution.

54. Dogmas, Sacraments and hierarchy, both their notion and reality, are only interpretations and evolutions of the Christian intelligence which have increased and perfected by an external series of additions the little germ latent in the Gospel.

55. Simon Peter never even suspected that Christ entrusted the primacy in the Church to him.

56. The Roman Church became the head of all the churches, not through the ordinance of Divine Providence, but merely through political conditions.

57. The Church has shown that she is hostile to the progress of the natural and theological sciences.

58. Truth is no more immutable than man himself, since it evolved with him, in him and through him.

59. Christ did not teach a determined body of doctrine applicable to all times and all men, but rather inaugurated a religious movement adapted or to be adapted to different times and places.

60. Christian doctrine was originally Judaic. Through successive

evolutions it became first Pauline, then Joannine, finally Hellenic and universal.

61. It may be said without paradox that there is no chapter of Scripture, from the first of Genesis to the last of the Apocalypse, which contains a doctrine absolutely identical with that which the Church teaches on the same matter. For the same reason, therefore, no chapter of Scripture has the same sense for the critic and the theologian.

62. The chief articles of the Apostles' Creed did not have the same sense for the Christians of the first ages as they have for the Christians of our time.

63. The Church shows that she is incapable of effectively maintaining evangelical ethics, since she obstinately clings to immutable doctrines which cannot be reconciled with modern progress.

64. Scientific progress demands that the concepts of Christian doctrine concerning God, creation, revelation, the Person of the Incarnate Word and Redemption be re-adjusted.

65. Modern Catholicism can be reconciled with true science only if it is transformed into a non-dogmatic Christianity; that is to say, into a broad and liberal Protestantism.

The following Thursday, the fourth day of the same month and year, all these matters were accurately reported to our Most Holy Lord, Pope Pius X. His Holiness approved and confirmed the decree of the Most Eminent Fathers and ordered that each and every one of the above-listed propositions be held by all as condemned and proscribed.

Peter Palombelli
Notary of the Holy Roman and Universal Inquisition

# On Modernism
## *(Pascendi Dominici Gregis)*

September 8, 1907

Venerable Brethren, Health and the Apostolic Blessing

### *Duty of the Apostolic See*

1. One of the primary obligations assigned by Christ to the office divinely committed to Us of feeding the Lord's flock is that of guarding with the greatest vigilance the Deposit of the Faith delivered to the Saints, rejecting the profane novelties of words and the gainsaying of knowledge falsely so called. There has never been a time when this watchfulness of the supreme pastor was not necessary to the Catholic body, for, owing to the efforts of the enemy of the human race, there have never been lacking "men speaking perverse things" (*Titus* 1:10), "vain talkers and seducers" (*Acts* 20:30), "erring and driving into error." (*2 Tim.* 3:13). It must, however, be confessed that these latter days have witnessed a notable increase in the number of the enemies of the Cross of Christ, who, by arts entirely new and full of deceit, are striving to destroy the vital energy of the Church, and, as far as in them lies, utterly to subvert the very Kingdom of Christ. Wherefore We may no longer keep silence, lest We should seem to fail in Our most sacred duty, and lest the kindness that, in the hope of wiser counsels, We have hitherto shown them, should be set down to lack of diligence in the discharge of Our office.

### Necessity of Immediate Action

2. That We should act without delay in this matter is made imperative especially by the fact that the partisans of error are to be sought not only among the Church's open enemies; but, what is to be most dreaded and deplored, in her very bosom, and are the more mischievous the less they keep in the open. We allude, Venerable Brethren, to many who belong to the Catholic laity, and, what is much more sad, to the ranks of the priesthood itself, who, animated by a false zeal for the Church, lacking the solid safeguards of philosophy and theology, nay more, thoroughly imbued with the poisonous doctrines taught by the enemies of the Church, and lost to all sense of modesty, put themselves forward as reformers of the Church; and, forming more boldly into line of attack, assail all that is most sacred in the work of Christ, not sparing even the Person of the Divine Redeemer, whom, with sacrilegious audacity, they degrade to the condition of a simple and ordinary man.

### Characteristics of the Modernists

3. Although they express their astonishment that We should number them among the enemies of the Church, no one will be reasonably surprised that We should do so, if, leaving out of account the internal disposition of the soul, of which God alone is the Judge, he considers their tenets, their manner of speech and their action. Nor indeed would he be wrong in regarding them as the most pernicious of all the adversaries of the Church. For, as We have said, they put into operation their designs for her undoing, not from without but from within. Hence, the danger is present almost in the very veins and heart of the Church, whose injury is the more certain from the very fact that their knowledge of her is more intimate. Moreover, they lay the ax not to the branches and shoots, but to the very root, that is, to the Faith and its deepest fibers. And once having struck at this root of immortality, they proceed to diffuse poison through the whole tree, so that there is no part of Catholic truth which they leave untouched, none that

they do not strive to corrupt. Further, none is more skillful, none more astute than they, in the employment of a thousand noxious devices; for they play the double part of rationalist and Catholic, and this so craftily that they easily lead the unwary into error; and as audacity is their chief characteristic, there is no conclusion of any kind from which they shrink or which they do not thrust forward with pertinacity and assurance. To this must be added the fact, which indeed is well calculated to deceive souls, that they lead a life of the greatest activity, of assiduous and ardent application to every branch of learning, and that they possess, as a rule, a reputation for irreproachable morality. Finally, there is the fact which is all but fatal to the hope of cure that their very doctrines have given such a bent to their minds, that they disdain all authority and brook no restraint; and relying upon a false conscience, they attempt to ascribe to a love of truth that which is in reality the result of pride and obstinacy.

## Previous Attempts Have Failed

Once indeed We had hopes of recalling them to a better mind, and to this end We first of all treated them with kindness as Our children, then with severity; and at last We have had recourse, though with great reluctance, to public reproof. It is known to you, Venerable Brethren, how unavailing have been Our efforts. For a moment they have bowed their head, only to lift it more arrogantly than before. If it were a matter which concerned them alone, We might perhaps have overlooked it; but the security of the Catholic name is at stake. Wherefore We must interrupt a silence which it would be criminal to prolong, that We may point out to the whole Church, as they really are, men who are badly disguised.

## Division of the Encyclical

4. It is one of the cleverest devices of the Modernists (as they are commonly and rightly called) to present their doctrines without order and systematic arrangement, in a scattered and dis-

jointed manner, so as to make it appear as if their minds were in doubt or hesitation, whereas in reality they are quite fixed and steadfast. For this reason it will be of advantage, Venerable Brethren, to bring their teachings together here into one group, and to point out their interconnection, and thus to pass to an examination of the sources of the errors, and to prescribe remedies for averting the evil results.

## The Modernist Personality

5. To proceed in an orderly manner in this somewhat abstruse subject, it must first of all be noted that the Modernist sustains and includes within himself a manifold personality; he is a philosopher, a believer, a theologian, an historian, a critic, an apologist, a reformer. These roles must be clearly distinguished one from another by all who would accurately understand their system and thoroughly grasp the principles and the outcome of their doctrines.

## Agnosticism

6. We begin, then, with the philosopher. Modernists place the foundation of religious philosophy in that doctrine which is commonly called *Agnosticism*. According to this teaching human reason is confined entirely within the field of *phenomena*, that is to say, to things that appear, and in the manner in which they appear: it has neither the right nor the power to overstep these limits. Hence it is incapable of lifting itself up to God, and of recognizing His existence, even by means of visible things. From this it is inferred that God can never be the direct object of science, and that, as regards history, He must not be considered as an historical subject. Given these premises, everyone will at once perceive what becomes of *Natural Theology*, of the *motives of credibility*, of *external revelation*. The Modernists simply sweep them entirely aside; they include them in *Intellectualism*, which they denounce as a system which is ridiculous and long since defunct. Nor does the fact that the Church has formally condemned these

portentous errors exercise the slightest restraint upon them. Yet the Vatican Council has defined, "If anyone says that the one true God, our Creator and Lord, cannot be known with certainty by the natural light of human reason by means of the things that are made, let him be anathema;"[1] and also, "If anyone says that it is not possible or not expedient that man be taught, through the medium of Divine Revelation, about God and the worship to be paid Him, let him be anathema;"[2] and finally, "If anyone says that Divine Revelation cannot be made credible by external signs, and that therefore men should be drawn to the faith only by their personal internal experience or by private inspiration, let him be anathema."[3] It may be asked, in what way do the Modernists contrive to make the transition from *Agnosticism*, which is a state of pure nescience, to scientific and historic *Atheism*, which is a doctrine of positive denial; and consequently, by what legitimate process of reasoning, they proceed from the fact of ignorance as to whether God has in fact intervened in the history of the human race or not, to explain this history, leaving God out altogether, as if He really had not intervened. Let him answer who can. Yet it is a fixed and established principle among them that both science and history must be atheistic: and within their boundaries there is room for nothing but *phenomena*; God and all that is divine are utterly excluded. We shall soon see clearly what, as a consequence of this most absurd teaching, must be held touching the most sacred Person of Christ, and the mysteries of His life and death and of His Resurrection and Ascension into Heaven.

### Vital Immanence

7. However, this *Agnosticism* is only the negative part of the system of the Modernists: the positive part consists in what they call *vital immanence*. Thus they advance from one to the other. Religion, whether natural or supernatural, must, like every other fact, admit of some explanation. But when natural theology has been destroyed, and the road to revelation closed by the rejection of the arguments of credibility, and all external revelation absolutely denied, it is clear that this explanation will be sought in

vain outside of man himself. It must, therefore, be looked for *in* man; and since religion is a form of life, the explanation must certainly be found in the life of man. In this way is formulated the principle of *religious immanence*. Moreover, the first actuation, so to speak, of every vital phenomenon—and religion, as noted above, belongs to this category—is due to a certain need or impulsion; but speaking more particularly of life, it has its origin in a movement of the heart, which movement is called a *sense*. Therefore, as God is the object of religion, we must conclude that faith, which is the basis and foundation of all religion, must consist in a certain interior sense, originating in a need of the divine. This need of the divine, which is experienced only in special and favorable circumstances, cannot of itself appertain to the domain of consciousness, but is first latent beneath consciousness, or, to borrow a term from modern philosophy, in the *subconsciousness*, where also its root lies hidden and undetected.

### The Need of the Divine

It may perhaps be asked how it is that this need of the divine which man experiences within himself resolves itself into religion? To this question the Modernist reply would be as follows: Science and history are confined within two boundaries, the one external, namely, the visible world, the other internal, which is consciousness. When one or other of these limits has been reached, there can be no further progress, for beyond is the *unknowable*. In presence of this *unknowable*, whether it is outside man and beyond the visible world of nature, or lies hidden within the subconsciousness, the need of the divine in a soul which is prone to religion excites—according to the principles of *Fideism*, without any previous advertence of the mind—a certain special sense, and this sense possesses, implied within itself both as its own object and as its intrinsic cause, the divine *reality* itself, and in a way unites man with God. It is this *sense* to which Modernists give the name of faith, and this is what they hold to be the beginning of religion.

### The Modernist's Revelation

8. But we have not yet reached the end of their philosophizing, or, to speak more accurately, of their folly. Modernists find in this *sense* not only faith, but in and with faith, as they understand it, they affirm that there is also to be found *revelation*. For, indeed, what more is needed to constitute a revelation? Is not that religious sense which is perceptible in the conscience, revelation, or at least the beginning of revelation? Nay, is it not God Himself manifesting Himself, indistinctly, it is true, in this same religious *sense*, to the soul? And they add: Since God is both the object and the cause of faith, this revelation is at the same time *of* God and *from* God, that is to say, God is both the Revealer and the Revealed.

### Religious Consciousness and Faith

From this, Venerable Brethren, springs that most absurd tenet of the Modernists, that every religion, according to the different aspect under which it is viewed, must be considered as both natural and supernatural. It is thus that they make consciousness and revelation synonymous. From this they derive the law laid down as the universal standard, according to which *religious consciousness* is to be put on an equal footing with revelation, and that to it all must submit, even the supreme authority of the Church, whether in the capacity of teacher, or in that of legislator in the province of sacred liturgy or discipline.

### Deformation of Religious History

9. In all this process, from which, according to the Modernists, faith and revelation spring, one point is to be particularly noted, for it is of capital importance on account of the historico-critical corollaries which they deduce from it. The *unknowable* they speak of does not present itself to faith as something solitary and isolated; but on the contrary in close conjunction with some phenomenon, which, though it belongs to the realms of science or

history, yet to some extent exceeds their limits. Such a phenomenon may be a fact of nature containing within itself something mysterious; or it may be a man, whose character, actions and words cannot, apparently, be reconciled with the ordinary laws of history. Then faith, attracted by the *unknowable* which is united with the phenomenon, seizes upon the whole phenomenon, and, as it were, permeates it with its own life. From this two things follow. The first is a sort of *transfiguration* of the phenomenon, by its elevation above its own true conditions, an elevation by which it becomes more adapted to clothe itself with the form of the divine character which faith will bestow upon it. The second consequence is a certain *disfiguration*—so it may be called—of the same phenomenon, arising from the fact that faith attributes to it, when stripped of the circumstances of place and time, characteristics which it does not really possess; and this takes place especially in the case of the phenomena of the past, and the more fully in the measure of their antiquity. From these two principles the Modernists deduce two laws, which, when united with a third which they have already derived from agnosticism, constitute the foundation of historic criticism. An example may be sought in the Person of Christ. In the Person of Christ, they say, science and history encounter nothing that is not human. Therefore, in virtue of the first canon deduced from agnosticism, whatever there is in His history suggestive of the divine must be rejected. Then, according to the second canon, the historical Person of Christ was *transfigured* by faith; therefore everything that raises it above historical conditions must be removed. Lastly, the third canon, which lays down that the Person of Christ has been *disfigured* by faith, requires that everything should be excluded, deeds and words and all else, that is not in strict keeping with His character, condition and education, and with the place and time in which He lived—a method of reasoning which is passing strange, but in it we have the Modernist criticism.

### The Religious Sense

10. It is thus that the *religious sense*, which through the agency

of *vital immanence* emerges from the lurking-places of the *sub-consciousness*, is the germ of all religion and the explanation of everything that has been or ever will be in any religion. This *sense*, which was at first only rudimentary and almost formless, under the influence of that mysterious principle from which it originated, gradually matured with the progress of human life, of which, as has been said, it is a certain form. This, then, is the origin of all, even of supernatural religion. For religions are mere developments of this *religious sense*. Nor is the Catholic religion an exception; it is quite on a level with the rest; for it was engendered, by the process of *vital immanence*, and by no other way, in the consciousness of Christ, who was a man of the choicest nature, whose like has never been, nor will be. In hearing these things we shudder indeed at so great an audacity of assertion and so great a sacrilege. And yet, Venerable Brethren, these are not merely the foolish babblings of unbelievers. There are Catholics, yea, and priests too, who say these things openly; and they boast that they are going to reform the Church by these ravings! The question is no longer one of the old error which claimed for human nature a sort of right to the supernatural. It has gone far beyond that, and has reached the point when it is affirmed that our most holy religion, in the man Christ as in us, emanated from nature spontaneously and of itself. Nothing assuredly could be more utterly destructive of the whole supernatural order. For this reason the Vatican Council most justly decreed: "If anyone says that man cannot be raised by God to a knowledge and perfection which surpasses nature, but that he can and should, by his own efforts and by a constant development, attain finally to the possession of all truth and good, let him be anathema."[4]

### The Intellect and Religious Sense

11. So far, Venerable Brethren, there has been no mention of the intellect. It also, according to the teaching of the Modernists, has its part in the act of faith. And it is of importance to see how. In that *sense* of which We have frequently spoken, since *sense* is not knowledge, they say God, indeed, presents Himself to man,

but in a manner so confused and indistinct that He can hardly be perceived by the believer. It is therefore necessary that a certain light should be cast upon this sense so that God may clearly stand out in relief and be set apart from it. This is the task of the intellect, whose office it is to reflect and to analyze; and by means of it, man first transforms into mental pictures the vital phenomena which arise within him, and then expresses them in words. Hence the common saying of Modernists: that the religious man must *think* his faith. The mind then, encountering this *sense*, throws itself upon it, and works in it after the manner of a painter who restores to greater clearness the lines of a picture that have been dimmed with age. The simile is that of one of the leaders of Modernism. The operation of the mind in this work is a double one: first, by a natural and spontaneous act it expresses its concept in a simple, popular statement; then, on reflection and deeper consideration, or, as they say, *by elaborating its thought*, it expresses the idea in *secondary* propositions, which are derived from the first, but are more precise and distinct. These *secondary* propositions, if they finally receive the approval of the supreme Magisterium of the Church, constitute *dogma*.

## The Origin of Dogma

12. We have thus reached one of the principal points in the Modernist's system, namely, the origin and the nature of dogma. For they place the origin of dogma in those primitive and simple formulas, which, under a certain aspect, are necessary to faith; for revelation, to be truly such, requires the clear knowledge of God in the consciousness. But dogma itself, they apparently hold, strictly consists in the *secondary* formulas.

## The Nature of Dogma

To ascertain the nature of dogma, we must first find the relation which exists between the *religious formulas* and the *religious sense*. This will be readily perceived by anyone who holds that these *formulas* have no other purpose than to furnish the believer with a means of giving to himself an account of his faith. These formulas therefore stand midway between the believer and his faith; in their relation to the faith they are the inadequate expression of its object, and are usually called *symbols*; in their relation to the believer they are mere *instruments*.

## Dogmas Are Symbols

Hence it is quite impossible to maintain that they absolutely contain the truth: for, in so far as they are *symbols*, they are the images of truth, and so must be adapted to the religious sense in its relation to man; and as *instruments*, they are the vehicles of truth, and must therefore in their turn be adapted to man in his relation to the religious sense. But the object of the *religious sense*, as something contained in the *absolute*, possesses an infinite variety of aspects, of which now one, now another, may present itself. In like manner he who believes can avail himself of varying conditions. Consequently, the formulas which we call dogma must be subject to these vicissitudes, and are, therefore, liable to change. Thus the way is open to the intrinsic *evolution* of dogma. Here we have an immense structure of sophisms which ruin and wreck all religion.

## Evolution of Dogma

13. Dogma is not only able, but ought to evolve and to be changed. This is strongly affirmed by the Modernists, and clearly flows from their principles. For among the chief points of their teaching is the following, which they deduce from the principle of *vital immanence*, namely, that *religious formulas* if they are to be really *religious* and not merely intellectual speculations, ought to be living and to live the life of the *religious sense*. This is not to be understood to mean that these formulas, especially if merely imaginative, were to be invented for the religious sense. Their origin matters nothing, any more than their number or quality. What is necessary is that the *religious sense*—with some modification when needful—should vitally assimilate them. In other words, it

is necessary that the *primitive formula* be accepted and sanctioned by the heart; and similarly the subsequent work from which are brought forth the *secondary formulas* must proceed under the guidance of the heart. Hence it comes that these formulas, in order to be living, should be, and should remain, adapted to the faith and to him who believes. Wherefore, if for any reason this adaptation should cease to exist, they lose their first meaning and accordingly need to be changed. In view of the fact that the character and lot of dogmatic formulas are so unstable, it is no wonder that Modernists should regard them so lightly and in such open disrespect, and have no consideration or praise for anything but the religious sense and for the religious life. In this way, with consummate audacity, they criticize the Church, as having strayed from the true path by failing to distinguish between the religious and moral sense of formulas and their surface meaning, and by clinging vainly and tenaciously to meaningless formulas, while religion itself is allowed to go to ruin. "Blind" they are, and "leaders of the blind" puffed up with the proud name of science, they have reached that pitch of folly at which they pervert the eternal concept of truth and the true meaning of religion; in introducing a new system in which "they are seen to be under the sway of a blind and unchecked passion for novelty, thinking not at all of finding some solid foundation of truth, but despising the holy and apostolic traditions, they embrace other and vain, futile, uncertain doctrines, unapproved by the Church, on which, in the height of their vanity, they think they can base and maintain truth itself."[5]

### The Modernist as a Believer

14. Thus far, Venerable Brethren, We have considered the Modernist as a philosopher. Now if We proceed to consider him as a believer, and seek to know how the believer, according to Modernism, is marked off from the philosopher, it must be observed that, although the philosopher recognizes the *reality of the divine* as the object of faith, still this *reality* is not to be found by him but in the heart of the believer, as an object of feeling and affirmation, and therefore confined within the sphere of phenom-

ena; but the question as to whether in itself it exists outside that feeling and affirmation is one which the philosopher passes over and neglects. For the Modernist believer, on the contrary, it is an established and certain fact that the reality of the divine does really exist in itself and quite independently of the person who believes in it. If you ask on what foundation this assertion of the believer rests, he answers: In the personal *experience* of the individual. On this head the Modernists differ from the Rationalists only to fall into the views of the Protestants and pseudo-mystics. The following is their manner of stating the question: In the *religious sense* one must recognize a kind of intuition of the heart which puts man in immediate contact with the *reality* of God, and infuses such a persuasion of God's existence and His action both within and without man as far to exceed any scientific conviction. They assert, therefore, the existence of a real experience, and one of a kind that surpasses all rational experience. If this experience is denied by some, like the Rationalists, they say that this arises from the fact that such persons are unwilling to put themselves in the moral state necessary to produce it. It is this *experience* which makes the person who acquires it to be properly and truly a believer.

### Destruction of One True Religion

How far this position is removed from that of Catholic teaching! We have already seen how its fallacies have been condemned by the Vatican Council. Later on, we shall see how these errors, combined with those which we have already mentioned, open wide the way to Atheism. Here it is well to note at once that, given this doctrine of *experience* united with that of *symbolism*, every religion, even that of paganism, must be held to be true. What is to prevent such experiences from being found in any religion? In fact, that they are so is maintained by not a few. On what grounds can Modernists deny the truth of an experience affirmed by a follower of Islam? Will they claim a monopoly of true experiences for Catholics alone? Indeed, Modernists do not deny, but actually maintain, some confusedly, others frankly, that all religions are true. That they cannot feel otherwise is obvious. For on what ground, according to their theories, could falsity be predicated of any religion whatsoever? Certainly it would be either on account of the falsity of the *religious sense* or on account of the falsity of the formula pronounced by the mind. Now the *religious sense*, although it maybe more perfect or less perfect, is always one and the same; and the intellectual formula, in order to be true, has but to respond to the *religious sense* and to the believer, whatever be the intellectual capacity of the latter. In the conflict between different religions, the most that Modernists can maintain is that the Catholic has more truth because it is more vivid, and that it deserves with more reason the name of Christian because it corresponds more fully with the origins of Christianity. No one will find it unreasonable that these consequences flow from the premises. But what is most amazing is that there are Catholics and priests, who, We would fain believe, abhor such enormities, and yet act as if they fully approved of them. For they lavish such praise and bestow such public honor on the teachers of these errors as to convey the belief that their admiration is not meant merely for the persons, who are perhaps not devoid of a certain merit, but rather for the sake of the errors which these persons openly profess and which they do all in their power to propagate.

### Religious Experience and Tradition

15. There is yet another element in this part of their teaching which is absolutely contrary to Catholic truth. For what is laid down as to *experience* is also applied with destructive effect to *tradition*, which has always been maintained by the Catholic Church. Tradition, as understood by the Modernists, is a communication with others of an *original experience*, through preaching by means of the intellectual formula. To this formula, in addition to its *representative* value they attribute a species of *suggestive* efficacy which acts firstly in the believer by stimulating the *religious sense*, should it happen to have grown sluggish, and by renewing the *experience* once acquired, and secondly, in those who do not yet believe by awakening in them for the first time the

*religious sense* and producing the *experience*. In this way is religious experience spread abroad among the nations; and not merely among contemporaries by preaching, but among future generations both by books and by oral transmission from one to another. Sometimes this communication of religious experience takes root and thrives, at other times it withers at once and dies. For the Modernists, to live is a proof of truth, since for them life and truth are one and the same thing. Thus we are once more led to infer that all existing religions are equally true, for otherwise they would not survive.

### Faith and Science

16.  We have proceeded sufficiently far, Venerable Brethren, to have before us enough, and more than enough, to enable us to see what are the relations which Modernists establish between faith and science—including, as they are wont to do under that name, history. And in the first place it is to be held that the object-matter of the one is quite extraneous to and separate from the object-matter of the other. For faith occupies itself solely with something which science declares to be for it *unknowable*. Hence each has a separate scope assigned to it: science is entirely concerned with phenomena, into which faith does not at all enter; faith, on the contrary, concerns itself with the divine, which is entirely unknown to science. Thus it is contended that there can never be any dissension between faith and science, for if each keeps on its own ground they can never meet and therefore never can be in contradiction. And if it be objected that in the visible world there are some things which appertain to faith, such as the human life of Christ, the Modernists reply by denying this. For though such things come within the category of phenomena, still in as far as they are *lived* by faith and in the way already described have been by faith *transfigured* and *disfigured*, they have been removed from the world of sense and transferred into material for the divine. Hence should it be further asked whether Christ has wrought real miracles, and made real prophecies, whether He rose truly from the dead and ascended into Heaven, the answer of agnostic sci-

ence will be in the negative and the answer of faith in the affir-
mative—yet there will not be, on that account, any conflict
between them. For it will be denied by the philosopher as a
philosopher speaking to philosophers and considering Christ only
in His *historical reality*; and it will be affirmed by the believer as
a believer speaking to believers and considering the life of Christ
as *lived again* by the faith and in the faith.

## Faith Subject to Science

17. It would be a great mistake, nevertheless, to suppose that,
according to these theories, one is allowed to believe that faith and
science are entirely independent of each other. On the side of science that is indeed quite true and correct, but it is quite otherwise
with regard to faith, which is subject to science, not on one but on
three grounds. For in the first place it must be observed that in
every religious fact, when one takes away the *divine reality* and
the *experience* of it which the believer possesses, everything else,
and especially the *religious formulas*, belongs to the sphere of
phenomena and therefore falls under the control of science. Let
the believer go out of the world if he will, but so long as he
remains in it, whether he like it or not, he cannot escape from the
laws, the observation, the judgments of science and of history.
Further, although it is contended that God is the object of faith
alone, the statement refers only to the *divine reality*, not to the
*idea* of God. The latter also is subject to science which, while it
philosophizes in what is called the logical order, soars also to the
absolute and the ideal. It is therefore the right of philosophy and
of science to form its knowledge concerning the idea of God, to
direct it in its evolution and to purify it of any extraneous elements
which may have entered into it. Hence we have the Modernist
axiom that the religious evolution ought to be brought into accord
with the moral and intellectual, or as one whom they regard as
their leader has expressed it, ought to be subject to it. Finally, man
does not suffer a dualism to exist in himself, and the believer
therefore feels within him an impelling need so to harmonize faith
with science that it may never oppose the general conception

which science sets forth concerning the universe.

Thus it is evident that science is to be entirely independent of faith, while on the other hand, and notwithstanding that they are supposed to be strangers to each other, faith is made subject to science. All this, Venerable Brethren, is in formal opposition to the teachings of Our predecessor, Pius IX, where he lays it down that: "In matters of religion it is the duty of philosophy not to command but to serve, not to prescribe what is to be believed, but to embrace what is to be believed with reasonable obedience, not to scrutinize the depths of the mysteries of God, but to venerate them devoutly and humbly."[6]

The Modernists completely invert the parts, and of them may be applied the words which another of Our predecessors, Gregory IX, addressed to some theologians of his time: "Some among you, puffed up like bladders with the spirit of vanity, strive by profane novelties to cross the boundaries fixed by the Fathers, twisting the meaning of the sacred text . . . to the philosophical teaching of the rationalists, not for the profit of their hearer but to make a show of science . . . these men, led away by various and strange doctrines, turn the head into the tail and force the queen to serve the handmaid."[7]

### The Methods of Modernists

18. This will appear more clearly to anybody who studies the conduct of Modernists, which is in perfect harmony with their teachings. In their writings and addresses they seem not infrequently to advocate doctrines which are contrary one to the other, so that one would be disposed to regard their attitude as double and doubtful. But this is done deliberately and advisedly, and the reason of it is to be found in their opinion as to the mutual separation of science and faith. Thus in their books one finds some things which might well be approved by a Catholic, but on turning over the page one is confronted by other things which might well have been dictated by a rationalist. When they write history they make no mention of the divinity of Christ, but when they are in the pulpit they profess it clearly; again, when they are dealing

with history they take no account of the Fathers and the Councils, but when they catechize the people, they cite them respectfully. In the same way they draw their distinctions between exegesis which is theological and pastoral and exegesis which is scientific and historical. So, too, when they treat of philosophy, history and criticism, acting on the principle that science in no way depends upon faith, they feel no especial horror in treading in the footsteps of Luther[8] and are wont to display a manifold contempt for Catholic doctrines, for the Holy Fathers, for the Ecumenical Councils, for the ecclesiastical Magisterium; and should they be taken to task for this, they complain that they are being deprived of their liberty. Lastly, maintaining the theory that faith must be subject to science, they continuously and openly rebuke the Church on the ground that she resolutely refuses to submit and accommodate her dogmas to the opinions of philosophy; while they, on their side, having for this purpose blotted out the old theology, endeavor to introduce a new theology which shall support the aberrations of philosophers.

### *The Modernist as Theologian*

19.  At this point, Venerable Brethren, the way is opened for us to consider the Modernists in the theological arena—a difficult task, yet one that may be disposed of briefly. It is a question of effecting the conciliation of faith with science, but always by making the one subject to the other. In this matter the Modernist theologian takes exactly the same principles which we have seen employed by the Modernist philosopher—the principles of *immanence* and *symbolism*—and applies them to the believer. The process is an extremely simple one. The philosopher has declared: *The principle of faith is immanent*; the believer has added: *This principle is God*; and the theologian draws the conclusion: *God is immanent in man*. Thus we have *theological immanence*. So, too, the philosopher regards it as certain that *the representations of the object of faith are merely symbolical*; the believer has likewise affirmed that *the object of faith is God in himself*; and the theologian proceeds to affirm that: *The representations of the divine*

*reality are symbolical.* And thus we have *theological symbolism.* These errors are truly of the gravest kind and the pernicious character of both will be seen clearly from an examination of their consequences. For, to begin with *symbolism,* since symbols are but symbols in regard to their objects and only instruments in regard to the believer, it is necessary first of all, according to the teachings of the Modernists, that the believer does not lay too much stress on the formula, as formula, but avail himself of it only for the purpose of uniting himself to the absolute truth which the formula at once reveals and conceals, that is to say, endeavors to express but without ever succeeding in doing so. They would also have the believer make use of the formulas only in as far as they are helpful to him, for they are given to be a help and not a hindrance; with proper regard, however, for the social respect due to formulas which the public magisterium has deemed suitable for expressing the common consciousness until such time as the same magisterium shall provide otherwise. Concerning *immanence* it is not easy to determine what Modernists precisely mean by it, for their own opinions on the subject vary. Some understand it in the sense that God working in man is more intimately present in him than man is even in himself; and this conception, if properly understood, is irreproachable. Others hold that the divine action is one with the action of nature, as the action of the first cause is one with the action of the secondary cause; and this would destroy the supernatural order. Others, finally, explain it in a way which savors of pantheism, and this, in truth, is the sense which best fits in with the rest of their doctrines.

### The Principle of Divine Permanence

20. With this principle of *immanence* is connected another which may be called the principle of *divine permanence.* It differs from the first in much the same way as the private *experience* differs from the *experience* transmitted by Tradition. An example illustrating what is meant will be found in the Church and the Sacraments. The Church and the Sacraments, according to the Modernists, are not to be regarded as having been instituted by

Christ Himself. This is barred by agnosticism, which recognizes in Christ nothing more than a man whose religious consciousness has been, like that of all men, formed by degrees; it is also barred by the law of immanence, which rejects what they call external *application*; it is further barred by the law of evolution, which requires, for the development of the germs, time and a certain series of circumstances; it is finally, barred by history, which shows that such in fact has been the course of things. Still it is to he held that both Church and Sacraments have been founded *mediately* by Christ. But how? In this way: All Christian consciences were, they affirm, in a manner virtually included in the conscience of Christ as the plant is included in the seed. But as the branches live the life of the seed, so, too, all Christians are to be said to live the life of Christ. But the life of Christ, according to faith, is divine, and so, too, is the life of Christians. And if this life produced, in the course of ages, both the Church and the Sacraments, it is quite right to say that their origin is from Christ and is divine. In the same way they make out that the Holy Scriptures and the dogmas are divine. And in this, the Modernist theology may be said to reach its completion. A slender provision, in truth, but more than enough for the theologian who professes that the conclusions of science, whatever they may be, must always be accepted! No one will have any difficulty in making the application of these theories to the other points with which We propose to deal.

### Dogma and the Sacraments

21. Thus far We have touched upon the origin and nature of faith. But as faith has many branches, and chief among them the Church, dogma, worship, devotions, the Books which we call "sacred," it concerns us to know what the Modernists teach concerning them. To begin with dogma, We have already indicated its origin and nature. Dogma is born of a sort of impulse or necessity by virtue of which the believer elaborates his thought so as to render it clearer to his own conscience and that of others. This elaboration consists entirely in the process of investigating and

refining the primitive mental *formula*, not indeed in itself and according to any logical explanation, but according to circumstances, or *vitally* as the Modernists somewhat less intelligibly describe it. Hence it happens that around this *primitive* formula *secondary* formulas, as We have already indicated, gradually continue to be formed, and these subsequently grouped into one body, or one doctrinal construction, and further sanctioned by the public magisterium as responding to the common consciousness, are called dogma. Dogma is to be carefully distinguished from the speculations of theologians which, although not alive with the life of dogma, are not without their utility as serving both to harmonize religion with science and to remove opposition between them, and to illumine and defend religion from without, and it may be even to prepare the matter for future dogma. Concerning worship there would not be much to be said, were it not that under this head are comprised the Sacraments, concerning which the Modernist errors are of the most serious character. For them the Sacraments are the resultant of a double impulse or need—for, as we have seen, everything in their system is explained by inner impulses or necessities. The first need is that of giving some sensible manifestation to religion; the second is that of expressing it, which could not be done without some sensible form and consecrating acts, and these are called Sacraments. But for the Modernists, Sacraments are bare symbols or signs, though not devoid of a certain efficacy—an efficacy, they tell us, like that of certain phrases vulgarly described as having caught the popular ear, inasmuch as they have the power of putting certain leading ideas into circulation, and of making a marked impression upon the mind. What the phrases are to the ideas, that the Sacraments are to the religious sense, that and nothing more. The Modernists would express their mind more clearly were they to affirm that the Sacraments are instituted solely to foster the faith—but this is condemned by the Council of Trent: *If anyone says that these Sacraments are instituted solely to foster the faith, let him be anathema.*[9]

### The Holy Scriptures

22. We have already touched upon the nature and origin of the Sacred Books. According to the principles of the Modernists they may be rightly described as a summary of *experiences*, not indeed of the kind that may now and again come to anybody, but those extraordinary and striking experiences which are the possession of every religion. And this is precisely what they teach about our books of the Old and New Testament. But to suit their own theories they note with remarkable ingenuity that, although experience is something belonging to the present, still it may draw its material in like manner from the past and the future inasmuch as the believer by memory *lives* the past over again after the manner of *the present*, and lives the future already by anticipation. This explains how it is that the historical and apocalyptic books are included among the Sacred Writings. God does indeed speak in these books through the medium of the believer, but according to Modernist theology, only by *immanence* and *vital permanence*. We may ask, what then becomes of inspiration? Inspiration, they reply, is in nowise distinguished from that impulse which stimulates the believer to reveal the faith that is in him by words of writing, except perhaps by its vehemence. It is something like that which happens in poetical inspiration, of which it has been said: There is a god in us, and when he stirreth he sets us afire. It is in this sense that God is said to be the origin of the inspiration of the Sacred Books. The Modernists, moreover, affirm concerning this inspiration that there is nothing in the Sacred Books which is devoid of it. In this respect some might be disposed to consider them as more orthodox than certain writers in recent times who somewhat restrict inspiration, as, for instance, in what have been put forward as so-called *tacit citations*. But in all this we have mere verbal conjuring. For if we take the Bible, according to the standards of agnosticism, namely, as a human work, made by men for men, albeit the theologian is allowed to proclaim that it is divine by *immanence*, what room is there left in it for inspiration? The Modernists assert a general inspiration of the Sacred Books, but they admit no inspiration in the Catholic sense.

## The Church

23. A wider field for comment is opened when we come to what the Modernist school has imagined to be the nature of the Church. They begin with the supposition that the Church has its birth in a double need; first, the need of the individual believer to communicate his faith to others, especially if he has had some original and special experience, and secondly, when the faith has become common to many, the need of the *collectivity* to form itself into a society and to guard, promote and propagate the common good. What, then, is the Church? It is the product of the *collective conscience*, that is to say, of the association of individual consciences which, by virtue of the principle of *vital permanence*, depend all on one first believer, who for Catholics is Christ. Now every society needs a directing authority to guide its members toward the common end, to foster prudently the elements of cohesion, which in a religious society are doctrine and worship. Hence the triple authority in the Catholic Church, *disciplinary, dogmatic, liturgical.* The nature of this authority is to be gathered from its origin, and its rights and duties from its nature. In past times it was a common error that authority came to the Church from without, that is to say directly from God; and it was then rightly held to be *autocratic.* But this conception has now grown obsolete. For in the same way as the Church is a vital emanation of the collectivity of consciences, so too authority emanates vitally from the Church itself. Authority, therefore, like the Church, has its origin in the religious conscience, and, that being so, is subject to it. Should it disown this dependence it becomes a tyranny. For we are living in an age when the sense of liberty has reached its highest development. In the civil order the public conscience has introduced popular government. Now there is in man only one conscience, just as there is only one life. It is for the ecclesiastical authority, therefore, to adopt a democratic form, unless it wishes to provoke and foment an intestine conflict in the consciences of mankind. The penalty of refusal is disaster. For it is madness to think that the sentiment of liberty, as it now obtains, can recede. Were it forcibly pent up and held in bonds, the more terrible

would be its outburst, sweeping away at once both Church and religion. Such is the situation in the minds of the Modernists, and their one great anxiety is, in consequence, to find a way of conciliation between the authority of the Church and the liberty of the believers.

### Relation of Church and State

24. But it is not only within her own household that the Church must come to terms. Besides her relations with those within, she has others with those who are outside. The Church does not occupy the world all by herself; there are other societies in the world, with which she must necessarily have dealings and contact. The rights and duties of the Church towards civil societies must, therefore, be determined, and determined, of course, by her own nature, that, to wit, which the Modernists have already described to us. The rules to be applied in this matter are clearly those which have been laid down for science and faith, though in the latter case the question turned upon the *object*, while in the present case we have one of *ends*. In the same way, then, as faith and science are alien to each other by reason of the diversity of their *objects*, Church and State are strangers by reason of the diversity of their ends, that of the Church being spiritual while that of the State is temporal. Formerly it was possible to subordinate the temporal to the spiritual and to speak of some questions as *mixed*, conceding to the Church the position of queen and mistress in all such, because the Church was then regarded as having been instituted immediately by God as the author of the supernatural order. But this doctrine is today repudiated alike by philosophers and historians. The State must, therefore, be separated from the Church, and the Catholic from the citizen. Every Catholic, from the fact that he is also a citizen, has the right and the duty to work for the common good in the way he thinks best, without troubling himself about the authority of the Church, without paying any heed to its wishes, its counsels, its orders—nay, even in spite of its rebukes. For the Church to trace out and prescribe for the citizen any line of action, on any pretext whatsoever, is to be guilty of an

abuse of authority, against which one is bound to protest with all one's might. Venerable Brethren, the principles from which these doctrines spring have been solemnly condemned by Our predecessor, Pius VI, in his Apostolic Constitution *Auctorem Fidei*.[10]

### The Church's Magisterium

25. But it is not enough for the Modernist school that the State should be separated from the Church. For as faith is to be subordinated to science as far as phenomenal elements are concerned, so too in temporal matters the Church must be subject to the State. This, indeed, Modernists may not yet say openly, but they are forced by the logic of their position to admit it. For granted the principle that in temporal matters the State possesses the sole power, it will follow that when the believer, not satisfied with merely internal acts of religion, proceeds to external acts—such for instance as the reception or administration of the Sacraments—these will fall under the control of the State. What will then become of ecclesiastical authority, which can only be exercised by external acts? Obviously it will be completely under the dominion of the State. It is this inevitable consequence which urges many among *liberal* Protestants to reject all external worship—nay, all external religious fellowship, and leads them to advocate what they call *individual* religion. If the Modernists have not yet openly proceeded so far, they ask the Church in the meantime to follow of her own accord in the direction in which they urge her and to adapt herself to the forms of the State. Such are their ideas about *disciplinary* authority. But much more evil and pernicious are their opinions on *doctrinal* and *dogmatic* authority. The following is their conception of the Magisterium of the Church: No religious society, they say, can be a real unit unless the religious conscience of its members be one, and also the formula which they adopt. But this double unity requires a kind of common mind whose office is to find and determine the formula that corresponds best with the common conscience; and it must have, moreover, an authority sufficient to enable it to impose on the community the formula which has been decided upon. From

the combination and, as it were, fusion of these two elements, the common mind which draws up the formula and the authority which imposes it, arises, according to the Modernists, the notion of the ecclesiastical Magisterium. And, as this Magisterium springs, in its last analysis, from the individual consciences and possesses its mandate of public utility for their benefit, it necessarily follows that the ecclesiastical Magisterium must be dependent upon them, and should therefore be made to bow to the popular ideals. To prevent individual consciences from expressing freely and openly the impulses they feel, to hinder criticism from urging forward dogma in the path of its necessary evolution, is not a legitimate use but an abuse of a power given for the public weal. So too a due method and measure must be observed in the exercise of authority. To condemn and proscribe a work without the knowledge of the author, without hearing his explanations, without discussion, is something approaching to tyranny. And here again it is a question of finding a way of reconciling the full rights of authority on the one hand and those of liberty on the other. In the meantime the proper course for the Catholic will be to proclaim publicly his profound respect for authority, while never ceasing to follow his own judgment. Their general direction for the Church is as follows: that the ecclesiastical authority, since its end is entirely spiritual, should strip itself of that external pomp which adorns it in the eyes of the public. In this, they forget that while religion is for the soul, it is not exclusively for the soul, and that the honor paid to authority is reflected back on Christ who instituted it.

### The Evolution of Doctrine

26. To conclude this whole question of faith and its various branches, we have still to consider, Venerable Brethren, what the Modernists have to say about the development of the one and the other. First of all they lay down the general principle that in a living religion everything is subject to change, and must in fact be changed. In this way they pass to what is practically their principal doctrine, namely, *evolution*. To the laws of evolution every-

thing is subject under penalty of death—dogma, Church, worship, the Books we revere as sacred, even faith itself. The enunciation of this principle will not be a matter of surprise to anyone who bears in mind what the Modernists have had to say about each of these subjects. Having laid down this law of evolution, the Modernists themselves teach us how it operates. And first, with regard to faith. The primitive form of faith, they tell us, was rudimentary and common to all men alike, for it had its origin in human nature and human life. Vital evolution brought with it progress, not by the accretion of new and purely adventitious forms from without, but by an increasing perfusion of the religious sense into the conscience. The progress was of two kinds: *negative*, by the elimination of all extraneous elements, such, for example, as those derived from the family or nationality; and *positive*, by that intellectual and moral refining of man, by means of which the idea of the divine became fuller and clearer, while the *religious sense* became more acute. For the progress of faith the same causes are to be assigned as those which are adduced above to explain its origin. But to them must be added those extraordinary men whom we call prophets—of whom Christ was the greatest—both because in their lives and their words there was something mysterious which faith attributed to the Divinity, and because it fell to their lot to have new and original *experiences* fully in harmony with the religious needs of their time. The progress of dogma is due chiefly to the fact that obstacles to the faith have to be surmounted, enemies have to be vanquished and objections have to be refuted. Add to this a perpetual striving to penetrate ever more profoundly into those things which are contained in the mysteries of faith. Thus, putting aside other examples, it is found to have happened in the case of Christ: in Him that divine something which faith recognized in Him was slowly and gradually expanded in such a way that He was at last held to be God. The chief stimulus of the evolution of worship consists in the need of accommodation to the manners and customs of peoples, as well as the need of availing itself of the value which certain acts have acquired by usage. Finally, evolution in the Church itself is fed by the need of adapting itself to historical conditions and of harmonizing itself with existing forms of society. Such is their view with regard to each. And here, before proceeding further, We wish to draw attention to this whole theory of *necessities* or *needs*, for beyond all that we have seen, it is, as it were, the base and foundation of that famous method which they describe as historical.

## Tradition and Progress

27. Although evolution is urged on by needs or necessities, yet, if controlled by these alone, it would easily overstep the boundaries of Tradition, and thus, separated from its primitive vital principle, would make for ruin instead of progress. Hence, by those who study more closely the ideas of the Modernists, evolution is described as a resultant from the conflict of two forces, one of them tending towards progress, the other towards conservation. The conserving force exists in the Church and is found in Tradition; Tradition is represented by religious authority, and this both by right and in fact. By right, for it is in the very nature of authority to protect Tradition: and in fact, since authority, raised as it is above the contingencies of life, feels hardly, or not at all, the spurs of progress. The progressive force, on the contrary, which responds to the inner needs, lies in the individual consciences and works in them—especially in such of them as are in more close and intimate contact with life. Already we observe, Venerable Brethren, the introduction of that most pernicious doctrine which would make of the laity the factor of progress in the Church. Now it is by a species of covenant and compromise between these two forces of conservation and progress, that is to say between authority and individual consciences, that changes and advances take place. The individual consciences, or some of them, act on the collective conscience, which brings pressure to bear on the depositaries of authority to make terms and to keep to them.

## The Modernist Complex

With all this in mind, one understands how it is that the Modernists express astonishment when they are reprimanded or punished. What is imputed to them as a fault they regard as a sacred duty. They understand the needs of consciences better than anyone else, since they come into closer touch with them than does the ecclesiastical authority. Nay, they embody them, so to speak, in themselves. Hence, for them to speak and to write publicly is a bounden duty. Let authority rebuke them if it pleases—they have their own conscience on their side and an intimate experience which tells them with certainty that what they deserve is not blame but praise. Then they reflect that, after all, there is no progress without a battle and no battle without its victims; and victims they are willing to be like the prophets and Christ Himself. They have no bitterness in their hearts against the authority which uses them roughly, for after all they readily admit that it is only doing its duty as authority. Their sole grief is that it remains deaf to their warnings, for in this way it impedes the progress of souls, but the hour will most surely come when further delay will be impossible, for if the laws of evolution may be checked for a while they cannot be finally evaded. And thus they go their way, reprimands and condemnations not withstanding, masking an incredible audacity under a mock semblance of humility. While they make a pretense of bowing their heads, their minds and hands are more boldly intent than ever on carrying out their purposes. And this policy they follow willingly and wittingly, both because it is part of their system that authority is to be stimulated but not dethroned, and because it is necessary for them to remain within the ranks of the Church in order that they may gradually transform the collective conscience. And in saying this, they fail to perceive that they are avowing that the collective conscience is not with them, and that they have no right to claim to be its interpreters.

### Previous Condemnations of Modernism

28. It is thus, Venerable Brethren, that for the Modernists, whether as authors or propagandists, there is to be nothing stable, nothing immutable in the Church. Nor, indeed, are they without forerunners in their doctrines, for it was of these that Our predecessor Pius IX wrote: "These enemies of divine revelation extol

human progress to the skies, and with rash and sacrilegious daring would have it introduced into the Catholic religion as if this religion were not the work of God but of man, or some kind of philosophical discovery susceptible of perfection by human efforts."[11] On the subject of revelation and dogma in particular, the doctrine of the Modernists offers nothing new. We find it condemned in the Syllabus of Pius IX, where it is enunciated in these terms: "Divine revelation is imperfect, and therefore subject to continual and indefinite progress, corresponding with the progress of human reason";[12] and condemned still more solemnly in the Vatican Council: "The doctrine of the faith which God has revealed has not been proposed to human intelligences to be perfected by them as if it were a philosophical system, but as a divine deposit entrusted to the Spouse of Christ to be faithfully guarded and infallibly interpreted. Hence also that sense of the sacred dogmas is to be perpetually retained which our Holy Mother the Church has once declared, nor is this sense ever to be abandoned on plea or pretext of a more profound comprehension of the truth."[13] Nor is the development of our knowledge, even concerning the faith, barred by this pronouncement; on the contrary, it is supported and maintained. For the same Council continues: "Let intelligence and science and wisdom, therefore, increase and progress abundantly and vigorously in individuals and in the mass, in the believer and in the whole Church, throughout the ages and the centuries—but only in its own kind, that is, according to the same dogma, the same sense, the same acceptation."[14]

### Further Examination of Modernism

29. We have studied the Modernist as philosopher, believer and theologian. It now remains for us to consider him as historian, critic, apologist and reformer.

### The Modernist as Historian

30. Some Modernists, devoted to historical studies, seem to be deeply anxious not to be taken for philosophers. About philoso-

phy they profess to know nothing whatever, and in this they display remarkable astuteness, for they are particularly desirous not to be suspected of any prepossession in favor of philosophical theories which would lay them open to the charge of not being, as they call it, *objective*. And yet the truth is that their history and their criticism are saturated with their philosophy, and that their historico-critical conclusions are the natural outcome of their philosophical principles. This will be patent to anyone who reflects. Their three first laws are contained in those three principles of their philosophy already dealt with: the principle of *agnosticism*, the theorem of the *transfiguration* of things by faith, and that other which may be called the principle of *disfiguration*. Let us see what consequences flow from each of these. *Agnosticism* tells us that history, like science, deals entirely with phenomena, and the consequence is that God, and every intervention of God in human affairs, is to be relegated to the domain of faith as belonging to it alone. Wherefore in things where there is combined a double element, the divine and the human, as, for example, in Christ, or the Church, or the Sacraments, or the many other objects of the same kind, a division and separation must be made and the human element must be left to history while the divine will be assigned to faith. Hence we have that distinction, so current among the Modernists, between the Christ of history and the Christ of faith; the Church of history and the Church of faith; the Sacraments of history and the Sacraments of faith, and so in similar matters. Next we find that the human element itself, which the historian has to work on, as it appears in the documents, is to be considered as having been transfigured by faith, that is to say, raised above its historical conditions. It becomes necessary, therefore, to eliminate also the accretions which faith has added, to relegate them to faith itself and to the history of faith. Thus, when treating of Christ, the historian must set aside all that surpasses man in his natural condition, according to what psychology tells us of him, or according to what we gather from the place and period of his existence. Finally, they require, by virtue of the third principle, that even those things which are not outside the sphere of history should pass through the sieve, excluding all and relegating to faith everything which, in their judgment, is not in harmony with what they call the *logic* of facts or not in character with the persons of whom they are predicated. Thus, they will not allow that Christ ever uttered those things which do not seem to be within the capacity of the multitudes that listened to Him. Hence they delete from His *real* history and transfer to faith all the allegories found in His discourses. We may peradventure inquire on what principle they make these divisions? Their reply is that they argue from the character of the man, from his condition of life, from his education, from the complexus of the circumstances under which the facts took place; in short, if We understand them aright, on a principle which in the last analysis is merely *subjective*. Their method is to put themselves into the position and person of Christ, and then to attribute to Him what they would have done under like circumstances. In this way, absolutely *a priori* and acting on philosophical principles which they hold but which they profess to ignore, they proclaim that Christ, according to what they call His *real* history, was not God and never did anything divine, and that as man He did and said only what they, judging from the time in which He lived, consider that He ought to have said or done.

### The Modernist as Critic

31. As history takes its conclusions from philosophy, so too criticism takes its conclusions from history. The critic on the data furnished him by the historian, makes two parts of all his documents. Those that remain after the triple elimination above described go to form the *real* history; the rest is attributed to the history of the faith or, as it is styled, to *internal* history. For the Modernists distinguish very carefully between these two kinds of history, and it is to be noted that they oppose the history of the faith to *real* history precisely as real. Thus, as we have already said, we have a twofold Christ: a real Christ, and a Christ, the one of faith, who never really existed; a Christ who has lived at a given time and in a given place, and a Christ who never lived outside the pious meditations of the believer—the Christ, for instance, whom

we find in the Gospel of St. John, which, according to them, is mere meditation from beginning to end.

### His Principles of Criticism

32. But the dominion of philosophy over history does not end here. Given that division, of which We have spoken, of the documents into two parts, the philosopher steps in again with his dogma of *vital immanence*, and shows how everything in the history of the Church is to be explained by *vital emanation*. And since the cause or condition of every vital emanation whatsoever is to be found in some need or want, it follows that no fact can be regarded as antecedent to the need which produced it—historically the fact must be posterior to the need. What, then, does the historian do in view of this principle? He goes over his documents again, whether they be contained in the Sacred Books or elsewhere, draws up from them his list of the particular needs of the Church, whether relating to dogma, or liturgy, or other matters which are found in the Church thus related, and then he hands his list over to the critic. The critic takes in hand the documents dealing with the history of faith and distributes them, period by period, so that they correspond exactly with the list of needs, always guided by the principle that the narration must follow the facts, as the facts follow the needs. It may at times happen that some parts of the Sacred Scriptures, such as the Epistles, themselves constitute the fact created by the need. Even so, the rule holds that the age of any document can only be determined by the age in which each need has manifested itself in the Church. Further, a distinction must be made between the beginning of a fact and its development, for what is born in one day requires time for growth. Hence the critic must once more go over his documents, ranged as they are through the different ages, and divide them again into two parts, separating those that regard the origin of the facts from those that deal with their development, and these he must again arrange according to their periods.

## Modernist Confusion

33. Then the philosopher must come in again to enjoin upon the historian the obligation of following in all his studies the precepts and laws of evolution. It is next for the historian to scrutinize his documents once more, to examine carefully the circumstances and conditions affecting the Church during the different periods, the conserving force she has put forth, the needs both internal and external that have stimulated her to progress, the obstacles she has had to encounter, in a word, everything that helps to determine the manner in which the laws of evolution have been fulfilled in her. This done, he finishes his work by drawing up a history of the development in its broad lines. The critic follows and fits in the rest of the documents. He sets himself to write. The history is finished. Now We ask here: Who is the author of this history? The historian? The critic? Assuredly neither of these but the philosopher. From beginning to end everything in it is *a priori*, and an apriorism that reeks of heresy. These men are certainly to be pitied, of whom the Apostle might well say: "They became vain in their thoughts . . . professing themselves to be wise, they became fools." (*Rom.* 1:21-22). At the same time, they excite resentment when they accuse the Church of arranging and confusing the texts after her own fashion, and for the needs of her cause. In this they are accusing the Church of something for which their own conscience plainly reproaches them.

## Modernist Treatment of the Bible

34. The result of this dismembering of the records, and this partition of them throughout the centuries is naturally that the Scriptures can no longer be attributed to the authors whose names they bear. The Modernists have no hesitation in affirming generally that these books, and especially the Pentateuch and the first three Gospels, have been gradually formed from a primitive brief narration, by additions, by interpolations of theological or allegorical interpretations, or parts introduced only

for the purpose of joining different passages together. This means, to put it briefly and clearly, that in the Sacred Books we must admit a *vital evolution*, springing from and corresponding with the evolution of faith. The traces of this evolution, they tell us, are so visible in the books that one might almost write a history of it. Indeed, this history they actually do write, and with such an easy assurance that one might believe them to have seen with their own eyes the writers at work through the ages amplifying the Sacred Books. To aid them in this they call to their assistance that branch of criticism which they call *textual*, and labor to show that such a fact or such a phrase is not in its right place, adducing other arguments of the same kind. They seem, in fact, to have constructed for themselves certain types of narration and discourses, upon which they base their assured verdict as to whether a thing is or is not out of place. Let him who can judge how far they are qualified in this way to make such distinctions. To hear them descant of their works on the Sacred Books, in which they have been able to discover so much that is defective, one would imagine that before them nobody ever even turned over the pages of Scripture. The truth is that a whole multitude of Doctors, far superior to them in genius, in erudition, in sanctity, have sifted the Sacred Books in every way, and so far from finding in them anything blameworthy have thanked God more and more heartily the more deeply they have gone into them, for His divine bounty in having vouchsafed to speak thus to men. Unfortunately, these great Doctors did not enjoy the same aids to study that are possessed by the Modernists for they did not have for their rule and guide a philosophy borrowed from the negation of God, and a criterion which consists of themselves.

## *Contrary to Catholic Teaching*

We believe, then, that We have set forth with sufficient clearness the historical method of the Modernists. The philosopher leads the way, the historian follows, and then in due order come the internal and textual critics. And since it is characteristic of the

primary cause to communicate its virtue to causes which are secondary, it is quite clear that the criticism with which We are concerned is not any kind of criticism, but that which is rightly called
*agnostic, immanentist* and *evolutionist* criticism. Hence anyone
who adopts it and employs it makes profession thereby of the
errors contained in it, and places himself in opposition to Catholic
teaching. This being so, it is much a matter for surprise that it
should have found acceptance to such an extent among certain
Catholics. Two causes may be assigned for this: first, the close
alliance which the historians and critics of this school have
formed among themselves independent of all differences of
nationality or religion; second, their boundless effrontery by
which, if one then makes any utterance, the others applaud him in
chorus, proclaiming that science has made another step forward,
while if an outsider should desire to inspect the new discovery for
himself, they form a coalition against him. He who denies it is
decried as one who is ignorant, while he who embraces and
defends it has all their praise. In this way they entrap not a few,
who, did they but realize what they are doing, would shrink back
with horror. The domineering overbearance of those who teach
the errors, and the thoughtless compliance of the more shallow
minds who assent to them, create a corrupted atmosphere which
penetrates everywhere, and carries infection with it. But let Us
pass to the apologist.

### The Modernist as Apologist

35. The Modernist apologist depends in two ways on the
philosopher. First, *indirectly*, inasmuch as his subject-matter is
history—history dictated, as we have seen, by the philosopher;
and, secondly, *directly*, inasmuch as he takes both his doctrines
and his conclusions from the philosopher. Hence that common
axiom of the Modernist school that in the new apologetics controversies in religion must be determined by psychological and
historical research. The Modernist apologists, then, enter the
arena, proclaiming to the rationalists that, though they are defending religion, they have no intention of employing the data of the

sacred books or the histories in current use in the Church, and written upon the old lines, but *real* history composed on modern principles and according to the modern method. In all this they assert that they are not using an *argumentum ad hominem*, because they are really of the opinion that the truth is to be found only in this kind of history. They feel that it is not necessary for them to make profession of their own sincerity in their writings. They are already known to and praised by the rationalists as fighting under the same banner, and they not only plume themselves on these encomiums, which would only provoke disgust in a real Catholic, but use them as a counter-compensation to the reprimands of the Church.

### Modernist Apologetic Methodology

Let us see how the Modernist conducts his apologetics. The aim he sets before himself is to make one who is still without faith attain that *experience* of the Catholic religion which, according to the system, is the sole basis of faith. There are two ways open to him, the *objective* and the *subjective*. The first of them starts from agnosticism. It tends to show that religion, and especially the Catholic religion, is endowed with such vitality as to compel every psychologist and historian of good faith to recognize that its history hides some element of the *unknown*. To this end it is necessary to prove that the Catholic religion, as it exists today, is that which was founded by Jesus Christ; that is to say, that it is nothing else than the progressive development of the germ which He brought into the world. Hence it is imperative first of all to establish what this germ was, and this the Modernist claims to be able to do by the following formula: Christ announced the coming of the Kingdom of God, which was to be realized within a brief lapse of time and of which He was to become the Messias, the divinely-given founder and ruler. Then it must be shown how this germ, always *immanent* and *permanent* in the Catholic religion, has gone on slowly developing in the course of history, adapting itself successively to the different circumstances through which it has passed, borrowing from them by *vital* assimilation all the doctrinal, cultural, ecclesiastical forms that served its purpose; while, on the other hand, it surmounted all obstacles, vanquished all enemies, and survived all assaults and all combats. Anyone who well and duly considers this mass of obstacles, adversaries, attacks, combats, and the vitality and fecundity which the Church has shown throughout them all, must admit that if the laws of evolution are visible in her life they fail to explain the whole of her history—the *unknown* rises forth from it and presents itself before us. Thus do they argue, not perceiving that their determination of the primitive germ is only an *a priori* assumption of agnostic and evolutionist philosophy, and that the germ itself has been gratuitously defined so that it may fit in with their contention.

### Modernist Confusion

36. But while they endeavor by this line of reasoning to prove and plead for the Catholic religion, these new apologists are more than willing to grant and to recognize that there are in it many things which are repulsive. Nay, they admit openly, and with ill-concealed satisfaction, that they have found that even its dogma is not exempt from errors and contradictions. They add also that this is not only excusable but—curiously enough—that it is even right and proper. In the Sacred Books there are many passages referring to science or history where, according to them, manifest errors are to be found. But, they say, the subject of these books is not science or history, but only religion and morals. In them history and science serve only as a species of covering to enable the religious and moral experiences wrapped up in them to penetrate more readily among the masses. The masses understood science and history as they are expressed in these books, and it is clear that the expression of science and history in a more perfect form would have proved not so much a help as a hindrance. Moreover, they add, the Sacred Books, being essentially religious, are necessarily quick with life. Now life has its own truths and its own logic—quite different from rational truth and rational logic, belonging as they do to a different order,

viz., truth of adaptation and of proportion both with what they call the *medium* in which it lives and with the end for which it lives. Finally, the Modernists, losing all sense of control, go so far as to proclaim as true and legitimate whatever is explained by life.

## The Simplicity of Truth

We, Venerable Brethren, for whom there is but one and only one truth, and who hold that the Sacred Books, "written under the inspiration of the Holy Ghost, have God for their author"[15] declare that this is equivalent to attributing to God Himself the lie of utility or officious lie, and We say with St. Augustine: "In an authority so high, admit but one officious lie, and there will not remain a single passage of those apparently difficult to practice or to believe, which on the same most pernicious rule may not be explained as a lie uttered by the author willfully and to serve a purpose."[16] And thus it will come about, the holy Doctor continues, that "everybody will believe and refuse to believe what he likes or dislikes in them," namely, the Scriptures. But the Modernists pursue their way eagerly. They grant also that certain arguments adduced in the Sacred Books in proof of a given doctrine, like those, for example, which are based on the prophecies, have no rational foundation to rest on. But they defend even these as artifices of preaching, which are justified by life. More than that, they are ready to admit, nay, to proclaim that Christ Himself manifestly erred in determining the time when the coming of the Kingdom of God was to take place; and they tell us that we must not be surprised at this since even He Himself was subject to the laws of life! After this what is to become of the dogmas of the Church? The dogmas bristle with flagrant contradictions, but what does it matter since, apart from the fact that vital logic accepts them, they are not repugnant to symbolical truth. Are we not dealing with the Infinite, and has not the Infinite an infinite variety of aspects? In short, to maintain and defend these theories they do not hesitate to declare that the noblest homage that can be paid to the Infinite is to make it the object of contradictory statements! But when they justify even contradictions, what is it that they will refuse to justify?

## Subjective Arguments

37. But it is not solely by *objective* arguments that the non-believer may be disposed to faith. There are also those that are *subjective*, and for this purpose the modernist apologists return to the doctrine of *immanence*. They endeavor, in fact, to persuade their non-believer that down in the very depths of his nature and his life lie hidden the need and the desire for some religion, and this not a religion of any kind, but the specific religion known as Catholicism, which, they say, is absolutely *postulated* by the perfect development of life. And here again We have grave reason to complain that there are Catholics who, while rejecting *immanence* as a doctrine, employ it as a method of apologetics, and who do this so imprudently that they seem to admit, not merely a capacity and a suitability for the supernatural, such as has at all times been emphasized, within due limits, by Catholic apologists, but that there is in human nature a true and rigorous need for the supernatural order. Truth to tell, it is only the moderate Modernists who make this appeal to an exigency for the Catholic religion. As for the others, who might be called *integralists*, they would show to the non-believer, as hidden in his being, the very germ which Christ Himself had in His consciousness, and which He transmitted to mankind. Such, Venerable Brethren, is a summary description of the apologetic method of the Modernists, in perfect harmony with their doctrines—methods and doctrines replete with errors, made not for edification but for destruction, not for the making of Catholics but for the seduction of those who are Catholics into heresy; and tending to the utter subversion of all religion.

## The Modernist as Reformer

38. It remains for Us now to say a few words about the Modernist as reformer. From all that has preceded, it is abundantly

clear how great and how eager is the passion of such men for innovation. In all Catholicism there is absolutely nothing on which it does not fasten. They wish philosophy to be reformed, especially in the ecclesiastical seminaries. They wish the scholastic philosophy to be relegated to the history of philosophy and to be classed among absolute systems, and the young men to be taught modern philosophy which alone is true and suited to the times in which we live. They desire the reform of theology: rational theology is to have modern philosophy for its foundation, and positive theology is to be founded on the history of dogma. As for history, it must be written and taught only according to their methods and modern principles. Dogmas and their evolution, they affirm, are to be harmonized with science and history. In the Catechism no dogmas are to be inserted except those that have been reformed and are within the capacity of the people. Regarding worship, they say, the number of external devotions is to be reduced, and steps must be taken to prevent their further increase, though, indeed, some of the admirers of symbolism are disposed to be more indulgent on this head. They cry out that ecclesiastical government requires to be reformed in all its branches, but especially in its disciplinary and dogmatic departments. They insist that both outwardly and inwardly it must be brought into harmony with the modern conscience, which now wholly tends toward democracy; a share in ecclesiastical government should therefore be given to the lower ranks of the clergy, and even to the laity, and authority, which is too much concentrated, should be decentralized. The Roman Congregations, and especially the *Index* and the *Holy Office*, must be likewise modified. The ecclesiastical authority must alter its line of conduct in the social and political world; while keeping outside political organizations, it must adapt itself to them, in order to penetrate them with its spirit. With regard to morals, they adopt the principle of the Americanists, that the active virtues are more important than the passive, and are to be more encouraged in practice. They ask that the clergy should return to their primitive humility and poverty, and that in their ideas and action they should admit the principles of Modernism; and there are some who, gladly listening to the teaching of their

Protestant masters, would desire the suppression of the celibacy of the clergy. What is there left in the Church which is not to be reformed by them and according to their principles?

## Modernism, Synthesis of All Heresies

39. It may, perhaps, seem to some, Venerable Brethren, that We have dealt at too great length on this exposition of the doctrines of the Modernists. But it was necessary that We should do so, both in order to meet their customary charge that We do not understand their ideas, and to show that their system does not consist in scattered and unconnected theories, but, as it were, in a closely connected whole, so that it is not possible to admit one without admitting all. For this reason, too, We have had to give to this exposition a somewhat didactic form, and not to shrink from employing certain unwonted terms which the Modernists have brought into use. And now with Our eyes fixed upon the whole system, no one will be surprised that We should define it to be the synthesis of all heresies. Undoubtedly, were anyone to attempt the task of collecting together all the errors that have been broached against the faith and to concentrate into one the sap and substance of them all, he could not succeed in doing so better than the Modernists have done. Nay, they have gone farther than this, for, as We have already intimated, their system means the destruction not of the Catholic religion alone, but of all religion. Hence the rationalists are not wanting in their applause, and the most frank and sincere among them congratulate themselves on having found in the Modernists the most valuable of all allies.

Let us turn for a moment, Venerable Brethren, to that most disastrous doctrine of *agnosticism*. By it every avenue to God on the side of the intellect is barred to man, while a better way is supposed to be opened from the side of a certain sense of the soul and action. But who does not see how mistaken is such a contention? For the sense of the soul is the response to the action of the thing which the intellect or the outward senses set before it. Take away the intelligence, and man, already inclined to follow the senses, becomes their slave. Doubly mistaken, from another point of view, for all these fantasies of the religious sense will never be able to destroy common sense, and common sense tells us that emotion and everything that leads the heart captive proves a hindrance instead of a help to the discovery of truth. We speak of truth in itself—for that other purely *subjective* truth, the fruit of the internal sense and action, if it serves its purpose for the play of words, is of no benefit to the man who wants above all things to know whether outside himself there is a God into whose hands he is one day to fall. True, the Modernists call in *experience* to eke out their system, but what does this *experience* add to that sense of the soul? Absolutely nothing beyond a certain intensity and a proportionate deepening of the conviction of the reality of the object. But these two will never make the sense of the soul into anything but sense, nor will they alter its nature, which is liable to deception when the intelligence is not there to guide it; on the contrary, they but confirm and strengthen this nature, for the more intense the sense is the more it is really sense. And as we are here dealing with religious sense and the experience involved in it, it is known to you, Venerable Brethren, how necessary in such a matter is prudence, and the learning by which prudence is guided. You know it from your own dealings with souls, and especially with souls in whom sentiment predominates; you know it also from your reading of works of ascetical theology—works for which the Modernists have but little esteem, but which testify to a science and a solidity far greater than theirs, and to a refinement and subtlety of observation far beyond any which the Modernists take credit to themselves for possessing. It seems to Us nothing short of madness, or at the least consummate temerity to accept for true, and without investigation, these incomplete experiences which are the vaunt of the Modernist. Let Us for a moment put the question: If experiences have so much force and value in their estimation, why do they not attach equal weight to the experience that so many thousands of Catholics have that the Modernists are on the wrong path? Is it that the Catholic experiences are the only ones which are false and deceptive? The vast majority of mankind holds and always will hold firmly that sense and experience alone, when not enlightened and guided by reason, cannot reach to the knowledge of God. What, then, remains but atheism and the absence of all religion? Certainly it is not the doctrine of *symbolism* that will save us from this. For if all the intellectual elements, as they call them, of religion are nothing more than mere symbols of God, will not the very name of God or of divine personality be also a symbol, and if this be admitted, the personality of God will become a matter of doubt and the gate will be opened to pantheism? And to pantheism pure and simple that other doctrine of the *divine immanence* leads directly. For this is the question which We ask: Does or does not this *immanence* leave God distinct from man? If it does, in what does it differ from the Catholic doctrine, and why does it reject the doctrine of external revelation? If it does not, it is pantheism. Now the doctrine of *immanence* in the Modernist acceptation holds and professes that every phenomenon of conscience proceeds from man as man. The rigorous conclusion from this is the identity of man with God, which means pantheism. The distinction which Modernists make between science and faith leads to the same conclusion. The object of science, they say, is the reality of the knowable; the object of faith, on the contrary, is the reality of the unknowable. Now, what makes the unknowable unknowable is the fact that there is no proportion between its object and the intellect—a defect of proportion which nothing whatever, even in the doctrine of the Modernist, can suppress. Hence the unknowable remains and will eternally remain unknowable to the believer as well as to the philosopher. Therefore if any religion at all is possible, it can only be the religion of an unknowable reality. And why this might not be that soul of the universe, of which certain rationalists speak, is something which certainly does not seem to Us apparent. These reasons suffice to show superabundantly by how many roads Modernism leads to atheism and to the annihilation of all religion. The error of Protestantism made the first step on this path; that of Modernism makes the second; atheism makes the next.

## The Danger of Curiosity

40. To penetrate still deeper into the meaning of Modernism

and to find a suitable remedy for so deep a sore, it behooves Us, Venerable Brethren, to investigate the causes which have engendered it and which foster its growth. That the proximate and immediate cause consists in an error of the mind cannot be open to doubt. We recognize that the remote causes may be reduced to two: curiosity and pride. Curiosity by itself, if not prudently regulated, suffices to account for all errors. Such is the opinion of Our predecessor, Gregory XVI, who wrote: "A lamentable spectacle is that presented by the aberrations of human reason when it yields to the spirit of novelty, when against the warning of the Apostle it seeks to know beyond what it is meant to know, and when relying too much on itself it thinks it can find the truth outside the Catholic Church wherein truth is found without the slightest shadow of error."[17]

### Pride Sits in the Modernist House

But it is pride which exercises an incomparably greater sway over the soul to blind it and lead it into error, and pride sits in Modernism as in its own house, finding sustenance everywhere in its doctrines and lurking in its every aspect. It is pride which fills Modernists with that self-assurance by which they consider themselves and pose as the rule for all. It is pride which puffs them up with that vainglory which allows them to regard themselves as the sole possessors of knowledge, and makes them say, elated and inflated with presumption, "We are not as the rest of men," and which, lest they should seem as other men, leads them to embrace and to devise novelties even of the most absurd kind. It is pride which rouses in them the spirit of disobedience and causes them to demand a compromise between authority and liberty. It is owing to their pride that they seek to be the reformers of others while they forget to reform themselves, and that they are found to be utterly wanting in respect for authority, even for the supreme authority. Truly there is no road which leads so directly and so quickly to Modernism as pride. When a Catholic layman or a priest forgets the precept of the Christian life which obliges us to renounce ourselves if we would follow Christ and neglects to tear pride from his heart, then it is he who most of all is a fully ripe subject for the errors of Modernism. For this reason, Venerable Brethren, it will be your first duty to resist such victims of pride, to employ them only in the lowest and obscurest offices. The higher they try to rise, the lower let them be placed, so that the lowliness of their position may limit their power of causing damage. Examine most carefully your young clerics by yourselves and by the directors of your seminaries, and when you find the spirit of pride among them reject them without compunction from the priesthood. Would to God that this had always been done with the vigilance and constancy which were required!

### Ignorance of Modernists

41. If we pass on from the moral to the intellectual causes of Modernism, the first and the chief which presents itself is ignorance. Yes, these very Modernists who seek to be esteemed as Doctors of the Church, who speak so loftily of modern philosophy and show such contempt for scholasticism, have embraced the one with all its false glamour, precisely because their ignorance of the other has left them without the means of being able to recognize confusion of thought and to refute sophistry. Their whole system, containing as it does errors so many and so great, has been born of the union between faith and false philosophy.

### Methods of Propagandism

42. Would that they had but displayed less zeal and energy in propagating it! But such is their activity and such their unwearying labor on behalf of their cause, that one cannot but be pained to see them waste such energy in endeavoring to ruin the Church when they might have been of such service to her had their efforts been better directed. Their artifices to delude men's minds are of two kinds, the first to remove obstacles from their path, the second to devise and apply actively and patiently every resource that can serve their purpose. They recognize that the three chief difficulties which stand in their way are the scholastic method of phi-

losophy, the authority and Tradition of the Fathers and the Magisterium of the Church, and on these they wage unrelenting war. Against scholastic philosophy and theology they use the weapons of ridicule and contempt. Whether it is ignorance or fear, or both, that inspires this conduct in them, certain it is that the passion for novelty is always united in them with hatred of scholasticism, and there is no surer sign that a man is tending to Modernism than when he begins to show his dislike for the scholastic method. Let the Modernists and their admirers remember the proposition condemned by Pius IX: "The method and principles which have served the ancient doctors of scholasticism when treating of theology no longer correspond with the exigencies of our time or the progress of science."[18] They exercise all their ingenuity in an effort to weaken the force and falsify the character of Tradition, so as to rob it of all its weight and authority. But for Catholics nothing will remove the authority of the second Council of Nicea, where it condemns those "who dare, after the impious fashion of heretics, to deride the ecclesiastical traditions, to invent novelties of some kind . . . or endeavor by malice or craft to overthrow any one of the legitimate traditions of the Catholic Church"; nor that of the declaration of the fourth Council of Constantinople: "We therefore profess to preserve and guard the rules bequeathed to the Holy Catholic and Apostolic Church, by the Holy and most illustrious Apostles, by the orthodox Councils, both general and local, and by every one of those divine interpreters, the Fathers and Doctors of the Church." Wherefore the Roman Pontiffs, Pius IV and Pius IX, ordered the insertion in the profession of faith of the following declaration: "I most firmly admit and embrace the apostolic and ecclesiastical traditions and other observances and constitutions of the Church."

## Modernist Contempt for the Fathers

The Modernists pass judgment on the holy Fathers of the Church even as they do upon Tradition. With consummate temerity they assure the public that the Fathers, while personally most worthy of all veneration, were entirely ignorant of history and criticism, for which they are only excusable on account of the time in which they lived. Finally, the Modernists try in every way to diminish and weaken the authority of the ecclesiastical Magisterium itself by sacrilegiously falsifying its origin, character and rights, and by freely repeating the calumnies of its adversaries. To the entire band of Modernists may be applied those words which Our predecessor sorrowfully wrote: "To bring contempt and odium on the mystic Spouse of Christ, who is the true light, the children of darkness have been wont to cast in her face before the world a stupid calumny, and perverting the meaning and force of things and words, to depict her as the friend of darkness and ignorance, and the enemy of light, science and progress."[19] This being so, Venerable Brethren, there is little reason to wonder that the Modernists vent all their bitterness and hatred on Catholics who zealously fight the battles of the Church. There is no species of insult which they do not heap upon them, but their usual course is to charge them with ignorance or obstinacy. When an adversary rises up against them with an erudition and force that renders them redoubtable, they seek to make a conspiracy of silence around him to nullify the effects of his attack. This policy towards Catholics is the more invidious in that they belaud with admiration which knows no bounds the writers who range themselves on their side, hailing their works, exuding novelty in every page, with a chorus of applause. For them the scholarship of a writer is in direct proportion to the recklessness of his attacks on antiquity, and of his efforts to undermine Tradition and the ecclesiastical Magisterium. When one of their number falls under the condemnations of the Church the rest of them, to the disgust of good Catholics, gather round him, loudly and publicly applaud him and hold him up in veneration as almost a martyr for truth. The young, excited and confused by all this clamor of praise and abuse, some of them afraid of being branded as ignorant, others ambitious to rank among the learned and both classes goaded internally by curiosity and pride, not infrequently surrender and give themselves up to Modernism.

## The Temerity of the Modernists

43. And here we have already some of the artifices employed by Modernists to exploit their wares. What efforts do they not make to win new recruits! They seize upon professorships in the seminaries and universities, and gradually make of them chairs of pestilence. In sermons from the pulpit they disseminate their doctrines, although possibly in utterances which are veiled. In congresses they express their teachings more openly. In their social gatherings they introduce them and commend them to others. Under their own names and under pseudonyms they publish numbers of books, newspapers, reviews and sometimes one and the same writer adopts a variety of pseudonyms to trap the incautious reader into believing in a multitude of Modernist writers. In short, with feverish activity they leave nothing untried in act, speech and writing. And with what result? We have to deplore the spectacle of many young men, once full of promise and capable of rendering great services to the Church, now gone astray. It is also a subject of grief to Us that many others who, while they certainly do not go so far as the former, have yet been so infected by breathing a poisoned atmosphere, as to think, speak and write with a degree of laxity which ill becomes a Catholic. They are to be found among the laity, and in the ranks of the clergy, and they are not wanting even in the last place where one might expect to meet them, in religious communities. If they treat of biblical questions, it is upon Modernist principles; if they write history, they carefully, and with ill-concealed satisfaction, drag into the light, on the plea of telling the whole truth, everything that appears to cast a stain upon the Church. Under the sway of certain *a priori* conceptions they destroy as far as they can the pious traditions of the people, and bring into disrespect certain relics highly venerable from their antiquity. They are possessed by the empty desire of having their names upon the lips of the public, and they know they would never succeed in this were they to say only what has always been said by all men. Meanwhile it may be that they have persuaded themselves that in all this they are really serving God and the Church. In reality they only offend both, less perhaps by their

works in themselves than by the spirit in which they write, and by the encouragement they thus give to the aims of the Modernists.

## Calls for Vigilance

44. Against this host of grave errors, and its secret and open advance, Our predecessor Leo XIII, of happy memory, worked strenuously, both in his words and his acts, especially as regards the study of the Bible. But, as we have seen, the Modernists are not easily deterred by such weapons. With an affectation of great submission and respect, they proceeded to twist the words of the Pontiff to their own sense, while they described his action as directed against others than themselves. Thus the evil has gone on increasing from day to day. We, therefore, Venerable Brethren, have decided to suffer no longer delay, and to adopt measures which are more efficacious. We exhort and conjure you to see to it that in this most grave matter no one shall be in a position to say that you have been in the slightest degree wanting in vigilance, zeal or firmness. And what We ask of you and expect of you, We ask and expect also of all other pastors of souls, of all educators and professors of clerics, and in a very special way of the superiors of religious communities.

## Scholastic Philosophy

45. In the first place, with regard to studies, We will and strictly ordain that scholastic philosophy be made the basis of the sacred sciences. It goes without saying that "if anything is met with among the scholastic doctors which may be regarded as something investigated with an excess of subtlety, or taught without sufficient consideration; anything which is not in keeping with the certain results of later times; anything, in short, which is altogether destitute of probability, We have no desire whatever to propose it for the imitation of present generations."[20] And let it be clearly understood above all things that when We prescribe scholastic philosophy We understand chiefly that which the Angelic Doctor has bequeathed to us, and We, therefore, declare

that all the ordinances of Our predecessor on this subject continue fully in force, and, as far as may be necessary, We do decree anew, and confirm, and order that they shall be strictly observed by all. In seminaries where they have been neglected it will be for the Bishops to exact and require their observance in the future; and let this apply also to the superiors of religious orders. Further, We admonish professors to bear well in mind that they cannot set aside St. Thomas, especially in metaphysical questions, without grave disadvantage.

## Promotion of Sound Theology

46. On this philosophical foundation the theological edifice is to be carefully raised. Promote the study of theology, Venerable Brethren, by all means in your power, so that your clerics on leaving the seminaries may carry with them a deep admiration and love of it, and always find in it a source of delight. For "in the vast and varied abundance of studies opening before the mind desirous of truth, it is known to everyone that theology occupies such a commanding place, that according to an ancient adage of the wise it is the duty of the other arts and sciences to serve it, and to wait upon it after the manner of handmaidens."[21] We will add that We deem worthy of praise those who with full respect for Tradition, the Fathers, and the ecclesiastical Magisterium, endeavor, with well-balanced judgment, and guided by Catholic principles (which is not always the case), to illustrate positive theology by throwing upon it the light of true history. It is certainly necessary that positive theology should be held in greater appreciation than it has been in the past, but this must be done without detriment to scholastic theology; and those are to be disapproved as Modernists who exalt positive theology in such a way as to seem to despise the scholastic.

## The Role of Profane Studies

47. With regard to secular studies, let it suffice to recall here what our predecessor has admirably said: "Apply yourselves

energetically to the study of natural sciences: in which department the things that have been so brilliantly discovered, and so
usefully applied, to the admiration of the present age, will be the
object of praise and commendation to those who come after us."[22]
But this is to be done without interfering with sacred studies, as
Our same predecessor prescribed in these most weighty words:
"If you carefully search for the cause of those errors you will find
that it lies in the fact that in these days when the natural sciences
absorb so much study, the more severe and lofty studies have
been proportionately neglected—some of them have almost
passed into oblivion, some of them are pursued in a half-hearted
or superficial way and, sad to say, now that the splendor of the
former estate is dimmed, they have been disfigured by perverse
doctrines and monstrous errors."[23] We ordain, therefore, that the
study of natural sciences in the seminaries be carried out according to this law.

## Practical Application

48. All these prescriptions, both Our own and those of Our
predecessor, are to be kept in view whenever there is question of
choosing directors and professors for seminaries and Catholic
Universities. Anyone who in any way is found to be tainted with
Modernism is to be excluded without compunction from these
offices, whether of government or of teaching, and those who
already occupy them are to be removed. The same policy is to be
adopted toward those who openly or secretly lend countenance to
Modernism either by extolling the Modernists and excusing their
culpable conduct, or by carping at scholasticism, and the Fathers,
and the magisterium of the Church, or by refusing obedience to
ecclesiastical authority in any of its depositories; and toward those
who show a love of novelty in history, archaeology, biblical exegesis; and finally toward those who neglect the sacred sciences or
appear to prefer to them the secular. In all this question of studies,
Venerable Brethren, you cannot be too watchful or too constant,
but most of all in the choice of professors, for as a rule the students are modeled after the pattern of their masters. Strong in the

consciousness of your duty, act always in this matter with prudence and with vigor.

### *"Do Not Lay Hands Hastily . . ."*

49. Equal diligence and severity are to be used in examining and selecting candidates for Holy Orders. Far, far from the clergy be the love of novelty! God hateth the proud and the obstinate mind. For the future the doctorate of theology and canon law must never be conferred on anyone who has not first of all made the regular course of scholastic philosophy; if conferred, it shall be held as null and void. The rules laid down in 1896 by the Sacred Congregation of Bishops and Regulars for the clerics, both secular and regular, of Italy, concerning the frequenting of the Universities, We now decree to be extended to all nations.[24] Clerics and priests inscribed in a Catholic Institute or University must not in the future follow in civil Universities those courses for which there are chairs in the Catholic Institutes to which they belong. If this has been permitted anywhere in the past, We ordain that it be not allowed for the future. Let the Bishops who form the Governing Board of such Catholic Institutes or Universities watch with all care that these Our commands be constantly observed.

### *Examine Publications Carefully*

50. It is also the duty of the Bishops to prevent writings of Modernists, or whatever savors of Modernism or promotes it, from being read when they have been published, and to hinder their publication when they have not. No books or papers or periodicals whatever of this kind are to be permitted to seminarists or university students. The injury to them would be not less than that which is caused by immoral reading—nay, it would be greater, for such writings poison Christian life at its very fount. The same decision is to be taken concerning the writings of some Catholics, who, though not evilly disposed themselves, are ill-instructed in theological studies and imbued with modern philosophy, and strive to make this harmonize with the faith, and, as they say, to

turn it to the profit of the faith. The name and reputation of these authors cause them to read without suspicion, and they are, therefore, all the more dangerous in gradually preparing the way for Modernism.

### *Imprimatur and Nihil Obstat*

51. To add some more general directions, Venerable Brethren, in a matter of such moment, We order that you do everything in your power to drive out of your dioceses, even by solemn interdict, any pernicious books that may be in circulation there. The Holy See neglects no means to remove writings of this kind, but their number has now grown to such an extent that it is hardly possible to subject them all to censure. Hence it happens sometimes that the remedy arrives too late, for the disease has taken root during the delay. We will, therefore, that the Bishops putting aside all fear and the prudence of the flesh, despising the clamor of evil men, shall, gently, by all means, but firmly, do each his own part in this work, remembering the injunctions of Leo XIII in the Apostolic Constitution *Officiorum*: "Let the Ordinaries, acting in this also as Delegates of the Apostolic See, exert themselves to proscribe and to put out of reach of the faithful injurious books or other writings printed or circulated in their dioceses."[25] In this passage the Bishops, it is true, receive an authorization, but they have also a charge laid upon them. Let no Bishop think that he fulfills his duty by denouncing to Us one or two books, while a great many others of the same kind are being published and circulated. Nor are you to be deterred by the fact that a book has obtained elsewhere the permission which is commonly called the *Imprimatur*, both because this may be merely simulated, and because it may have been granted through carelessness or too much indulgence or excessive trust placed in the author, which last has perhaps sometimes happened in the religious orders. Besides, just as the same food does not agree with everyone, it may happen that a book, harmless in one place, may, on account of the different circumstances, be hurtful in another. Should a Bishop, therefore, after having taken the advice of pru-

dent persons, deem it right to condemn any of such books in his diocese, We give him ample faculty for the purpose and We lay upon him the obligation of doing so. Let all this be done in a fitting manner, and in certain cases it will suffice to restrict the prohibition to the clergy; but in all cases it will be obligatory on Catholic booksellers not to put on sale books condemned by the Bishop. And while We are treating of this subject, We wish the Bishops to see to it that booksellers do not, through desire for gain, engage in evil trade. It is certain that in the catalogs of some of them the books of the Modernists are not infrequently announced with no small praise. If they refuse obedience, let the Bishops, after due admonition, have no hesitation in depriving them of the title of Catholic booksellers. This applies, and with still more reason, to those who have the title of Episcopal booksellers. If they have that of Pontifical booksellers, let them be denounced to the Apostolic See. Finally, We remind all of Article XXVI of the above-mentioned Constitution *Officiorum*: "All those who have obtained an apostolic faculty to read and keep forbidden books, are not thereby authorized to read and keep books and periodicals forbidden by the local Ordinaries unless the apostolic faculty expressly concedes permission to read and keep books condemned by anyone whomsoever."

### Censorship

52. It is not enough to hinder the reading and the sale of bad books—it is also necessary to prevent them from being published. Hence, let the Bishops use the utmost strictness in granting permission to print. Under the rules of the Constitution *Officiorum*, many publications require the authorization of the Ordinary, and in certain dioceses (since the Bishop cannot personally make himself acquainted with them all) it has been the custom to have a suitable number of official censors for the examination of writings. We have the highest esteem for this institution of censors, and We not only exhort, but We order that it be extended to all dioceses. In all episcopal Curias, therefore, let censors be appointed for the revision of works intended for

publication, and let the censors be chosen from both ranks of the clergy—secular and regular—men whose age, knowledge and prudence will enable them to follow the safe and golden mean in their judgments. It shall be their office to examine everything which requires permission for publication according to Articles XLI and XLII of the above-mentioned Constitution. The censor shall give his verdict in writing. If it be favorable, the Bishop will give the permission for publication by the word *Imprimatur*, which must be preceded by the *Nihil obstat* and the name of the censor. In the Roman Curia official censors shall be appointed in the same way as elsewhere, and the duty of nominating them shall appertain to the Master of the Sacred Palace, after they have been proposed to the Cardinal Vicar and have been approved and accepted by the Sovereign Pontiff. It will also be the office of the Master of the Sacred Palace to select the censor for each writing. Permission for publication will be granted by him as well as by the Cardinal Vicar or his Vicegerent, and this permission, as above prescribed, must be preceded by the *Nihil obstat* and the name of the censor. Only on a very rare and exceptional occasion, and on the prudent decision of the Bishop, shall it be possible to omit mention of the censor. The name of the censor shall never be made known to the authors until he shall have given a favorable decision, so that he may not have to suffer inconvenience either while he is engaged in the examination of a writing or in case he should withhold his approval. Censors shall never be chosen from the religious orders until the opinion of the Provincial, or in Rome, of the General, has been privately obtained, and the Provincial or the General must give a conscientious account of the character, knowledge and orthodoxy of the candidate. We admonish religious superiors of their most solemn duty never to allow anything to be published by any of their subjects without permission from themselves and from the Ordinary. Finally, We affirm and declare that the title of censor with which a person may be honored has no value whatever, and can never be adduced to give credit to the private opinions of him who holds it.

*Priests as Editors*

53. Having said this much in general, We now ordain in particular a more careful observance of Article XLII of the above-mentioned Constitution *Officiorum*, according to which "it is forbidden
to secular priests, without the previous consent of the Ordinary, to
undertake the editorship of papers or periodicals." This permission
shall be withdrawn from any priest who makes a wrong use of it
after having received an admonition thereupon. With regard to
priests who are *correspondents* or *collaborators* of periodicals, as
it happens not infrequently that they contribute matter infected
with Modernism to their papers or periodicals, let the Bishops see
to it that they do not offend in this manner; and if they do, let them
warn the offenders and prevent them from writing. We solemnly
charge in like manner the superiors of religious orders that they
fulfill the same duty, and should they fail in it, let the Bishops
make due provision with authority from the Supreme Pontiff. Let
there be, as far as this is possible, a special censor for newspapers
and periodicals written by Catholics. It shall be his office to read
in due time each number after it has been published, and if he find
anything dangerous in it let him order that it be corrected as soon
as possible. The Bishop shall have the same right even when the
censor has seen nothing objectionable in a publication.

*Congresses*

54. We have already mentioned congresses and public gatherings as among the means used by the Modernists to propagate and
defend their opinions. In the future, Bishops shall not permit congresses of priests except on very rare occasions. When they do
permit them it shall only be on condition that matters appertaining to the Bishops or the Apostolic See be not treated in them, and
that no resolutions or petitions be allowed that would imply a
usurpation of sacred authority, and that absolutely nothing be said
in them which savors of Modernism, presbyterianism or laicism.
At congresses of this kind, which can only be held after permission in writing has been obtained in due time and for each case, it

shall not be lawful for priests of other dioceses to be present without the written permission of their Ordinary. Further, no priest must lose sight of the solemn recommendation of Leo XIII: "Let priests hold as sacred the authority of their pastors, let them take it for certain that the sacerdotal ministry, if not exercised under the guidance of the Bishops, can never be either holy, or very fruitful, or worthy of respect."[26]

## Diocesan Vigilance Committees

55. But of what avail, Venerable Brethren, will be all Our commands and prescriptions if they be not dutifully and firmly carried out? In order that this may be done it has seemed expedient to us to extend to all dioceses the regulations which the Bishops of Umbria, with great wisdom, laid down for theirs many years ago. "In order," they say, "to extirpate the errors already propagated and to prevent their further diffusion, and to remove those teachers of impiety through whom the pernicious effects of such diffusion are being perpetuated, this sacred Assembly, following the example of St. Charles Borromeo, has decided to establish in each of the dioceses a Council consisting of approved members of both branches of the clergy, which shall be charged with the task of noting the existence of errors and the devices by which new ones are introduced and propagated, and to inform the Bishop of the whole, so that he may take counsel with them as to the best means for suppressing the evil at the outset and preventing it spreading for the ruin of souls or, worse still, gaining strength and growth."[27] We decree, therefore, that in every diocese a council of this kind, which We are pleased to name the "Council of Vigilance," be instituted without delay. The priests called to form part in it shall be chosen somewhat after the manner above prescribed for the censors, and they shall meet every two months on an appointed day in the presence of the Bishop. They shall be bound to secrecy as to their deliberations and decisions, and in their functions shall be included the following: they shall watch most carefully for every trace and sign of Modernism both in publications and in teaching, and to preserve the clergy and the young from it they

shall take all prudent, prompt and efficacious measures. Let them combat novelties of words, remembering the admonitions of Leo XIII: "It is impossible to approve in Catholic publications a style inspired by unsound novelty which seems to deride the piety of the faithful and dwells on the introduction of a new order of Christian life, on new directions of the Church, on new aspirations of the modern soul, on a new social vocation of the clergy, on a new Christian civilization, and many other things of the same kind."[28] Language of the kind here indicated is not to be tolerated either in books or in lectures. The Councils must not neglect the books treating of the pious traditions of different places or of sacred relics. Let them not permit such questions to be discussed in journals or periodicals destined to foster piety, either with expressions savoring of mockery or contempt, or by dogmatic pronouncements, especially when, as is often the case, what is stated as a certainty either does not pass the limits of probability or is based on prejudiced opinion. Concerning sacred relics, let this be the rule: if Bishops, who alone are judges in such matters, know for certain that a relic is not genuine, let them remove it at once from the veneration of the faithful; if the authentications of a relic happen to have been lost through civil disturbances, or in any other way, let it not be exposed for public veneration until the Bishop has verified it. The argument of prescription or well-founded presumption is to have weight only when devotion to a relic is commendable by reason of its antiquity, according to the sense of the Decree issued in 1896 by the Congregation of Indulgences and Sacred Relics: "Ancient relics are to retain the veneration they have always enjoyed except when in individual instances there are clear arguments that they are false or supposititious." In passing judgment on pious traditions let it always be borne in mind that in this matter the Church uses the greatest prudence, and that she does not allow traditions of this kind to be narrated in books except with the utmost caution and with the insertion of the declaration imposed by Urban VIII; and even then she does not guarantee the truth of the fact narrated; she simply does not forbid belief in things for which human evidence is not wanting. On this matter the Sacred Congregation of Rites, thirty years ago, decreed as follows: "These apparitions or revelations have neither been approved nor condemned by the Holy See, which has simply allowed them to be believed on purely human faith, on the tradition which they relate, corroborated by testimony and documents worthy of credence."[29] Anyone who follows this rule has no cause to fear. For the devotion based on any apparition, in so far as it regards the fact itself, that is to say, in so far as the devotion is *relative*, always implies the condition of the fact being true; while in so far as it is *absolute*, it is always based on the truth, seeing that its object is the persons of the Saints who are honored. The same is true of relics. Finally, We entrust to the Councils of Vigilance the duty of overseeing assiduously and diligently social institutions as well as writings on social questions so that they may harbor no trace of Modernism, but obey the prescriptions of the Roman Pontiffs.

### *Triennial Returns*

56. Lest what We have laid down thus far should pass into oblivion, We will and ordain that the Bishops of all dioceses, a year after the publication of these letters and every three years thenceforward, furnish the Holy See with a diligent and sworn report on the things which have been decreed in this Our Letter, and on the doctrines that find currency among the clergy, and especially in the seminaries and other Catholic institutions, those not excepted which are not subject to the Ordinary, and We impose the like obligation on the Generals of religious orders with regard to those who are under them.

### *Conclusion*

57. This, Venerable Brethren, is what We have thought it Our duty to write to you for the salvation of all who believe. The adversaries of the Church will doubtless abuse what We have said to refurbish the old calumny by which We are traduced as the enemy of science and of the progress of humanity. As a fresh answer to such accusations, which the history of the Christian

religion refutes by never-failing evidence, it is Our intention to establish by every means in our power a special Institute in which, through the co-operation of those Catholics who are most eminent for their learning, the advance of science and every other department of knowledge may be promoted under the guidance and teaching of Catholic truth. God grant that We may happily realize Our design with the assistance of all those who bear a sincere love for the Church of Christ. But of this We propose to speak on another occasion.

*Apostolic Blessing*

Meanwhile, Venerable Brethren, fully confident in your zeal and energy, We beseech for you with Our whole heart the abundance of heavenly light, so that in the midst of this great danger to souls from the insidious invasions of error upon every hand, you may see clearly what ought to be done, and labor to do it with all your strength and courage. May Jesus Christ, the author and finisher of our faith, be with you in His power; and may the Immaculate Virgin, the destroyer of all heresies, be with you by her prayers and aid. And We, as a pledge of Our affection and of the Divine solace in adversity, most lovingly grant to you, your clergy and people, the Apostolic Benediction.

58.  Given at St. Peter's, Rome, September 8, 1907, in the fifth year of Our Pontificate.

Pius X, Pope

NOTES

1. Vatican Council I, *De Revelatione,* can. 1.
2. *Ibid.,* can. 2.
3. Vatican Council I, *De Fide,* can. 3.
4. *De Revelatione,* can. 3.
5. Gregory XVI, encyclical of June 25, 1834, *Singulari Nos.*
6. Brief to the Bishop of Breslau, June 15, 1857.

7. Gregory IX, *Epist. ad Magistros theol. paris.*, July 7, 1223.

8. Proposition 29, condemned by Leo X in the bull of May 16, 1520, *Exsurge Domine:* "A way has been made for us for weakening the authority of Councils, and for freely contradicting their actions, and judging their decrees, and boldly confessing whatever seems true, whether it has been approved, or disapproved by any Council whatsoever."

9. Sess. VII, *De Sacramentis in genere,* can. 5.

10. Proposition 2: "The proposition which states 'that power has been given by God to the Church, that it might be communicated to the pastors who are its ministers for the salvation of souls'; if thus understood that the power of ecclesiastical ministry and of rule is derived from the COMMUNITY of the faithful to the pastors: heretical." Proposition 3: "In addition, the proposition which states 'that the Roman Pontiff is the ministerial head,' if it is so explained that the Roman Pontiff does not receive from Christ in the person of blessed Peter, but from the Church, the power of ministry, which as successor of Peter, true Vicar of Christ and head of the whole Church he possesses in the universal Church: heretical."

11. Pius IX, encyclical of November 9, 1846, *Qui pluribus.*

12. Syllabus, Prop. 5.

13. Vatican Council I, Constitution *Dei Filius*, chap. 4.

14. *Loc. cit.*

15. Vatican Council, *De Revelatione, can.* 2.

16. *Epist.* 28.

17. Gregory XVI, encyclical of June 25, 1834, *Singulari Nos.*

18. Syllabus, Prop. 13.

19. *Motu Proprio* of March 14, 1891, *Ut mysticam.*

20. Leo XIII, encyclical of August 4, 1879, *Aeterni Patris.*

21. Leo XIII, Apostolic letter of December 10, 1889, *In magna.*

22. Leo XIII, allocution of March 7, 1880.

23. *Loc. cit.*

24. Cf. *AAS*, 29:359ff

25. Cf. *AAS*, 30:39ff.

26. Leo XIII, encyclical of February 10, 1884, *Nobilissima Gallorum.*

27. Acts of the Congress of the Bishops of Umbria, November, 1849, *tit.* 2, *art.* 6

28. Instruction of the Sacred Congregation of Extraordinary Ecclesiastical Affairs, January 27, 1902.

29. Decree of May 2, 1877.

# OUR APOSTOLIC MANDATE
*(On the "Sillon")*

August 25, 1910

To the French Archbishops and Bishops:
To Our Well-Beloved Sons Peter Hector Coulié,
Cardinal-Priest of the Holy Roman Church, Archbishop of
Lyons; Lewis Henry Lucon, Cardinal-Priest of the
Holy Roman Church, Archbishop of Rheims;
Paulin Peter Andrieu, Cardinal-Priest of the Holy Roman
Church, Archbishop of Bordeaux; and to all Our Other
Venerable Brethren, the French Archbishops and Bishops.

Venerable Brethren,

1. Our Apostolic mandate requires from Us that We watch over
the purity of the Faith and the integrity of Catholic discipline. It
requires from Us that We protect the faithful from evil and error;
especially so when evil and error are presented in dynamic language which, concealing vague notions and ambiguous expressions with emotional and high-sounding words, is likely to set
ablaze the hearts of men in the pursuit of ideals which, while
attractive, are nonetheless nefarious. Such were not so long ago
the doctrines of the so-called philosophers of the 18th century,
doctrines of the Revolution[1] and Liberalism which have been so
often condemned; such are even today the theories of the Sillon[2]
which, under the glowing appearance of generosity, are all too
often wanting in clarity, logic and truth. These theories do not

belong to the Catholic, or for that matter, to the French spirit.

### *Credit Is Given to Sillonists for Their Dedication*

2. We have long debated, Venerable Brethren, before We decided to solemnly and publicly speak Our mind on the Sillon. Only when your concern augmented Our own did We decide to do so. For We love, indeed, the valiant young people who fight under the Sillon's banner, and We deem them worthy of praise and admiration in many respects. We love their leaders, whom We are pleased to acknowledge as noble souls on a level above vulgar passions and inspired with the noblest form of enthusiasm in their quest for goodness. You have seen, Venerable Brethren, how, imbued with a living realization of the brotherhood of men and supported in their selfless efforts by their love of Jesus Christ and a strict observance of their religious duties, they sought out those who labor and suffer in order to set them on their feet again.

### *The Origin of the Sillon—The Courage of Its Members*

3. This was shortly after Our Predecessor Leo XIII of happy memory had issued his remarkable Encyclical on the condition of the working class. Speaking through her supreme leader, the Church had just poured out the tenderness of her motherly love over the humble and the lowly; and it looked as though she was calling out for an ever growing number of people to labor for the restoration of order and justice in our uneasy society. Was it not opportune, then, for the leaders of the Sillon to come forward and place at the service of the Church their troops of young believers who could fulfill her wisdom and her hopes? And in fact, the Sillon did raise among the workers the standard of Jesus Christ, the sign of salvation for peoples and nations. Nourishing its social action at the fountain of divine grace, it did impose a respect for religion upon the least willing groups, accustoming the ignorant and the impious to hearing the Word of God. And not seldom, during public debates, stung by a question or sarcasm, you saw them jumping to their feet and proudly proclaiming their faith in the

face of a hostile audience. This was the heyday of the Sillon; its brighter side accounts for the encouragement and tokens of approval which the bishops and the Holy See gave liberally when this religious fervor was still obscuring the true nature of the Sillonist movement.

### Straying from the Right Path

4. For it must be said, Venerable Brethren, that Our expectations have been frustrated in large measure. The day came when perceptive observers could discern alarming trends within the Sillon; the Sillon was losing its way. Could it have been otherwise? Its leaders were young, full of enthusiasm and self-confidence. But they were not adequately equipped with historical knowledge, sound philosophy and solid theology to tackle without danger the difficult social problems in which their work and their inclinations were involving them. They were not sufficiently equipped to be on their guard against the penetration of liberal and Protestant concepts on doctrine and obedience.

### Ignoring Advice and Admonition Calls for Censure

5. They were given no small measure of advice. Admonition came after the advice, but, to Our sorrow, both advice and reproaches ran off the sheath of their elusive souls and were of no avail. Things came to such a pass that We should be failing in Our duty if We kept silent any longer. We owe the truth to Our dear sons of the Sillon who are carried away by their generous ardor along a path strewn with errors and dangers. We owe the truth to a large number of seminarians and priests who have been drawn away by the Sillon, if not from the authority, at least from the guidance and influence of the bishops. We owe it also to the Church in which the Sillon is sowing discord and whose interests it endangers.

### The Claim of Sillonists for Independence

6. In the first place, We must take up sharply the pretension of the Sillon to escape the jurisdiction of ecclesiastical authority. Indeed, the leaders of the Sillon claim that they are working in a field which is not that of the Church; they claim that they are pursuing aims in the temporal order only and not those of the spiritual order; that the Sillonist is simply a Catholic devoted to the betterment of the working class and to democratic endeavors by drawing from the practices of his faith the energy for his selfless efforts. They claim that, neither more nor less than a Catholic craftsman, farmer, economist or politician, the Sillonist is subject to common standards of behavior, yet without being bound in a special manner by the authority of the Church.

### Their Claim Is Unjustified

7. To reply to these fallacies is only too easy: for whom will they make believe that the Catholic Sillonists, the priests and seminarians enrolled in their ranks, have in sight in their social work only the temporal interests of the working class? To maintain this We think would be an insult to them. The truth is that the Sillonist leaders are self-confessed and irrepressible idealists: they claim to regenerate the working class by first elevating the conscience of man; they have a social doctrine, and they have religious and philosophical principles for the reconstruction of society upon new foundations; they have a particular conception of human dignity, freedom, justice and brotherhood; and in an attempt to justify their social dreams, they put forward the Gospel, but interpreted in their own way; and what is even more serious, they call to witness Christ, but a diminished and distorted Christ. Further, they teach these ideas in their study groups and inculcate them upon their friends, and they also introduce them into their working procedures. Therefore they are really professors of social, civic and religious morals; and whatever modifications they may introduce in the organization of the Sillonist movement, We have the right to say that the aims of the Sillon, its character

and its action, belong to the field of morals, which is the proper domain of the Church. In view of all this, the Sillonists are deceiving themselves when they believe that they are working in a field that lies outside the limits of Church authority and of its doctrinal and directive power.

### They Teach Positive Errors

8. Even if their doctrines were free from errors, it would still be a very serious breach of Catholic discipline to decline obstinately the direction of those who have received from Heaven the mission to guide individuals and communities along the straight path of truth and goodness. But, as We have already said, the evil lies far deeper: The Sillon, carried away by an ill-conceived love for the weak, has fallen into error.

### They Strive after a Condemned Democratic Ideal

9. Indeed, the Sillon proposes to raise up and re-educate the working class. But in this respect, the principles of Catholic doctrine have been defined, and the history of Christian civilization bears witness to their beneficent fruitfulness. Our Predecessor of happy memory re-affirmed them in masterly documents, and all Catholics dealing with social questions have the duty to study them and to keep them in mind. He taught, among other things, that "Christian Democracy must preserve the diversity of classes, which is assuredly the attribute of a soundly constituted State, and it must seek to give human society the form and character which God, its Author, has imparted to it." Our Predecessor denounced "a certain Democracy which goes so far in wickedness as to place sovereignty in the people and aims at the suppression of classes and their levelling down." At the same time, Leo XIII laid down for Catholics a program of action, the only program capable of putting society back onto its centuries-old Christian basis.[3] But what have the leaders of the Sillon done? Not only have they adopted a program and teaching different from that of Leo XIII (which would be of itself a singularly auda-

cious decision on the part of laymen, thus taking up, concurrent with the Sovereign Pontiff, the role of director of social action in the Church), but they have openly rejected the program laid out by Leo XIII on the essential principles of society; they place authority in the people, or gradually suppress it and strive, as their ideal, to effect the levelling down of the classes. In opposition to Catholic doctrine, therefore, they are proceeding toward a condemned ideal.

### They Ignore the Natural Laws Governing Human Nature

10. We know well that they flatter themselves with the idea of raising human dignity and the discredited condition of the working class. We know that they wish to render just and perfect the labor laws and the relations between employers and employees, thus causing a more complete justice and a greater measure of charity to prevail upon earth, and causing also a profound and fruitful transformation in society by which mankind would make an undreamed-of progress. Certainly, We do not blame these efforts; they would be excellent in every respect if the Sillonists did not forget that a person's progress consists in developing his natural abilities by fresh motivations to operate within the frame of, and in conformity with, the laws of human nature. But on the contrary, by ignoring the laws governing human nature and by breaking the bounds within which they operate, the human person is led not toward progress but toward death. This, nevertheless, is what they want to do with human society; they dream of a Future City built on different principles, and they dare to proclaim these more fruitful and more beneficial than the principles upon which the present Christian City rests.

### Human Society Must Be Built According to God's Plan

11. No, Venerable Brethren, We must repeat with the utmost energy in these times of social and intellectual anarchy when everyone takes it upon himself to teach as a teacher and lawmaker—the City cannot be built otherwise than as God has built

it; society cannot be set up unless the Church lays the foundations and supervises the work; no, civilization is not something yet to be found, nor is the New City to be built on hazy notions. It has been in existence and still is: it is Christian civilization, it is the Catholic City. It has only to be set up and restored continually against the unremitting attacks of insane dreamers, rebels and miscreants. *Omnia Instaurare in Christo*.[4]

### The Main Points of the Sillonist Doctrine

12. Now, lest We be accused of judging too hastily and with unjustified rigor the social doctrines of the Sillon, We wish to examine their essential points.

### Liberty and Equality

13. The Sillon has a praiseworthy concern for human dignity. But it understands human dignity in the manner of some philosophers of whom the Church does not at all feel proud. The first condition of that dignity is liberty, but viewed in the sense that, except in religious matters, each man is autonomous. This is the basic principle from which the Sillon draws further conclusions: Today the people are in tutelage under an authority distinct from themselves; they must liberate themselves: *political emancipation*. They are also dependent upon employers who own the means of production, exploit, oppress and degrade the workers; they must shake off the yoke: *economic emancipation*. Finally, they are ruled by a caste called *Intelligentsia* which, by its very nature, enjoys undue preponderance in the direction of affairs.[5] The people must break away from this domination: *intellectual emancipation*. The levelling-down of differences from this three-fold point of view will bring about equality among men, and such equality is viewed as true human justice. A socio-political setup resting on these two pillars of Liberty and Equality, to which Fraternity will presently be added, is what they call Democracy.

## Government by the People

14. However, liberty and equality are, so to speak, no more than a negative side. The distinctive and positive aspect of Democracy is to be found in the largest possible participation of everyone in the government of public affairs.[6] And this, in turn, comprises a threefold aspect, that is, political, economic and moral.

### The Political Aspect: Authority in the People

15. At first, the Sillon does not wish to abolish political authority. On the contrary, it considers it necessary; but it wishes to divide it, or rather to multiply it in such a way that each citizen will become a kind of king. Authority, so they concede, comes from God, but it resides primarily in the people and expresses itself by means of elections or, better still, by selection. However, it still remains in the hands of the people; it does not escape their control.[7] It will be an external authority, yet only in appearance; in fact, it will be internal because it will be an authority assented to.

### The Economic Aspect: Guild-Socialism

16. All other things being equal, the same principle will apply to economics. Taken away from a specific group, management will be so well multiplied that each worker will himself become a kind of employer. The system by which the Sillon intends to actualize this economic ideal is not Socialism, they say; it is a system of guilds in a number large enough to induce a healthy competition and to protect the workers' independence; in this manner they will not be bound to any guild in particular.

### The Moral Aspect: The Community First

17. We come now to the principal aspect, the moral aspect. Since, as we have seen, authority is much reduced, another force is necessary to supplement it and to provide a permanent counter-

weight against individual selfishness. This new principle, this force, is the love of professional interest and of public interest, that is to say, the love of the very end of the profession and of society. Visualize a society in which, in the soul of everyone, along with the innate love of personal interest and family welfare prevails love for one's occupation and for the welfare of the community. Imagine this society in which, in the conscience of everyone, personal and family interests are so subordinate that a superior interest always takes precedence over them. Could not such a society almost do without any authority? And would it not be the embodiment of the ideal of human dignity, with each citizen having the soul of a king, and each worker the soul of a master? Snatched away from the pettiness of private interests and raised up to the interests of the profession and, even higher, to those of the whole nation and, higher still, to those of the human race (for the Sillon's field of vision is not bound by national borders, it encompasses all men even to the ends of the earth), the human heart, enlarged by the love of the commonwealth, would embrace all comrades of the same profession, all compatriots, all men. Such is the ideal of human greatness and nobility to be attained through the famous popular trilogy: *Liberty, Equality, Fraternity.*

### The Three Aspects are Interrelated

18. These three elements, that is, political, economic and moral, are interdependent, and, as We have said, the moral element is dominant. Indeed, no political Democracy can survive if it is not solidly anchored to an economic Democracy. But neither one nor the other is possible if it is not rooted in an awareness by the human conscience of being invested with moral responsibilities and energies mutually commensurate. But granted the existence of that awareness, so created by conscious responsibilities and moral forces, the kind of Democracy arising from it will naturally reflect in deeds the consciousness and moral forces from which it flows. In the same manner, political Democracy will also issue from the trade-guild system. Thus,

both political and economic Democracies, the latter bearing the former, will be fastened to unshakeable bases in the very consciousness of the people.

### Democratic Education of the People: A Dream

19. To sum up, such is the theory, one could say the dream, of the Sillon; and that is what its teaching aims at, which it calls the democratic education of the people, that is, raising to its maximum the conscience and civic responsibility of every one, from which will result economic and political Democracy and the reign of Justice, Liberty, Equality, Fraternity.

### A Doctrine Contrary to Catholic Truth

20. This brief explanation, Venerable Brethren, will show you clearly how much reason We have for saying that the Sillon opposes doctrine to doctrine, that it seeks to build its City on a theory contrary to Catholic truth, and that it falsifies the basic and essential notions which regulate social relations in human society. The following considerations will make this opposition even more evident.

### The Real Source of Authority

21. The Sillon places public authority primarily in the people, from whom it then flows into the government in such a manner, however, that it continues to reside in the people. But Leo XIII absolutely condemned this doctrine in his Encyclical *Diuturnum Illud,* on political government, in which he said: "Modern writers in great numbers, following in the footsteps of those who called themselves philosophers in the last century, declare that all power comes from the people; consequently, those who exercise power in society do not exercise it from their own authority, but from an authority delegated to them by the people, and on the condition that it can be revoked by the will of the people from whom they hold it. Quite contrary is the sentiment of Catholics, who hold that

the right of governing derives from God as its natural and necessary principle."

Admittedly, the Sillon holds that authority—which it first
places in the people—descends from God, but in such a way "as
to return from below upward, while in the organization of the
Church, power descends from above downward."[8]

But besides its being abnormal for the delegation of power to
ascend, since it is in its nature to descend, Leo XIII refuted in
advance this attempt to reconcile Catholic doctrine with the error
of philosophism. For he continues: "It is necessary to remark here
that those who preside over the government of public affairs may
indeed, in certain cases, be chosen by the will and judgement of
the multitude without repugnance or opposition to Catholic doctrine. But while this choice marks out the ruler, it does not confer
upon him the authority to govern; it does not delegate the power,
it designates the person who will be invested with it."

## Authority, Liberty and Obedience

22. For the rest, if the people remain the holders of power,
what becomes of authority? A shadow, a myth; there is no more
law properly so called, no more obedience. The Sillon acknowledges this: indeed, since it demands that threefold political, economic and intellectual emancipation in the name of human
dignity, the Future City which it is engaged in forming will have
no masters and no servants. All citizens will be free, all comrades, all kings. A command, a precept, would be viewed as an
attack upon their freedom; subordination to any form of superiority would be a diminishment of the human person, and obedience a disgrace. Is it in this manner, Venerable Brethren, that the
traditional doctrine of the Church represents social relations,
even in the most perfect society? Has not every community of
people, dependent and unequal by nature, need of an authority to
direct its activity toward the common good and to enforce its
laws? And if perverse individuals are to be found in a community
(and there always are), should not authority be all the stronger as
the selfishness of the wicked is more threatening? Further, unless

one greatly deceives oneself in the conception of liberty, can it be said with an atom of reason that authority and liberty are incompatible? Can one teach that obedience is contrary to human dignity and that the ideal would be to replace it by "accepted authority"? Did not St. Paul the Apostle foresee human society in all its possible stages of development when he bade the faithful to be subject to every authority? Does obedience to men as the legitimate representatives of God, that is to say, in the final analysis, obedience to God, degrade man and reduce him to a level unworthy of himself? Is the religious life, which is based on obedience, contrary to the ideal of human nature? Were the Saints, the most obedient of men, just slaves and degenerates? Finally, can you imagine social conditions in which Jesus Christ, if He returned to earth, would not give an example of obedience, and further, would no longer say: "Render unto Caesar the things that are Caesar's and to God the things that are God's?"

## Justice and Equality

23. Teaching such doctrines, and applying them to its internal organization, the Sillon therefore sows erroneous and fatal notions on authority, liberty and obedience among your Catholic youth. The same is true of justice and equality. The Sillon says that it is striving to establish an era of equality which, by that very fact, would be also an era of greater justice. Thus, to the Sillon, every inequality of condition is an injustice, or at least a diminution of justice. Here we have a principle that conflicts sharply with the nature of things, a principle conducive to jealousy, to injustice, and subversive of any social order. Thus, Democracy alone will bring about the reign of perfect justice! Is this not an insult to other forms of government which are thereby debased to the level of sterile makeshifts? Besides, the Sillonists once again clash on this point with the teaching of Pope Leo XIII. In the Encyclical on political government which We have already quoted, they could read this: "Justice being preserved, it is not forbidden to the people to choose for themselves the form of government which best corresponds with their character or with the

institutions and customs handed down by their forefathers."

And the Encyclical alludes to the three well-known forms of government, thus implying that justice is compatible with any of them. And does not the Encyclical on the condition of the working class state[9] clearly that justice can be restored within the existing social setup, since it indicates the means of doing so? Undoubtedly, Pope Leo XIII did not mean to speak of some form of justice, but of perfect justice. Therefore, when he said that justice could be found in any of the three aforesaid forms of government, he was teaching that in this respect Democracy does not enjoy a special privilege.[10] The Sillonists who maintain the opposite view either turn a deaf ear to the teaching of the Church or form for themselves an idea of justice and equality which is not Catholic.

### Fraternity vs. Charity

24. The same applies to the notion of Fraternity, which they found on the love of common interest or, beyond all philosophies and religions, on the mere notion of humanity, thus embracing with an equal love and tolerance all human beings and their miseries, whether these are intellectual, moral, or physical and temporal. But Catholic doctrine tells us that the primary duty of charity does not lie in the toleration of false ideas, however sincere they may be; nor in theoretical or practical indifference toward the errors and vices in which we see our brethren plunged, but in zeal for their intellectual and moral improvement as well as for their material well-being. Catholic doctrine further tells us that love for our neighbor flows from our love for God, who is Father to all, and goal of the human family; and in Jesus Christ, whose members we are, to the point that in doing good to others, we are doing good to Jesus Christ Himself. Any other kind of love is sheer illusion, sterile and fleeting.

Indeed, we have the human experience of pagan and secular societies of ages past to show that concern for common interests or affinities of nature weigh very little against the passions and wild desires of the heart. No, Venerable Brethren, there is no genuine fraternity outside Christian charity. Through love of God and His Son Jesus Christ our Saviour, Christian charity embraces all men, comforts all and leads all to the same faith and same heavenly happiness.

By separating fraternity from Christian charity thus understood, Democracy, far from being a progress, would mean a disastrous step backward for civilization. If, as We desire with all Our heart, the highest possible peak of well-being for society and its members is to be attained through fraternity, or, as it is also called, universal solidarity, all minds must be united in the knowledge of Truth, all wills united in morality and all hearts in the love of God and His Son Jesus Christ. But this union is attainable only by Catholic charity, and that is why Catholic charity alone can lead the people in the march of progress toward the ideal civilization.

### Human Dignity

25. Finally, at the root of all their fallacies on social questions lie the false hopes of the Sillonists on human dignity. According to them, man will be a man truly worthy of the name only when he has acquired a strong, enlightened and independent consciousness, able to do without a master, obeying only himself, and able to assume the most demanding responsibilities without faltering. Such are the big words by which human pride is exalted, like the dream carrying man away without light, without guidance and without help into the realm of illusion in which he will be destroyed by his errors and passions while awaiting the glorious day of his full consciousness. And that great day, when will it come? Unless human nature can be changed, which is not within the power of the Sillonists, will that day ever come? Did the Saints, who brought human dignity to its highest point, possess that kind of dignity? And what of the lowly of this earth, who are unable to rise so high but are content to plow their furrow modestly at the level where Providence placed them? They who are diligently discharging their duties with Christian humility, obedience and patience, are they not also worthy of being called men?

Will not Our Lord take them one day out of their obscurity and place them in Heaven among the princes of His people?

### Effect of the Sillonists' Errors on Their Policy

26. We close here Our observations on the errors of the Sillon. We do not claim to have exhausted the subject, for We should yet draw your attention to other points that are equally false and dangerous, for example, on the manner to interpret the concept of the coercive power of the Church. But We must now examine the influence of these errors upon the practical conduct and upon the social action of the Sillon.

### The Sillonist Organization

27. The Sillonist doctrines are not kept within the domain of abstract philosophy; they are taught to Catholic youth, and even worse, efforts are made to apply them in everyday life. The Sillon is regarded as the nucleus of the Future City, and, accordingly, it is being made to its image as much as possible. Indeed, the Sillon has no hierarchy. The governing elite has emerged from the rank and file by selection, that is, by imposing itself through its moral authority and its virtues. People join it freely, and freely they may leave it. Studies are carried out without a master, at the very most with an adviser. The study groups are really intellectual pools in which each member is at once both master and student. The most complete fellowship prevails among its members and draws their souls into close communion; hence the common soul of the Sillon. It has been called a "friendship." Even the priest, on entering, lowers the eminent dignity of his priesthood and, by a strange reversal of roles, becomes a student, placing himself on a level with his young friends, and is no more than a comrade.

### Lack of Respect and Obedience

28. In these democratic practices and in the theories of the Ideal City from which they flow, you will recognize, Venerable

Brethren, the hidden cause of the lack of discipline with which you have so often had to reproach the Sillon. It is not surprising that you do not find among the leaders and their comrades trained on these lines, whether seminarians or priests, the respect, the docility and the obedience which are due to your authority and to yourselves; nor is it surprising that you should be conscious of an underlying opposition on their part, and that, to your sorrow, you should see them withdraw altogether from works which are not those of the Sillon, or, if compelled under obedience, that they should comply with distaste. You are the past; they are the pioneers of the civilization of the future. You represent the hierarchy, social inequalities, authority and obedience, worn-out institutions to which their hearts, captured by another ideal, can no longer submit. Occurrences so sad as to bring tears to Our eyes bear witness to this frame of mind. And We cannot, with all Our patience, overcome a just feeling of indignation. Now then! Distrust of the Church, their Mother, is being instilled into the minds of Catholic youth; they are being taught that after nineteen centuries she has not yet been able to build up in this world a society on true foundations; she has not understood the social notions of authority, liberty, equality, fraternity and human dignity; they are told that the great Bishops and Kings, who have made France what it is and governed so gloriously, have not been able to give their people true justice and true happiness because they did not possess the Sillonist ideal!

### A Legacy from the Revolution of 1789

29. The breath of the Revolution has passed this way, and We can conclude that, while the social doctrines of the Sillon are erroneous, its spirit is dangerous and its education disastrous.

### A Reprovable Doctrine and a Reprovable Action

30. But then what are We to think of its action in the Church? What are We to think of a movement so punctilious in its brand of Catholicism that unless you embrace its cause you would almost

be regarded as an internal enemy of the Church and one who understands nothing of the Gospel and of Jesus Christ! We deem it necessary to insist on that point because it is precisely its Catholic ardor which has secured for the Sillon until quite recently valuable encouragements and the support of distinguished persons. Well now, judging the words and deeds, We feel compelled to say that in this action as well as in its doctrine the Sillon does not give satisfaction to the Church.

## The Church Does Not Promote Democracy

31. In the first place, its brand of Catholicism accepts only the democratic form of government, which it considers the most favorable to the Church and, so to speak, identifies it with her. The Sillon, therefore, subjects its religion to a political party. We do not have to demonstrate here that the advent of universal Democracy is of no concern to the action of the Church in the world; We have already recalled that the Church has always left to nations the care of giving themselves the form of government which they think most suited to their needs. What We wish to affirm once again, after Our Predecessor, is that it is an error and a danger to bind down Catholicism by principle to a particular form of government. This error and this danger are all the greater when religion is associated with a kind of democracy whose doctrines are false. But this is what the Sillon is doing. For the sake of a particular political form, it compromises the Church, it sows division among Catholics, snatches away young people, and even priests and seminarians, from purely Catholic action, and is wasting away as a dead loss part of the living forces of the nation.

## Sillonists Abstain from Defending the Church

32. And behold, Venerable Brethren, an astounding contradiction: It is precisely because religion ought to transcend all parties, and it is in appealing to this principle, that the Sillon abstains from defending the beleaguered Church. Certainly, it is not the Church that has gone into the political arena: They have dragged

her there to mutilate and to despoil her. Is it not the duty of every Catholic, then, to use the political weapons which he holds to defend her? Is it not a duty to confine politics to its own domain and to leave the Church alone except in order to give her that which is her due? Well, at the sight of the violences thus done to the Church, We are often grieved to see the Sillonists folding their arms except when it is to their advantage to defend her; We see them dictate or maintain a program which nowhere and in no degree can be called Catholic. Yet this does not prevent the same men, when fully engaged in political strife and spurred by a provocation, from publicly proclaiming their faith. What are We to say except that there are two different men in the Sillonist: the individual who is Catholic, and the Sillonist, the man of action, who is neutral.

## Cooperation among Workers of All Religions

33. There was a time when the Sillon as such was truly Catholic. It recognized but one moral force—Catholicism; and the Sillonists were wont to proclaim that Democracy would have to be Catholic or would not exist at all. A time came when they changed their minds. They left to each one his religion or his philosophy. They ceased to call themselves Catholics, and for the formula "Democracy will be Catholic," they substituted "Democracy will not be anti-Catholic," any more than it will be anti-Jewish or anti-Buddhist. This was the time of the "Greater Sillon." For the construction of the Future City they appealed to the workers of all religions and all sects. These were asked but one thing: to share the same social ideal, to respect all creeds and to bring with them a certain supply of moral force. Admittedly, they declared that "The leaders of the Sillon place their religious faith above everything. But can they deny others the right to draw their moral energy from whence they can? In return, they expect others to respect their right to draw their own moral energy from the Catholic Faith. Accordingly, they ask all those who want to change today's society in the direction of Democracy not to oppose each other on account of the philosophical or religious

convictions which may separate them, but to march hand in hand, not renouncing their convictions, but trying to provide on the ground of practical realities the proof of the excellence of their personal convictions. Perhaps a union will be effected on this ground of emulation between souls holding different religious or philosophical convictions."[11] And they added at the same time (but how could this be accomplished?) that "The Little Catholic Sillon will be the soul of the Greater Cosmopolitan Sillon."

### Catholics, Protestants and Freethinkers

34. Recently, the term "Greater Sillon" was discarded and a new organization was born, without modifying—quite the contrary—the spirit and the substratum of things: "In order to organize in an orderly manner the different forces of activity, the Sillon still remains as a Soul, a Spirit, which will pervade the groups and inspire their work." Thus, a host of new groups, Catholic, Protestant, Freethinking,[12] now apparently autonomous, are invited to set to work:

"Catholic comrades will work among themselves in a special organization and will learn and educate themselves. Protestant and Freethinking Democrats will do likewise on their own side. But all of us, Catholics, Protestants and Freethinkers will have at heart to arm young people, not in view of the fratricidal struggle, but in view of a disinterested emulation in the field of social and civic virtues."[13]

### Very Serious Remarks

35. These declarations and this new organization of the Sillonist action call for very serious remarks.

### An Interdenominational Association to Reform Civilization

36. Here we have, founded by Catholics, an interdenominational association that is to work for the reform of civilization, an undertaking which is, above all, religious in character; for there is

no true civilization without a moral civilization, and no true moral civilization without the true religion: it is a proven truth, an historical fact. The new Sillonists cannot pretend that they are merely working on "the ground of practical realities" where differences of belief do not matter. Their leader is so conscious of the influence which the convictions of the mind have upon the result of the action that he invites them, whatever religion they may belong to, "to provide on the ground of practical realities the proof of the excellence of their personal convictions." And with very good reason: all practical results reflect the nature of one's religious convictions, just as the limbs of a man, down to his fingertips, owe their very shape to the principle of life that dwells in his body.

### Catholics, Protestants and Skeptics

37. This being said, what must be thought of the indiscriminate mingling in which young Catholics will be caught up with heterodox and unbelieving folk in a work of this nature? Is it not a thousandfold more dangerous for them than a neutral association? What are we to think of this appeal to all the heterodox, and to all the unbelievers, to prove the excellence of their convictions in the social sphere in a sort of apologetic contest? Has not this contest lasted for nineteen centuries in conditions less dangerous for the faith of Catholics? And was it not all to the credit of the Catholic Church? What are we to think of this respect for all errors and of this strange invitation made by a Catholic to all the dissidents to strengthen their convictions through study so that they may have more and more abundant sources of fresh forces? What are we to think of an association in which all religions and even Free Thought may express themselves openly and in complete freedom? For the Sillonists who, in public lectures and elsewhere, proudly proclaim their personal faith, certainly do not intend to silence others, nor do they intend to prevent a Protestant from asserting his Protestantism and the skeptic from affirming his skepticism. Finally, what are we to think of a Catholic who, on entering his study group, leaves his Catholicism outside the door so as not to alarm his comrades who, "dreaming of disinterested

social action, are not inclined to make it serve the triumph of interests, coteries and even convictions, whatever they may be"? Such is the profession of faith of the new Democratic Committee for Social Action which has taken over the main objective of the previous organization and which, they say, "breaking the ambiguity which surrounded the Greater Sillon both in reactionary and anticlerical circles," is now open to all men "who respect moral and religious forces and who are convinced that no genuine social emancipation is possible without the leaven of generous idealism."

### Putting Aside Religious Convictions

38. Alas! Yes, the ambiguity has been broken: the social action of the Sillon is no longer Catholic. The Sillonist, as such, does not work for a coterie, and "the Church," he says, "cannot in any sense benefit from the sympathies that his action may stimulate." A strange situation indeed! They fear lest the Church should profit for a selfish and interested end by the social action of the Sillon, as if everything that benefited the Church did not benefit the whole human race! A curious reversal of notions! The Church might benefit from social action! As if the greatest economists had not recognized and proved that it is social action alone which, if serious and fruitful, must benefit by the Church! But stranger still, alarming and saddening at the same time, are the audacity and frivolity of men who call themselves Catholics and dream of re-shaping society under such conditions and of establishing on earth, over and beyond the pale of the Catholic Church, "the reign of love and justice" with workers coming from everywhere, of all religions and of no religion, with or without beliefs, so long as they forego what might divide them—their religious and philosophical convictions; and so long as they share what unites them—a "generous idealism and moral force; drawn from whence they can." When we consider the forces, knowledge and supernatural virtues which were necessary to establish the Christian City, and the sufferings of millions of martyrs, and the light given by the Fathers and Doctors of the Church, and the self-sacrifice of all

the heroes of charity, and a powerful hierarchy ordained in Heaven, and the streams of divine grace—the whole having been built up, bound together and impregnated by the life and spirit of Jesus Christ, the Wisdom of God, the Word made Man—when we think, I say, of all this, it is frightening to behold new apostles eagerly attempting to do better by a common interchange of vague idealism and civic virtues. What are they going to produce? What is to come out of this collaboration? A mere verbal and chimerical construction in which we see, glowing in a jumble and in seductive confusion, the words of Liberty, Justice, Fraternity, Love, Equality and human exaltation, all resting upon an ill-understood human dignity. It will be a tumultuous agitation, sterile for the end proposed, but which will benefit the less utopian exploiters of the people. Yes, we can truly say that the Sillon, its eyes fixed on a chimera, brings Socialism in its train.

## A Humanitarian Dream

39.  We fear that worse is to come: the end result of this developing promiscuousness, the beneficiary of this cosmopolitan social action, can only be a Democracy which will be neither Catholic, nor Protestant, nor Jewish. It will be a religion (for Sillonism, so the leaders have said, is a religion) more universal than the Catholic Church, uniting all men to become brothers and comrades at last in the "Kingdom of God": "We do not work for the Church, we work for mankind."

## Toward a One-World Church

40.  And now, overwhelmed with the deepest sadness, We ask Ourselves, Venerable Brethren, what has become of the Catholicism of the Sillon? Alas! This organization, which formerly afforded such promising expectations, this limpid and impetuous stream, has been harnessed in its course by the modern enemies of the Church and is now no more than a miserable affluent of the great movement of apostasy being organized in every country for the establishment of a One-World Church which shall have nei-

ther dogmas, nor hierarchy; neither discipline for the mind, nor
curb for the passions; and which, under the pretext of freedom and
human dignity, would bring back to the world (if such a church
could overcome) the reign of legalized cunning and force, and the
oppression of the weak and of those who toil and suffer.

## The Gospel of the Revolution

41. We know only too well the dark workshops in which are
elaborated these mischievous doctrines which ought not to seduce
clear-thinking minds. The leaders of the Sillon have not been able
to guard against these doctrines. The exaltation of their sentiments, the undiscriminating good will of their hearts, their philosophical mysticism, mixed with a measure of illuminism, have
carried them away toward another Gospel, which they thought
was the true Gospel of Our Saviour, to such an extent that they
speak of Our Lord Jesus Christ with a familiarity supremely dis-
respectful, and that—their ideal being akin to the Revolution—
they fear not to draw between the Gospel and the Revolution
blasphemous comparisons for which the excuse cannot be made
that they are due to some confused and over-hasty composition.

## Distortion of the Gospel

42. We wish to draw your attention, Venerable Brethren, to this
distortion of the Gospel and of the sacred character of Our Lord
Jesus Christ, God and Man, prevailing within the Sillon and elsewhere. As soon as the social question is being approached, it is a
fashion in some quarters to first put aside the divinity of Jesus
Christ, and then to mention only His unlimited clemency, His
compassion for all human miseries and His pressing exhortations
to the love of our neighbor and to the brotherhood of men. True,
Jesus has loved us with an immense, infinite love, and He came
on earth to suffer and die so that, gathered around Him in justice
and love, motivated by the same sentiments of mutual charity, all
men might live in peace and happiness. But for the realization of
this temporal and eternal happiness, He has laid down with

supreme authority the condition that we must belong to His flock, that we must accept His doctrine, that we must practice virtue, and that we must accept the teaching and guidance of Peter and his successors. Further, while Jesus was kind to sinners and to those who went astray, He did not respect their false ideas, however sincere they might have appeared. He loved them all, but He instructed them in order to convert them and save them. While He called to Himself, in order to comfort them, those who toiled and suffered, it was not to preach to them the jealousy of a chimerical equality. While He lifted up the lowly, it was not to instill in them the sentiment of a dignity independent from, and rebellious against the duty of obedience. While His heart overflowed with gentleness toward the souls of good will, He could also arm Himself with holy indignation against the profaners of the House of God, against the wretched men who scandalized the little ones, against the authorities who crush the people with the weight of heavy burdens without putting out a hand to lift them. He was as strong as He was gentle. He reproved, threatened, chastised; knowing and teaching us that fear is the beginning of wisdom and that it is sometimes proper for a man to cut off an offending limb to save his body. Finally, He did not announce for future society the reign of an ideal happiness from which suffering would be banished; but, by His lessons and by His example, He traced the path of the happiness which is possible on earth and of perfect happiness in Heaven: the royal way of the Cross. These are teachings that it would be wrong to apply only to one's personal life in order to win eternal salvation; these are eminently social teachings, and they show in Our Lord Jesus Christ something quite different from an inconsistent and impotent humanitarianism.

## Be at Once Gentle and Fearless

43. As for you, Venerable Brethren, carry on diligently with the work of the Saviour of men by emulating His gentleness and His strength. Minister to every misery; let no sorrow escape your pastoral solicitude; let no lament find you indifferent. But, on the other hand, preach fearlessly their duties to the powerful and to the

lowly; it is your function to form the conscience of the people and of the public authorities. The social question will be much nearer a solution when all those concerned, less demanding as regards their respective rights, shall fulfill their duties more exactingly.

### A Constructive Catholic Alternative

44. Moreover, since in the clash of interests, and especially in the struggle against dishonest forces, the virtue of a man, and even his holiness, are not always sufficient to guarantee him his daily bread, and since social structures, through their natural interplay, ought to be devised to thwart the efforts of the unscrupulous and enable all men of good will to attain their legitimate share of temporal happiness, We earnestly desire that you should take an active part in the organization of society with this objective in mind. And, to this end, while your priests will zealously devote their efforts to the sanctification of souls, to the defense of the Church and also to works of charity in the strict sense, you shall select a few of them, level-headed and of active disposition, holders of Doctors' degrees in philosophy and theology, thoroughly acquainted with the history of ancient and modern civilizations, and you shall set them to the not-so-lofty but more practical study of social science, so that you may place them at the opportune time at the helm of your works of Catholic action. However, let not these priests be misled in the maze of current opinions by the mirage of a false Democracy. Let them not borrow from the rhetoric of the worst enemies of the Church and of the people the high-flown phrases, full of promises, which are as high-sounding as they are unattainable. Let them be convinced that the social question and social science did not arise only yesterday; that the Church and the State, at all times and in happy concert, have raised up fruitful organizations to this end; that the Church, which has never betrayed the happiness of the people by consenting to dubious alliances, does not have to free herself from the past; that all that is needed is to take up again, with the help of the true workers for a social restoration, the organisms which the Revolution shattered, and to adapt them, in the same Christian spirit that

inspired them, to the new environment arising from the material development of today's society. Indeed, the true friends of the people are neither revolutionaries, nor innovators, they are promoters of tradition.

### Open to Sillonists

45. We desire that the Sillonist youth, freed from their errors, far from impeding this work, which is eminently worthy of your pastoral care, should bring to it their loyal and effective contribution in an orderly manner and with befitting submission.

### Practical Measures regarding the Sillon

46. We now turn to the leaders of the Sillon with the confidence of a father who speaks to his children, and We ask them, for their own good and for the good of the Church and of France, to turn their leadership over to you. We are certainly aware of the extent of the sacrifice that We request from them, but We know them to be of a sufficiently generous disposition to accept it; and, in advance, in the name of Our Lord Jesus Christ, whose representative We are, We bless them for this. As to the rank and file of the Sillon, We wish that they group themselves according to diocese in order to work, under the authority of their respective bishops, for the Christian and Catholic regeneration of the people, as well as for the improvement of their lot. These diocesan groups will be independent from one another for the time being. And, in order to show clearly that they have broken with the errors of the past, they will take the name of "Catholic Sillon," and each of the members will add to his Sillonist title the Catholic qualification. It goes without saying that each Catholic Sillonist will remain free to retain his political preferences, provided they are purified of everything that is not entirely conformable to the doctrine of the Church. Should some groups refuse, Venerable Brethren, to submit to these conditions, you should consider by that very fact that they are refusing to submit to your authority. Then you will have to examine whether they stay within the limits of pure politics or

economics, or persist in their former errors. In the former case, it is clear that you will have no more to do with them than with the general body of the faithful; in the latter case, you will have to take appropriate measures, with prudence but with firmness also. Priests will have to keep entirely out of the dissident groups, and they shall be content to extend the help of their sacred ministry to each member individually, applying to them in the tribunal of penitence the common rules of morals in respect to doctrine and conduct. As for the Catholic groups, while the priests and the seminarians may favor and help them, they shall abstain from joining them as members; for it is fitting that the priestly phalanx should remain above lay associations, even when these are most useful and inspired by the best spirit.

### A Prayer and a Wish

47. Such are the practical measures with which We have deemed necessary to confirm this letter on the Sillon and the Sillonists. From the depths of Our soul We pray that the Lord may cause these men and young people to understand the grave reasons which have prompted it. May He give them the docility of heart and the courage to show to the Church the sincerity of their Catholic fervor. As for you, Venerable Brethren, may the Lord inspire in your hearts toward them, since they will be yours henceforth, the sentiments of a true fatherly love.

### Apostolic Benediction

48. In expressing this hope, and to obtain these results which are so desirable, We grant to you, to your clergy and to your people, Our Apostolic Benediction with all Our heart.

49. Given at St. Peter's, Rome, on August 25, 1910, the eighth year of Our Pontificate.

Pius X, Pope

NOTES

1. The Revolution referred to in this and other paragraphs is the French Revolution of 1789, which dismantled existing social structures and was largely responsible for the dissemination of modern errors throughout the world. Other historical background: Following the Franco Prussian war in 1871, leftist elements gradually gained strength in France. By 1886, Freemasons had succeeded in controlling the French government. It was their avowed aim to eradicate the Catholic Faith. Textbooks, and even works of classical literature, were "doctored" to exclude all references to God. Church property was confiscated, and monks and nuns were forcibly driven out of their monasteries and convents, many of them seeking refuge in neighboring countries. By 1910 the Masonic French government had achieved its aim: the working class had been all but completely de-Christianized.

2. The French word *sillon* (pronounced *seé ohn*) literally means "furrow," the row which is plowed. It was adopted as the name of a movement. Rough equivalents would be "workshop" or "study group."

3. See in particular *Rerum Novarum* and *Graves De Communi Re*.

4. "To organize all things in Christ" or "To re-establish all things in Christ."

5. Literally: "They are dominated finally by a caste called directing, to whom its intellectual development guarantees an undue preponderance in the direction of affairs."

6. Literally: "The thing public"; Latin "*Res Publica*," from which the word "Republic" has been formed.

7. Literally: "Without leaving the people and becoming independent from them."

8. The Pope was quoting from a speech made by Marc Sangnier, a prominent leader, at Rouen in 1907.

9. This is the Encyclical *Rerum Novarum*.

10. Leo XIII also taught the real meaning of the term "Christian Democracy" in his Encylical *Graves de Communi Re*.

11. This passage comes from Marc Sangnier's speech at Rouen in 1907.

12. A "freethinker" is one who accepts no authority outside himself in the matter of religious belief. The term is roughly synonymous with *skeptic, rationalist, unbeliever* or *deist*.

13. Marc Sangnier speaking in Paris, May 1910.

Issued by Pope St. Pius X

# THE OATH AGAINST MODERNISM

September 1, 1910

To be sworn to by all clergy, pastors, confessors,
preachers, religious superiors, and professors
in philosophical-theological seminaries.

I . . . firmly embrace and accept each and every definition that
has been set forth and declared by the unerring teaching authority
of the Church, especially those principal truths which are directly
opposed to the errors of this day. And first of all, I profess that
God, the origin and end of all things, can be known with certainty
by the natural light of reason from the created world (see *Rom.*
1:20), that is, from the visible works of creation, as a cause from
its effects, and that, therefore, His existence can also be demonstrated: Secondly, I accept and acknowledge the external proofs of
revelation, that is, divine acts and especially miracles and prophecies as the surest signs of the divine origin of the Christian religion and I hold that these same proofs are well adapted to the
understanding of all eras and all men, even of this time. Thirdly, I
believe with equally firm faith that the Church, the guardian and
teacher of the revealed word, was personally instituted by the real
and historical Christ, when he lived among us, and that the
Church was built upon Peter, the prince of the apostolic hierarchy,
and his successors for the duration of time. Fourthly, I sincerely
hold that the doctrine of faith was handed down to us from the
Apostles through the orthodox Fathers in exactly the same meaning and always in the same purport. Therefore, I entirely reject the
heretical misrepresentation that dogmas evolve and change from

one meaning to another different from the one which the Church held previously. I also condemn every error according to which, in place of the divine deposit which has been given to the spouse of Christ to be carefully guarded by her, there is put a philosophical figment or product of a human conscience that has gradually been developed by human effort and will continue to develop indefinitely. Fifthly, I hold with certainty and sincerely confess that faith is not a blind sentiment of religion welling up from the depths of the subconscious under the impulse of the heart and the motion of a will trained to morality; but faith is a genuine assent of the intellect to truth received by hearing from an external source. By this assent, because of the authority of the supremely truthful God, we believe to be true that which has been revealed and attested to by a personal God, our Creator and Lord.

Furthermore, with due reverence, I submit and adhere with my whole heart to the condemnations, declarations and all the prescripts contained in the Encyclical *Pascendi* and in the decree *Lamentabili*, especially those concerning what is known as the history of dogmas. I also reject the error of those who say that the faith held by the Church can contradict history, and that Catholic dogmas, in the sense in which they are now understood, are irreconcilable with a more realistic view of the origins of the Christian religion. I also condemn and reject the opinion of those who say that a well-educated Christian assumes a dual personality—that of a believer and at the same time of a historian; as if it were permissible for a historian to hold things that contradict the faith of the believer, or to establish premises which, provided there be no direct denial of dogmas, would lead to the conclusion that dogmas are either false or doubtful. Likewise, I reject that method of judging and interpreting Sacred Scripture which, departing from the tradition of the Church, the analogy of faith and the norms of the Apostolic See, embraces the misrepresentations of the rationalists and with no prudence or restraint adopts textual criticism as the one and supreme norm. Furthermore, I reject the opinion of those who hold that a professor lecturing or writing on a historico-theological subject should first put aside any preconceived opinion about the supernatural origin of Catholic Tradition or about the divine promise of help to preserve all revealed truth forever; and that they should then interpret the writings of each of the Fathers solely by scientific principles, excluding all sacred authority, and with the same liberty of judgment that is common in the investigation of all ordinary historical documents.

Finally, I declare that I am completely opposed to the error of the Modernists who hold that there is nothing divine in sacred Tradition; or what is far worse, say that there is, but in a pantheistic sense, with the result that there would remain nothing but this plain simple fact—one to be put on a par with the ordinary facts of history—the fact, namely, that a group of men by their own labor, skill and talent have continued through subsequent ages a school begun by Christ and His Apostles. I firmly hold, then, and shall hold to my dying breath the belief of the Fathers in the charism of truth, which certainly is, was and always will be in the succession of the episcopacy from the Apostles. The purpose of this is, then, not that dogma may be tailored according to what seems better and more suited to the culture of each age; rather, that the absolute and immutable truth preached by the Apostles from the beginning may never be believed to be different, may never be understood in any other way.

I promise that I shall keep all these articles faithfully, entirely and sincerely, and guard them inviolate, in no way deviating from them in teaching or in any way in word or in writing. Thus I promise, thus I swear, so help me God . . .

Pius X, Pope

Encyclical Letter of Pope Pius XI

# ON THE FEAST OF CHRIST THE KING
## *(Quas Primas)*

December 11, 1925

To Our Venerable Brethren the Patriarchs, Primates,
Archbishops, Bishops, and other Ordinaries in Peace and
Communion with the Apostolic See

Venerable Brethren, Greeting and the Apostolic Benediction

1. In the first Encyclical Letter which We addressed at the
beginning of Our Pontificate to the Bishops of the universal
Church, We referred to the chief causes of the difficulties under
which mankind was laboring. And We remember saying that these
manifold evils in the world were due to the fact that the majority
of men had thrust Jesus Christ and His holy law out of their lives;
that these had no place either in private affairs or in politics: and
We said further, that as long as individuals and states refused to
submit to the rule of Our Saviour, there would be no really hope-
ful prospect of a lasting peace among nations. Men must look for
the *peace of Christ in the Kingdom of Christ*; and that We
promised to do as far as lay in Our power. *In the Kingdom of
Christ*, that is, it seemed to Us that peace could not be more effectually restored nor fixed upon a firmer basis than through the
restoration of the Empire of Our Lord. We were led in the meantime to indulge the hope of a brighter future at the sight of a more
widespread and keener interest evinced in Christ and His Church,

the one Source of Salvation, a sign that men who had formerly spurned the rule of our Redeemer and had exiled themselves from His Kingdom were preparing, and even hastening, to return to the duty of obedience.

### Holy Year Has Glorified Christ the King

2. The many notable and memorable events which have occurred during this Holy Year have given great honor and glory to Our Lord and King, the Founder of the Church.

### Missionary Zeal in the Church

3. At the Missionary Exhibition men have been deeply impressed in seeing the increasing zeal of the Church for the spread of the Kingdom of her Spouse to the most far distant regions of the earth. They have seen how many countries have been won to the Catholic name through the unremitting labor and self-sacrifice of missionaries, and the vastness of the regions which have yet to be subjected to the sweet and saving yoke of our King. All those who in the course of the Holy Year have thronged to this city under the leadership of their Bishops or priests had but one aim—namely, to expiate their sins—and at the tombs of the Apostles and in Our presence to promise loyalty to the rule of Christ.

### Eternal Bliss in the Kingdom of Heaven

4. A still further light of glory was shed upon His Kingdom when, after due proof of their heroic virtue, We raised to the honors of the altar six confessors and virgins. It was a great joy, a great consolation, that filled Our heart when in the majestic basilica of St. Peter Our decree was acclaimed by an immense multitude with the hymn of thanksgiving, *Tu Rex gloriae Christe.* We saw men and nations cut off from God, stirring up strife and discord and hurrying along the road to ruin and death, while the Church of God carries on her work of providing food for the spir-

itual life of men, nurturing and fostering generation after generation of men and women dedicated to Christ, faithful and subject to Him in His earthly kingdom, called by Him to eternal bliss in the Kingdom of Heaven.

### Nicene Creed Affirms the Kingship of Christ

5. Moreover, since this Jubilee Year marks the sixteenth centenary of the Council of Nicaea, We commanded that event to be celebrated, and We have done so in the Vatican basilica. There is a special reason for this in that the Nicene Synod defined and proposed for Catholic belief the dogma of the Consubstantiality of the Only-begotten with the Father, and added to the Creed the words "of whose kingdom there shall be no end," thereby affirming the kingly dignity of Christ.

### Establishing a Feast of Christ's Kingship

6. Since this Holy Year therefore has provided more than one opportunity to enhance the glory of the Kingdom of Christ, We deem it in keeping with Our Apostolic office to accede to the desire of many of the Cardinals, Bishops and faithful, made known to Us both individually and collectively, by closing this Holy Year with the insertion into the Sacred Liturgy of a special feast of the Kingship of Our Lord Jesus Christ. This matter is so dear to Our heart, Venerable Brethren, that I would wish to address to you a few words concerning it. It will be for you later to explain in a manner suited to the understanding of the faithful what We are about to say concerning the Kingship of Christ, so that the annual feast which We shall decree may be attended with much fruit and produce beneficial results in the future.

### Reasons for Giving Christ the Title of King

7. It has long been a common custom to give to Christ the metaphorical title of "King," because of the high degree of perfection whereby He excels all creatures. So He is said to reign "in

the hearts of men," both by reason of the keenness of His intellect and the extent of His knowledge, and also because He is very truth, and it is from Him that truth must be obediently received by all mankind. He reigns, too, *in the wills of men*, for in Him the human will was perfectly and entirely obedient to the Holy Will of God, and further by His grace and inspiration He so subjects our free-will as to incite us to the most noble endeavors. He is *King of hearts*, too, by reason of His "charity which surpasseth all knowledge." (*Eph.* 3:19). And His mercy and kindness which draw all men to Him, for never has it been known, nor will it ever be, that man be loved so much and so universally as Jesus Christ. But if we ponder this matter more deeply, we cannot but see that the title and the power of King belongs to Christ as Man in the strict and proper sense too. For it is only as Man that He may be said to have received from the Father "power, and glory, and a kingdom" (*Dan.* 7:14), since the Word of God, as consubstantial with the Father, has all things in common with Him, and therefore has necessarily supreme and absolute dominion over all things created.

### Evidence from the Old Testament

8. Do we not read throughout the Scriptures that Christ is the King? He it is that shall come out of Jacob to rule (*Num.* 24:19), who has been set by the Father as king over Sion, His holy mount, and shall have the Gentiles for His inheritance, and the utmost parts of the earth for His possession. (*Ps.* 2). In the nuptial hymn, where the future King of Israel is hailed as a most rich and powerful monarch, we read: "Thy throne, O God, is for ever and ever: the sceptre of thy kingdom is a sceptre of uprightness." (*Ps.* 44:7). There are many similar passages, but there is one in which Christ is even more clearly indicated. Here it is foretold that His Kingdom will have no limits, and will be enriched with justice and peace: "In His days shall justice spring up, and abundance of peace . . . And He shall rule from sea to sea, and from the river unto the ends of the earth." (*Ps.* 71:7-8).

### *Prophets Refer to the Saviour as King*

9. The testimony of the Prophets is even more abundant. That of Isaias is well known: "For a child is born to us, and a son is given to us, and the government is upon his shoulder: and his name shall be called, Wonderful, Counsellor, God the Mighty, the Father of the world to come, the Prince of Peace. His empire shall be multiplied, and there shall be no end of peace: he shall sit upon the throne of David, and upon his kingdom; to establish it and strengthen it with judgment and with justice, from henceforth and for ever." (*Is.* 9:6-7). With Isaias the other Prophets are in agreement. So Jeremias foretells the "just seed" that shall rest from the house of David—the Son of David that shall reign as king, "and shall be wise: and shall execute judgment and justice in the earth." (*Jer.* 23:5). So, too, Daniel, who announces the Kingdom that the God of Heaven shall found, "that shall never be destroyed…. and shall stand for ever." (*Dan.* 2:44). And again he says: "I beheld therefore in the vision of the night, and lo, one like the son of man came with the clouds of heaven, and he came even to the Ancient of days: and they presented him before him. And he gave him power, and glory, and a kingdom: and all peoples, tribes, and tongues shall serve him: his power is an everlasting power that shall not be taken away: and his kingdom shall not be destroyed." (*Dan.* 7:13-14). The prophecy of Zachary concerning the merciful King "riding upon an ass, and upon a colt the foal of an ass" entering Jerusalem as "the just and saviour" (*Zach.* 9:9), amid the acclamations of the multitude, was recognized as fulfilled by the holy Evangelists themselves.

### *Announcement by the Archangel Gabriel*

10. This same doctrine of the Kingship of Christ which we have found in the Old Testament is even more clearly taught and confirmed in the New Testament. The Archangel, announcing to the Virgin that she should bear a Son, says that "the Lord God shall give unto him the throne of David his father; and he shall reign in the house of Jacob for ever. And of his kingdom there

shall be no end." (*Luke* 1:32-33).

### Christ Speaks of His Own Kingly Authority

11. Moreover, Christ Himself speaks of His own kingly
authority: in His last discourse, speaking of the rewards and punishments that will be the eternal lot of the just and the damned; in
His reply to the Roman magistrate, who asked Him publicly
whether He were a king or not; after His Resurrection, when giving to His Apostles the mission of teaching and baptizing all
nations, He took the opportunity to call Himself King (*Matt.*
25:31-40), confirming the title publicly (*John* 18:37), and
solemnly proclaimed that all power was given Him in Heaven and
on earth. (*Matt.* 28:18). These words can only be taken to indicate
the greatness of His power, the infinite extent of His Kingdom.
What wonder, then, that He whom St. John calls the "prince of the
kings of the earth" (*Apoc.* 1:5) appears in the Apostle's vision of
the future as He who "hath on his garment, and on his thigh written: KING OF KINGS AND LORD OF LORDS!" (*Apoc.*
19:16). It is Christ whom the Father "hath appointed heir of all
things" (*Heb.* 1:2); "for he must reign, *until he hath put all his
enemies under his feet.*" (Cf. *1 Cor.* 15:25).

### The Church Continues to Call Christ King

12. It was surely right, then, in view of the common teaching
of the sacred books, that the Catholic Church, which is the Kingdom of Christ on earth, destined to be spread among all men and
all nations, should with every token of veneration salute her
Author and Founder in her annual liturgy as King and Lord, and
as King of kings. And, in fact, she used these titles, giving expression with wonderful variety of language to one and the same concept, both in ancient psalmody and in the Sacramentaries. She
uses them daily now in the prayers publicly offered to God, and in
offering the Immaculate Victim. The perfect harmony of the Eastern liturgies with our own in this continual praise of Christ the
King shows once more the truth of the axiom: *Legem credendi lex*

*statuit supplicandi*—The rule of faith is indicated by the law of our worship.

### Christ Has Dominion over All Creatures

13. The foundation of this power and dignity of Our Lord is rightly indicated by Cyril of Alexandria. "Christ," he says, "has dominion over all creatures, a dominion not seized by violence nor usurped, but His by essence and by nature."[1] His kingship is founded upon the ineffable Hypostatic Union. From this it follows not only that Christ is to be adored by Angels and men, but that to Him as Man, Angels and men are subject and must recognize His empire; by reason of the Hypostatic Union Christ has power over all creatures. But a thought that must give us even greater joy and consolation is this, that Christ is our King by acquired, as well as by natural right, for He is our Redeemer. Would that they who forget what they have cost their Saviour might recall the words: "You were not redeemed with corruptible things. . . . But with the precious blood of Christ, as of a lamb unspotted and undefiled." (*1 Peter* 1:18-19). We are no longer our own property, for Christ has purchased us "with a great price" (*1 Cor.* 6:20); our very bodies are the "members of Christ." (*1 Cor.* 6:15).

### Christ Is a Law-Giver

14. Let Us explain briefly the nature and meaning of this Lordship of Christ. It consists, We need scarcely say, in a threefold power which is essential to lordship. This is sufficiently clear from the scriptural testimony already adduced concerning the universal dominion of our Redeemer, and moreover it is a dogma of faith that Jesus Christ was given to man, not only as our Redeemer, but also as a law-giver, to whom obedience is due.[2] Not only do the Gospels tell us that He made laws, but they present Him to us in the act of making them. Those who keep them show their love for their Divine Master, and He promises that they shall remain in His love. (*John* 14:15, 15:10). He claimed judicial power as received from His Father when the Jews accused Him of

breaking the Sabbath by the miraculous cure of a sick man. "For neither doth the Father judge any man, but hath given all judgment to the Son." (*John* 5:22). In this power is included the right of rewarding and punishing all men living, for this right is inseparable from that of judging. Executive power, too, belongs to Christ, for all must obey His commands; none may escape them, nor the sanctions He has imposed.

### His Kingdom Is Concerned with Spiritual Things

15. This Kingdom is spiritual and is concerned with spiritual things. That this is so the above quotations from Scripture amply prove, and Christ by His own action confirms it. On many occasions, when the Jews and even the Apostles wrongly supposed that the Messias would restore the liberties and the kingdom of Israel, He repelled and denied such a suggestion. When the populace thronged around Him in admiration and would have acclaimed Him king, He shrank from the honor and sought safety in flight. Before the Roman magistrate He declared that His Kingdom was *not of this world*. The Gospels present this Kingdom as one which men prepare to enter by penance, and cannot actually enter except by faith and by Baptism, which, though an external rite, signifies and produces an interior regeneration. This Kingdom is opposed to none other than to that of Satan and to the power of darkness. It demands of its subjects a spirit of detachment from riches and earthly things, and a spirit of gentleness. They must hunger and thirst after justice, and more than this, they must deny themselves and carry the Cross.

### Christ Is Victim for Our Sins

16. Christ as our Redeemer purchased the Church at the price of His own Blood; as priest He offered Himself, and continues to offer Himself as a victim for our sins. Is it not evident, then, that His kingly dignity partakes in a manner of both these offices?

### Church Authority Is Christ's Authority

17. It would be a grave error, on the other hand, to say that Christ has no authority whatever in civil affairs, since, by virtue of the absolute empire over all creatures committed to Him by the Father, all things are in His power. Nevertheless, during His life on earth He refrained from the exercise of such authority, and although He Himself disdained to possess or to care for earthly goods, He did not, nor does He today, interfere with those who possess them. *Non eripit mortalia qui regna dat caelestia.*[3]

### Public Duty of Obedience to Christ

18. Thus the Empire of our Redeemer embraces all men. To use the words of Our immortal Predecessor, Pope Leo XIII: "His Empire includes not only Catholic nations, not only baptized persons who, though of right belonging to the Church, have been led astray by error, or have been cut off from her by schism, but also all those who are outside the Christian faith; so that truly the whole of mankind is subject to the power of Jesus Christ."[4] Nor is there any difference in this matter between the individual and the family or the State; for all men, whether collectively or individually, are under the dominion of Christ. In Him is the salvation of the individual, in Him is the salvation of society. "Neither is there salvation in any other. For there is no other name under heaven given to men, whereby we must be saved." (*Acts* 4:12). He is the author of happiness and true prosperity for every man and for every nation. "For a nation is happy when its citizens are happy. What else is a nation but a number of men living in concord?"[5] If, therefore, the rulers of nations wish to preserve their authority, to promote and increase the prosperity of their countries, they will not neglect the public duty of reverence and obedience to the rule of Christ. What We said at the beginning of Our Pontificate concerning the decline of public authority, and the lack of respect for the same, is equally true at the present day. "With God and Jesus Christ," We said, "excluded from political life, with authority derived not from God but from man, the very basis of that author-

ity has been taken away, because the chief reason of the distinction between ruler and subject has been eliminated. The result is that human society is tottering to its fall, because it has no longer a secure and solid foundation."[6]

## Christ the King of Public and Private Life

19. When once men recognize, both in private and in public life, that Christ is King, society will at last receive the great blessings of real liberty, well-ordered discipline, peace and harmony. Our Lord's regal office invests the human authority of princes and rulers with a religious significance; it ennobles the citizen's duty of obedience. It is for this reason that St. Paul, while bidding wives revere Christ in their husbands, and slaves respect Christ in their masters, warns them to give obedience to them not as men, but as the vicegerents of Christ; for it is not meet that men redeemed by Christ should serve their fellow-men. "You are bought with a price; be not made the bondslaves of men." (*1 Cor.* 7:23). If princes and magistrates duly elected are filled with the persuasion that they rule, not by their own right, but by the mandate and in the place of the Divine King, they will exercise their authority piously and wisely, and they will make laws and administer them, having in view the common good and also the human dignity of their subjects. The result will be a stable peace and tranquility, for there will be no longer any cause of discontent. Men will see in their king or in their rulers men like themselves, perhaps unworthy or open to criticism, but they will not on that account refuse obedience if they see reflected in them the authority of Christ, God and Man. Peace and harmony, too, will result; for with the spread and the universal extent of the Kingdom of Christ men will become more and more conscious of the link that binds them together, and thus many conflicts will be either prevented entirely or at least their bitterness will be diminished.

## Reign of Christ Would Bring True Peace

20. If the Kingdom of Christ, then, receives, as it should, all

nations under its way, there seems no reason why we should despair of seeing that peace which the King of Peace came to bring on earth—He who came *to reconcile all things, who came not to be ministered unto but to minister*, who, though *Lord of all*, gave Himself to us as a model of humility, and with His principal law united the precept of charity; who said also: "My yoke is sweet and my burden light." Oh, what happiness would be Ours if all men, individuals, families and nations, would but let themselves be governed by Christ! "Then at length," to use the words addressed by Our Predecessor, Pope Leo XIII, twenty-five years ago to the bishops of the Universal Church, "then at length will many evils be cured; then will the law regain its former authority; peace with all its blessings be restored. Men will sheathe their swords and lay down their arms when all freely acknowledge and obey the authority of Christ, and every tongue confesses that the Lord Jesus Christ is in the glory of God the Father."[7]

### Church Feasts Affect Both Mind and Heart

21. That these blessings may be abundant and lasting in Christian society, it is necessary that the Kingship of Our Saviour should be as widely as possible recognized and understood, and to the end nothing would serve better than the institution of a special feast in honor of the Kingship of Christ. For people are instructed in the truths of faith, and brought to appreciate the inner joys of religion far more effectually by the annual celebration of our sacred mysteries than by any official pronouncement of the teaching of the Church. Such pronouncements usually reach only a few and the more learned among the faithful; feasts reach them all; the former speak but once, the latter speak every year—in fact, forever. The Church's teaching affects the mind primarily; her feasts affect both mind and heart, and have a salutary effect upon the whole of man's nature. Man is composed of body and soul, and he needs these external festivities so that the sacred rites, in all their beauty and variety, may stimulate him to drink more deeply of the fountain of God's teaching, that he may make it a part of himself, and use it with profit for his spiritual life.

### Feasts Encourage Widespread Devotion

22. History, in fact, tells us that in the course of ages these festivals have been instituted one after another according as the needs or the advantage of the people of Christ seemed to demand: as when they needed strength to face a common danger, when they were attacked by insidious heresies, when they needed to be urged to the pious consideration of some mystery of faith or of some divine blessing. Thus in the earliest days of the Christian era, when the people of Christ were suffering cruel persecution, the cult of the martyrs was begun in order, says St. Augustine, "that the feasts of the martyrs might incite men to martyrdom."[8] The liturgical honors paid to confessors, virgins and widows produced wonderful results in an increased zest for virtue, necessary even in times of peace. But more fruitful still were the feasts instituted in honor of the Blessed Virgin. As a result of these men grew not only in their devotion to the Mother of God as an ever-present advocate, but also in their love of her as a mother bequeathed to them by their Redeemer. Not least among the blessings which have resulted from the public and legitimate honor paid to the Blessed Virgin and the Saints is the perfect and perpetual immunity of the Church from error and heresy. We may well admire in this the admirable wisdom of the Providence of God, who, ever bringing good out of evil, has from time to time suffered the faith and piety of men to grow weak, and allowed Catholic truth to be attacked by false doctrines, but always with the result that truth has afterward shone out with greater splendor, and that men's faith, aroused from its lethargy, has shown itself more vigorous than before.

### New Feasts Minister to the Needs of Souls

23. The festivals that have been introduced into the liturgy in more recent years have had a similar origin, and have been attended with similar results. When reverence and devotion to the Blessed Sacrament had grown cold, the feast of Corpus Christi was instituted, so that by means of solemn processions and prayer of eight days' duration, men might be brought once more to ren-

der public homage to Christ. So, too, the feast of the Sacred Heart of Jesus was instituted at a time when men were oppressed by the sad and gloomy severity of Jansenism, which had made their hearts grow cold, and shut them out from the love of God and the hope of salvation.

### The Plague of Anti-clericalism

24. If We ordain that the whole Catholic world shall revere Christ as King, We shall minister to the need of the present day, and at the same time provide an excellent remedy for the plague which now infects society. We refer to the plague of anti-clericalism,[9] its errors and impious activities. This evil spirit, as you are well aware, Venerable Brethren, has not come into being in one day; it has long lurked beneath the surface. The Empire of Christ over all nations was rejected. The right which the Church has from Christ Himself, to teach mankind, to make laws, to govern peoples in all that pertains to their eternal salvation, that right was denied. Then gradually the religion of Christ came to be likened to false religions and to be placed ignominiously on the same level with them. It was then put under the power of the State and tolerated more or less at the whim of princes and rulers. Some men went even further, and wished to set up in the place of God's religion a natural religion consisting in some instinctive affection of the heart. There were even some nations who thought they could dispense with God, and that their religion should consist in impiety and the neglect of God. The rebellion of individuals and States against the authority of Christ has produced deplorable consequences. We lamented these in the Encyclical *Ubi Arcano*; We lament them today: the seeds of discord sown far and wide; those bitter enmities and rivalries between nations, which still hinder so much the cause of peace; that insatiable greed which is so often hidden under a pretense of public spirit and patriotism, and gives rise to so many private quarrels; a blind and immoderate selfishness, making men seek nothing but their own comfort and advantage, and measure everything by these; no peace in the home, because men have forgotten or neglect their duty; the unity and

stability of the family undermined; society in a word, shaken to its foundations and on the way to ruin. We firmly hope, however, that the feast of the Kingship of Christ, which in future will be yearly observed, may hasten the return of society to our loving Saviour. It would be the duty of Catholics to do all they can to bring about this happy result. Many of these, however, have neither the station in society nor the authority which should belong to those who bear the torch of truth. This state of things may perhaps be attributed to a certain slowness and timidity in good people, who are reluctant to engage in conflict or oppose but a weak resistance; thus the enemies of the Church become bolder in their attacks. But if the faithful were generally to understand that it behooves them ever to fight courageously under the banner of Christ their King, then, fired with apostolic zeal, they would strive to win over to their Lord those hearts that are bitter and estranged from Him, and would valiantly defend His rights.

## Nations Suppress All Mention of Christ's Name

25. Moreover, the annual and universal celebration of the feast of the Kingship of Christ will draw attention to the evils which anti-clericalism has brought upon society in drawing men away from Christ, and will also do much to remedy them. While nations insult the beloved Name of our Redeemer by suppressing all mention of it in their conferences and parliaments, we must all the more loudly proclaim His kingly dignity and power, all the more universally affirm His rights.

## Christ's Kingship Recognized in Pious Customs

26. The way has been happily and providentially prepared for the celebration of this feast ever since the end of the last century. It is well known that this cult has been the subject of learned disquisitions in many books published in every part of the world, written in many different languages. The Kingship and Empire of Christ have been recognized in the pious custom, practiced by many families, of dedicating themselves to the Sacred Heart of

Jesus; not only families have performed this act of dedication, but nations, too, and kingdoms. In fact, the whole of the human race was at the instance of Pope Leo XIII, in the Holy Year 1900, consecrated to the Divine Heart. It should be remarked also that much has been done for the recognition of Christ's authority over society by the frequent Eucharistic Congresses which are held in our age. These give an opportunity to the people of each diocese, district or nation, and to the whole world of coming together to venerate and adore Christ the King hidden under the Sacramental species. Thus by sermons preached at meetings and in churches, by public adoration of the Blessed Sacrament exposed and by solemn processions, men unite in paying homage to Christ, whom God has given them for their King. It is by a divine inspiration that the people of Christ bring forth Jesus from His silent hiding-place in the church and carry Him in triumph through the streets of the city, so that He whom men refused to receive when He came unto His own, may now receive in full His kingly rights.

### Fruits of the Past Holy Year

27. For the fulfillment of the plan of which We have spoken, the Holy Year, which is now speeding to its close, offers the best possible opportunity. For during this year the God of mercy has raised the minds and hearts of the faithful to the consideration of heavenly blessings *which are above all understanding*, has either restored them once more to His grace, or inciting them anew to strive for higher gifts, has set their feet more firmly in the path of righteousness. Whether, therefore, We consider the many prayers that have been addressed to Us, or look to the events of the Jubilee Year, just past, We have every reason to think that the desired moment has at length arrived for enjoining that Christ be venerated by a special feast as King of all mankind. In this year, as We said at the beginning of this Letter, the Divine King, *truly wonderful in all His works, has been gloriously magnified*, for another company of His soldiers has been added to the list of Saints. In this year men have looked upon strange things and strange labors, from which they have understood and admired the victories won

by missionaries in the work of spreading His Kingdom. In this year, by solemnly celebrating the centenary of the Council of Nicaea, We have commemorated the definition of the divinity of the Word Incarnate, the foundation of Christ's Empire over all men.

### Feast of Christ the King Established

28. Therefore by Our Apostolic Authority We institute the Feast of the Kingship of Our Lord Jesus Christ to be observed yearly throughout the whole world on the last Sunday of the month of October—the Sunday, that is, which immediately precedes the Feast of All Saints. We further ordain that the dedication of mankind to the Sacred Heart of Jesus, which Our Predecessor of saintly memory, Pope Pius X, commanded to be renewed yearly, be made annually on that day. This year, however, We desire that it be observed on the thirty-first day of the month, on which day We Ourselves shall celebrate pontifically in honor of the Kingship of Christ, and shall command that the same dedication be performed in Our presence. It seems to Us that We cannot in a more fitting manner close this Holy Year, nor better signify Our gratitude and that of the whole of the Catholic world to Christ the immortal King of Ages, for the blessings showered upon Us, upon the Church and upon the Catholic world during this holy period.

### Crowning Glory upon the Mysteries of Christ's Life

29. It is not necessary, Venerable Brethren, that We should explain to you at any length why We have decreed that this feast of the Kingship of Christ should be observed in addition to those other feasts in which His kingly dignity is already signified and celebrated. It will suffice to remark that although in all the feasts of Our Lord the material object of worship is Christ, nevertheless their formal object is something quite distinct from His royal title and dignity. We have commanded its observance on a Sunday in order that not only the clergy may perform their duty by saying

Mass and reciting the Office, but that the laity too, free from their daily tasks, may in a spirit of holy joy give ample testimony of their obedience and subjection to Christ. The last Sunday of October seemed the most convenient of all for this purpose, because it is at the end of the liturgical year, and thus the feast of the Kingship of Christ sets the crowning glory upon the mysteries of the life of Christ already commemorated during the year, and, before celebrating the triumph of all the Saints, we proclaim and extol the glory of Him who triumphs in all the Saints and in all the Elect. Make it your duty and your task, Venerable Brethren, to see that sermons are preached to the people in every parish to teach them the meaning and the importance of this feast, that they may so order their lives as to be worthy of faithful and obedient subjects of the Divine King.

### Blessings We Desire

30. We would now, Venerable Brethren, in closing this Letter, briefly enumerate the blessings which We hope and pray may accrue to the Church, to society and to each one of the faithful as a result of the public veneration of the Kingship of Christ.

### Reminding Men of the Rights of the Church

31. When we pay honor to the princely dignity of Christ, men will doubtless be reminded that the Church, founded by Christ as a perfect society, has a natural and inalienable right to perfect freedom and immunity from the power of the State; and that in fulfilling the task committed to her by God of teaching, ruling and guiding to eternal bliss those who belong to the Kingdom of Christ, she cannot be subject to any external power. The State is bound to extend similar freedom to the orders and communities of religious of either sex, who give most valuable help to the Bishops of the Church by laboring for the extension and the establishment of the Kingdom of Christ. By their sacred vows they fight against the threefold concupiscence of the world; by making profession of a more perfect life they render the holiness which her

divine Founder willed should be a mark and characteristic of His Church more striking and more conspicuous in the eyes of all.

### Rulers Bound to Give Public Honor and Obedience to Christ

32. Nations will be reminded by the annual celebration of this feast that not only private individuals but also rulers and princes are bound to give public honor and obedience to Christ. It will call to their minds the thought of the Last Judgment, wherein Christ, who has been cast out of public life, despised, neglected and ignored, will most severely avenge these insults; for His kingly dignity demands that the State should take account of the Commandments of God and of Christian principles, both in making laws and in administering justice, and also in providing for the young a sound moral education.

### None of Our Faculties Exempt from His Empire

33. The faithful, moreover, by meditating upon these truths, will gain much strength and courage, enabling them to form their lives after the true Christian ideal. If to Christ Our Lord is given all power in Heaven and on earth; if all men, purchased by His Precious Blood, are by a new right subjected to His dominion; if this power embraces all men, it must be clear that not one of our faculties is exempt from His Empire. He must reign in our minds, which should assent with perfect submission and firm belief to revealed truths and to the doctrines of Christ. He must reign in our wills, which should obey the laws and precepts of God. He must reign in our hearts, which should spurn natural desires and love God above all things, and cleave to Him alone. He must reign in our bodies and in our members, which should serve as instruments for the interior sanctification of our souls, or to use the words of the Apostle Paul, "as instruments of justice unto God." (*Rom.* 6:13). If all these truths are presented to the faithful for their consideration, they will prove a powerful incentive to perfection. It is Our fervent desire, Venerable Brethren, that those who are without the fold may seek after and accept the sweet yoke

of Christ, and that we, who by the mercy of God are of the household of the Faith, may bear that yoke, not as a burden but with joy, with love, with devotion; that having lived our lives in accordance with the laws of God's Kingdom, we may receive full measure of good fruit, and counted by Christ good and faithful servants, we may be rendered partakers of eternal bliss and glory with Him in His heavenly Kingdom.

### The Apostolic Benediction

34. Let this letter, Venerable Brethren, be a token to you of Our fatherly love as the Feast of the Nativity of Our Lord Jesus Christ draws near; and receive the Apostolic Benediction as a pledge of divine blessings, which with loving heart, We impart to you, Venerable Brethren, to your clergy and to your people.

Given at St. Peter's, Rome, on the eleventh day of the month of December, in the Holy Year 1925, the fourth of Our Pontificate.

Pius XI, Pope

## NOTES

1. In huc. x.
2. *Conc. Trid.*, Sess. Vl, can. 21.
3. Hymn for the Epiphany.
4. Encyclical *Annum Sacrum*, May 25, 1899.
5. S. Aug., Ep. *ad Macedonium*, c. iii.
6. Encyclical *Ubi Arcano.*
7. Encyclical *Annum Sanctum*, May 25, 1899.
8. Sermo 47 *de Sanctis.*
9. Anti-clericalism: Opposition to Catholicism directed particularly against the clergy, using the civil law to suppress or secularize Catholic schools, hospitals, convents, etc. Anti-clericalism was epidemic in 19th and early 20th-century France, Italy, Spain and Portugal, being characteristic of Freemasonry. (Cf. Attwater, *A Catholic Dictionary*, 1961 ed.; TAN, 1997), p. 24.

# On Fostering True Religious Unity
## *(Mortalium Animos)*

January 6, 1928

Venerable Brethren,
Greetings and Apostolic Benediction

1. Never perhaps in the past have the minds of men been so engrossed as they are today with the desire to strengthen and extend for the common good of mankind that tie of brotherhood—the result of our common origin and nature—which binds us all so closely together. The world does not yet fully enjoy the fruits of peace; on the contrary, dissensions old and new in various lands still issue in rebellions and conflict. Such disputes, affecting the tranquil prosperity of nations, can never be settled without the combined and active goodwill of those who are responsible for their government, and hence it is easy to understand—especially now that the unity of mankind is no longer called into question—the widespread desire that all nations, in view of this universal kinship, should daily find closer union with one another.

*Inter-Religious Meetings based on an Erroneous*
*View of Religion*

2. It is with a similar motive that efforts are being made by some, in connection with the New Law promulgated by Christ

Our Lord. Assured that there exist few men who are entirely devoid of the religious sense, they seem to ground on this belief a hope that all nations, while differing indeed in religious matters, may yet without great difficulty be brought to fraternal agreement on certain points of doctrine which will form a common basis of the spiritual life. With this object, congresses, meetings and addresses are arranged, attended by a large concourse of hearers, where all without distinction, unbelievers of every kind as well as Christians, even those who unhappily have rejected Christ and denied His divine nature or mission, are invited to join in the discussion. Now, such efforts can meet with no kind of approval among Catholics. They presuppose the erroneous view that all religions are more or less good and praiseworthy, inasmuch as all give expression, under various forms, to that innate sense which leads men to God and to the obedient acknowledgement of His rule. Those who hold such a view are not only in error; they distort the true idea of religion, and thus reject it, falling gradually into naturalism and atheism. To favor this opinion, therefore, and to encourage such undertakings is tantamount to abandoning the religion revealed by God.

### *Desire for Unity Cloaks a Most Grave Error*

3. Nevertheless, when there is a question of fostering unity among Christians, it is easy for many to be misled by the apparent excellence of the object to be achieved. Is it not right, they ask, is it not the obvious duty of all who invoke the name of Christ to refrain from mutual reproaches and at last to be united in charity? Dare anyone say that he loves Christ and yet not strive with all his might to accomplish the desire of Him who asked His Father that His disciples might be "one"? (*John* 17:21). Did not Christ will that mutual charity should be the distinguishing characteristic of His disciples? "By this shall all men know that you are my disciples, if you have love one for another." (*John* 13:35). If only all Christians were "one," it is contended, then they might do so much more to drive out the plague of irreligion which, with its insidious and far-reaching advance, is threatening to sap the

strength of the Gospel. These and similar arguments, with ampli-
fications, are constantly on the lips of the "pan-Christians" who,
so far from being a few isolated individuals, have formed an entire
class and grouped themselves into societies of extensive member-
ship, usually under the direction of non-Catholics, who also disagree in matters of faith. The energy with which this scheme is
being promoted has won for it many adherents, and even many
Catholics are attracted by it, since it holds out the hope of a union
apparently consonant with the wishes of Holy Mother Church,
whose chief desire it is to recall her erring children and to bring
them back to her bosom. In reality, however, these fair and allur-
ing words cloak a most grave error, subversive of the foundations
of the Catholic Faith.

## A Plea to Bishops for Vigilance

4. Conscious, therefore, of Our Apostolic office, which warns
Us not to allow the flock of Christ to be led astray by harmful fallacies, We invoke your zeal, Venerable Brethren, to avert this evil.
We feel confident that each of you, by written and spoken word,
will explain clearly to the people the principles and arguments
that We are about to set forth, so that Catholics may know what
view and what course of action they should adopt regarding
schemes for the promiscuous union into one body of all who call
themselves Christians.

## Christ Founded Only One Church

5. God, the Creator of all things, made us that we might know
Him and serve Him; to our service, therefore, He has a full right.
He might indeed have been contented to prescribe for man's government the natural law alone, that is, the law which in creation
He has written upon man's heart, and might have regulated the
progress of that law by His ordinary Providence. He willed, however, to make positive laws which we should obey, and progres-
sively, from the beginnings of the human race until the coming
and preaching of Jesus Christ, He Himself taught mankind the

duties which a rational creature owes to his Creator. "God, who, at sundry times and in divers manners, spoke in times past to the fathers by the prophets, last of all, in these days hath spoken to us by his Son." (*Heb.* 1:1-2). Evidently, therefore, no religion can be true save that which rests upon the revelation of God, a revelation begun from the very first, continued under the Old Law and brought to completion by Jesus Christ Himself under the New. Now, if God has spoken—and it is historically certain that He has in fact spoken—then it is clearly man's duty implicitly to believe His revelation and to obey His commands. That we might rightly do both, for the glory of God and for our own salvation, the only-begotten Son of God founded His Church on earth. None, we think, of those who claim to be Christians will deny that a Church, and one sole Church, was founded by Christ.

### Christ's Church Is a Perfect Society

6. On the further question, however, as to what in the intention of its Founder was to be the precise nature of that Church, there is not the same agreement. Many of them, for example, deny that the Church of Christ was intended to be visible and manifest, at any rate in the sense that it was to be visibly the one body of the faithful, agreeing in one and the same doctrine under one teaching and governing authority. They conceive the visible Church as nothing more than a federation of the various Christian communities, even though these may hold different and mutually exclusive doctrines. The truth is that Christ founded His Church as a perfect society, of its nature external and perceptible to the senses, which in the future should carry on the work of the salvation of mankind under one head, with a living teaching authority, administering the Sacraments which are the sources of heavenly grace. (*John* 3:5, 6:48-59, 20:22-23 cf. *Matt.* 18:18, etc.). Wherefore He compared His Church to a kingdom (*Matt.* 8), to a house (cf. *Matt.* 16:18), to a sheepfold (*John* 10:16), and to a flock. (*John* 21:15-17). The Church thus wondrously instituted could not cease to exist with the death of its Founder and of the Apostles, the pioneers of its propagation; for its mission was to lead all men to salvation, with-

out distinction of time or place: "Going therefore, teach ye all nations." (*Matt.* 28:19). Nor could the Church ever lack the effective strength necessary for the continued accomplishment of its task, since Christ Himself is perpetually present with it, according to His promise: "Behold, I am with you all days, even to the consummation of the world." (*Matt.* 28:20). Hence not only must the Church still exist today and continue always to exist, but it must ever be exactly the same as it was in the days of the Apostles. Otherwise we must say—which God forbid—that Christ has failed in His purpose, or that He erred when He asserted of His Church that the gates of Hell would never prevail against it. (*Matt.* 16:18).

### A False Understanding of the Church Christ Founded

7. And here it will be opportune to expound and to reject a certain false opinion which lies at the root of this question and of that complex movement by which non-Catholics seek to bring about the union of Christian churches. Those who favor this view constantly quote the words of Christ, "That they all may be one . . . And there shall be one fold and one shepherd" (*John* 17:21, 10:16), in the sense that Christ thereby merely expressed a desire or a prayer which as yet has not been granted. For they hold that the unity of faith and government which is a note of the one true Church of Christ has up to the present time hardly ever existed, and does not exist today. They consider that this unity is indeed to be desired and may even, by cooperation and good will, be actually attained, but that meanwhile it must be regarded as a mere ideal. The Church, they say, is of its nature divided into sections, composed of several churches or distinct communities which still remain separate, and although holding in common some articles of doctrine, nevertheless differ concerning the remainder; that all these enjoy the same rights; and that the Church remained one and undivided at the most only from the Apostolic age until the first ecumenical councils. Hence, they say, controversies and long-standing differences which today still keep asunder the members of the Christian family must be entirely set aside, and from the residue of doctrines a common form of faith must be drawn up

and proposed for belief, in the profession of which all may not only know but also feel themselves to be brethren. If the various churches or communities were united in some kind of universal federation, they would then be in a position to oppose resolutely and successfully the progress of irreligion.

### *Non-Catholics Reject Papal Authority*

8. Such, Venerable Brethren, is the common contention. There are indeed some who recognize and affirm that Protestantism has with inconsiderate zeal rejected certain articles of faith and external ceremonies which are in fact useful and attractive, and which the Roman Church still retains. But they immediately go on to say that the Roman Church, too, has erred, and corrupted the primitive religion by adding to it and proposing for belief doctrines not only alien to the Gospel but contrary to its spirit. Chief among these they count that of the primacy of jurisdiction granted to Peter and to his successors in the See of Rome. There are actually some, though few, who grant to the Roman Pontiff a primacy of honor and even a certain power or jurisdiction; this, however, they consider to arise not from the divine law but merely from the consent of the faithful. Others, again, even go so far as to desire the Pontiff himself to preside over their mixed assemblies. For the rest, while you may hear many non-Catholics loudly preaching brotherly communion in Jesus Christ, yet not one will you find to whom it even occurs to obey the Vicar of Jesus Christ with devout submission in his capacity of teacher or ruler. Meanwhile, they assert their readiness to treat with the Church of Rome, but on equal terms, as equals with an equal. But even if they could so treat, there seems little doubt that they would do so only on condition that no pact into which they might enter should compel them to retract those opinions which still keep them outside the one fold of Christ.

### *The Catholic Church Still Teaches the Truth*

9. This being so, it is clear that the Apostolic See can by no

means take part in these assemblies, nor is it in any way lawful for Catholics to give to such enterprises their encouragement or support. If they did so, they would be giving countenance to a false Christianity quite alien to the one Church of Christ. Shall we commit the iniquity of suffering the truth, the truth revealed by God, to be made a subject for compromise? For it is indeed a question of defending revealed truth. Jesus Christ sent His Apostles into the whole world to declare the faith of the Gospel to every nation, and, to save them from error, He willed that the Holy Ghost should first teach them all truth. Has this doctrine, then, disappeared, or at any time been obscured, in the Church of which God Himself is the ruler and guardian? Our Redeemer plainly said that His Gospel was intended not only for the Apostolic age but for all time. Can the object of faith, then, have become in the process of time so dim and uncertain that today we must tolerate contradictory opinions? If this were so, then we should have to admit that the coming of the Holy Ghost upon the Apostles, the perpetual indwelling of the same Spirit in the Church, nay, the very preaching of Jesus Christ, have centuries ago lost their efficacy and value. To affirm this would be blasphemy. The only-begotten Son of God not only bade His representatives to teach all nations; He also obliged all men to give credence to whatever was taught them by "witnesses preordained by God." (*Acts* 10:41). Moreover, He enforced His command with this sanction: "He that believeth and is baptized, shall be saved: but he that believeth not shall be condemned." (*Mark* 16:16). These two commands for salvation, the one to teach, the other to believe, must be obeyed. But they cannot even be understood unless the Church proposes an inviolate and clear teaching and in proposing it is immune from all danger of error. It is also false to say that, although the deposit of truth does indeed exist, yet it is to be found only with such laborious effort and after such lengthy study and discussion that a man's life is hardly long enough for its discovery and attainment. This would be equivalent to saying that the most merciful God spoke through the prophets and through His only-begotten Son merely in order that some few men, and those advanced in years, might learn what He had revealed, and not in order to inculcate a doctrine of faith and morals by which man should be guided throughout the whole of his life.

## St. John Forbade Interaction with Heretics

10. These pan-Christians who strive for the union of the churches would appear to pursue the noblest of ideals in promoting charity among all Christians. But how should charity tend to the detriment of faith? Everyone knows that John himself, the Apostle of love, who seems in his Gospel to have revealed the secrets of the Sacred Heart of Jesus and who never ceased to impress upon the memory of his disciples the new commandment "to love one another," nevertheless strictly forbade any intercourse with those who professed a mutilated and corrupt form of Christ's teaching: "If any man come to you, and bring not this doctrine, receive him not into the house, nor say to him, God speed you." (*2 John* 1:10).

## Belief in the True Faith Establishes Genuine Unity

11. Therefore, since the foundation of charity is faith pure and inviolate, it is chiefly by the bond of one faith that the disciples of Christ are to be united. A federation of Christians, then, is inconceivable in which each member retains his own opinions and private judgment in matters of faith, even though they differ from the opinions of all the rest. How can men with opposite convictions belong to one and the same federation of the faithful: those who accept sacred Tradition as a source of revelation and those who reject it; those who recognize as divinely constituted the hierarchy of bishops, priests and ministers in the Church, and those who regard it as gradually introduced to suit the conditions of the time; those who adore Christ really present in the Most Holy Eucharist through that wonderful conversion of the bread and wine, Transubstantiation, and those who assert that the body of Christ is there only by faith or by the signification and virtue of the Sacrament; those who in the Eucharist recognize both Sacrament and Sacrifice, and those who say that it is nothing more than the

memorial of the Lord's Supper; those who think it right and useful to pray to the Saints reigning with Christ, especially to Mary the Mother of God, and to venerate their images, and those who refuse such veneration as derogatory to the honor due Jesus Christ, "the one mediator of God and men." (Cf. *1 Tim.* 2:5).

### *A Variety of Opinions Leads to Religious Indifference*

12. How so great a variety of opinions can clear the way for the unity of the Church, We know not. That unity can arise only from one teaching authority, one law of belief and one faith of Christians. But we do know that from such a state of affairs it is but an easy step to the neglect of religion or "indifferentism," and to the error of the Modernists, who hold that dogmatic truth is not absolute but relative, that is, that it changes according to the varying necessities of time and place and the varying tendencies of the mind; that it is not contained in an immutable tradition, but can be altered to suit the needs of human life.

### *Unlawful Distinction among Articles of Faith*

13. Furthermore, it is never lawful to employ in connection with articles of faith the distinction invented by some between "fundamental" and "non-fundamental" articles, the former to be accepted by all, the latter being left to the free acceptance of the faithful. The supernatural virtue of faith has as its formal motive the authority of God revealing, and this allows of no such distinction. All true followers of Christ, therefore, will believe the dogma of the Immaculate Conception of the Mother of God with the same faith as they believe the mystery of the august Trinity, the infallibility of the Roman Pontiff in the sense defined by the Ecumenical Vatican Council with the same faith as they believe the Incarnation of Our Lord. That these truths have been solemnly sanctioned and defined by the Church at various times, some of them even quite recently, makes no difference to their certainty, nor to our obligation of believing them. Has not God revealed them all?

## *The Church Protects Divine Revelation*

14. The teaching authority of the Church, in the divine wisdom, was constituted on earth in order that the revealed doctrines might remain forever intact and might be brought with ease and security to the knowledge of men. This authority is indeed daily exercised through the Roman Pontiff and the Bishops who are in communion with him; but it has the further office of defining some truth with solemn decree whenever it is opportune, and whenever this is necessary either to oppose the errors or the attacks of heretics, or again to impress the minds of the faithful with a clearer and more detailed explanation of the articles of sacred doctrine. But in the use of this extraordinary teaching authority no fresh invention is introduced, nothing new is ever added to the number of those truths which are at least implicitly contained within the deposit of Revelation divinely committed to the Church; but truths which to some perhaps may still seem obscure are rendered clear, or a truth which some may have called into question is declared to be of faith.

## *Taking Part in Non-Catholic Assemblies Forbidden*

15. Thus, Venerable Brethren, it is clear why this Apostolic See has never allowed its subjects to take part in the assemblies of non-Catholics. There is but one way in which the unity of Christians may be fostered, and that is by furthering the return to the one true Church of Christ of those who are separated from it; for from that one true Church they have in the past fallen away. The one Church of Christ is visible to all, and will remain, according to the will of its Author, exactly the same as He instituted it. The mystical Spouse of Christ has never in the course of centuries been contaminated, nor in the future can she ever be, as Cyprian bears witness: "The Bride of Christ cannot become false to her Spouse; she is inviolate and pure. She knows but one dwelling, and chastely and modestly she guards the sanctity of the nuptial chamber."[1] The same holy martyr marvelled that anyone could believe that "this unity of the Church built upon a divine founda-

tion, knit together by heavenly Sacraments, could ever be rent asunder by the conflict of wills."² For since the Mystical Body of Christ, like His physical body, is one (*1 Cor.* 12:12), compacted and fitly joined together (*Eph.* 4:16), it were foolish to say that the Mystical Body is composed of disjointed and scattered members. Whosoever therefore is not united with the body is no member thereof, neither is he in communion with Christ its Head.

### *All Must Return to the Catholic Church*

16. Furthermore, in this one Church of Christ no man can be or remain who does not accept, recognize and obey the authority and supremacy of Peter and his legitimate successors. Did not the ancestors of those who are now entangled in the errors of Photius and of the Reformers³ obey the Bishop of Rome, the chief shepherd of souls? Their children, alas! have left the home of their fathers; but that house did not therefore fall to the ground and perish forever, for it was supported by God. Let them, then, return to their Father, who, forgetting the insults in the past heaped upon the Apostolic See, will accord them a most loving welcome. If, as they constantly say, they long to be united with Us and Ours, why do they not hasten to enter the Church, "the mother and mistress of all Christ's faithful."⁴ Let them heed the words of Lactantius: "The Catholic Church is alone in keeping the true worship. This is the fount of truth, this the house of faith, this the temple of God; if any man enter not here, or if any man go forth from it, he is a stranger to the hope of life and salvation. Let none delude himself with obstinate wrangling. For life and salvation are here concerned, and these will be lost forever unless their interests be carefully and assiduously kept in mind."⁵

### *May the Separated Children Return to Rome*

17. Let Our separated children, therefore, draw nigh to the Apostolic See, set up in the City which Peter and Paul, Princes of the Apostles, consecrated by their blood; to the See which is "the root and womb whence issues the Church of God";⁶ and let them

come, not with any intention or hope that "the church of the living God, the pillar and ground of the truth" (*1 Tim.* 3:15) will cast aside the integrity of the faith and tolerate their errors, but to submit themselves to its teaching and government. Would that the happy lot, denied to so many of Our Predecessors, might at last be Ours, to embrace with fatherly affection those children whose unhappy separation from Us We now deplore. Would that God our Saviour, "Who will have all men to be saved, and to come to the knowledge of the truth" (*1 Tim.* 2:4), might hear our humble prayer and vouchsafe to recall to the unity of the Church all that are gone astray. To this all-important end We implore, and We desire that others should implore, the intercession of the Blessed Virgin Mary, Mother of divine grace, Help of Christians, victorious over all heresies, that she may entreat for Us the speedy coming of that longed-for day, when all men shall hear the voice of her divine Son, and shall be "careful to keep the unity of the Spirit in the bond of peace." (*Eph.* 4:3).

### *Hope That All May Enter the One True Church of Christ*

18. You, Venerable Brethren, know how dear to Our heart is this desire, and We wish that Our children also should know, not only those belonging to the Catholic fold, but also those separated from Us. If these will humbly beg light from Heaven, there is no doubt but that they will recognize the one true Church of Jesus Christ, and entering therein, will at last be united with Us in perfect charity. In the hope of this fulfillment, and as a pledge of Our fatherly goodwill, We impart most lovingly to you, Venerable Brethren, and to your clergy and people, the Apostolic Benediction.

Given at St. Peter's, Rome, on the 6th day of January, the Feast of the Epiphany of Our Lord Jesus Christ in the year 1928, the sixth of Our Pontificate.

Pius XI, Pope

## NOTES

1. *De Cath. Ecclesiae unitate*, 6.
2. *Ibid.*
3. That is, the Orthodox and Protestants.
4. *Conc. Lateran*, iv. c. 5.
5. *Divin. Inst.* lv. 30, 11-12.
6. Cypr., *Ep.* 48 *ad Cornelium*, 3.

# ON ATHEISTIC COMMUNISM
## (*Divini Redemptoris*)

March 19, 1937

To the Patriarchs, Primates, Archbishops, Bishops, and other
Ordinaries in Peace and Communion with the Apostolic See

Venerable Brothers,
Health and Apostolic Benediction

1. The promise of a Redeemer brightens the first page of the
history of mankind, and the confident hope aroused by this
promise softened the keen regret for a paradise which had been
lost. It was this hope that accompanied the human race on its
weary journey, until in the fullness of time the expected Saviour
came to begin a new universal civilization, the Christian civilization, far superior even to that which up to this time had been labo-
riously achieved by certain more privileged nations.

*Violent Revolutions Threaten Christianity*

2. Nevertheless, the struggle between good and evil remained
in the world as a sad legacy of the original fall. Nor has the
ancient tempter ever ceased to deceive mankind with false
promises. It is on this account that one convulsion following upon
another has marked the passage of the centuries, down to the revolution of our own days. This modern revolution, it may be said,
has actually broken out or threatens everywhere, and it exceeds in

amplitude and violence anything yet experienced in the preceding persecutions launched against the Church. Entire peoples find themselves in danger of falling back into a barbarism worse than that which oppressed the greater part of the world at the coming of the Redeemer.

### Atheistic Communism an Imminent Danger

3. This all too imminent danger, Venerable Brethren, as you have already surmised, is bolshevistic and atheistic Communism, which aims at upsetting the social order and at undermining the very foundations of Christian civilization.

### The Church Has Condemned Communism Many Times

4. In the face of such a threat, the Catholic Church could not and does not remain silent. This Apostolic See, above all, has not refrained from raising its voice, for it knows that its proper and special mission is to defend truth, justice and all those eternal values which Communism ignores or attacks. Ever since the days when groups of "intellectuals" were formed in an arrogant attempt to free civilization from the bonds of morality and religion, Our Predecessors overtly and explicitly drew the attention of the world to the consequences of the dechristianization of human society. With reference to Communism, Our Venerable Predecessor, Pius IX, of holy memory, as early as 1846 pronounced a solemn condemnation, which he confirmed in the words of the Syllabus directed against "that infamous doctrine of so-called Communism which is absolutely contrary to the natural law itself, and if once adopted would utterly destroy the rights, property and possessions of all men, and even society itself."[1] Later on, another of Our predecessors, the immortal Leo XIII, in his Encyclical *Quod Apostolici Muneris*, defined Communism as "the fatal plague which insinuates itself into the very marrow of human society only to bring about its ruin."[2] With clear intuition he pointed out that the atheistic movements existing among the masses of the Machine Age had their origin in that school of phi-

losophy which for centuries had sought to divorce science from the life of the Faith and of the Church.

## The Papacy Has Been a Strong Voice

5. During Our Pontificate We too have frequently and with urgent insistence denounced the current trend to atheism which is alarmingly on the increase. In 1924 when Our relief mission returned from the Soviet Union, We condemned Communism in a special Allocution[3] which We addressed to the whole world. In Our Encyclicals *Miserentissimus Redemptor*,[4] *Quadragesimo Anno*,[5] *Caritate Christi*,[6] *Acerba Animi*[7] and *Dilectissima Nobis*,[8] We raised a solemn protest against the persecutions unleashed in Russia, in Mexico and now in Spain. Our two Allocutions of last year, the first on the occasion of the opening of the International Catholic Press Exposition and the second during Our audience to the Spanish refugees, along with Our message of last Christmas, have evoked a worldwide echo which is not yet spent. In fact, the most persistent enemies of the Church, who from Moscow are directing the struggle against Christian civilization, themselves bear witness, by their unceasing attacks in word and act, that even to this hour the Papacy has continued faithfully to protect the sanctuary of the Christian religion, and that it has called public attention to the perils of Communism more frequently and more effectively than any other public authority on earth.

## This Is a Most Solemn Condemnation

6. To Our great satisfaction, Venerable Brethren, you have, by means of individual and even joint Pastoral Letters, accurately transmitted and explained to the Faithful these admonitions. Yet despite Our frequent and paternal warnings, the peril only grows greater from day to day because of the pressure exerted by clever agitators. Therefore We believe it to be Our duty to raise Our voice once more, in a still more solemn missive, in accord with the tradition of this Apostolic See, the Teacher of Truth, and in accord with the desire of the whole Catholic world, which makes

the appearance of such a document but natural. We trust that the echo of Our voice will reach every mind free from prejudice and every heart sincerely desirous of the good of mankind. We wish this the more because Our words are now receiving sorry confirmation from the spectacle of the bitter fruits of subversive ideas, which We foresaw and foretold, and which are in fact multiplying fearfully in the countries already stricken, or threatening every other country of the world.

### False Principles Will Be Examined

7. Hence We wish to expose once more in a brief synthesis the principles of atheistic Communism as they are manifested chiefly in Bolshevism. We wish also to indicate its method of action and to contrast with its false principles the clear doctrine of the Church, in order to inculcate anew and with greater insistence the means by which Christian civilization, the true *civitas humana*, can be saved from the satanic scourge, and not merely saved, but better developed for the well-being of human society.

### Communism Has an Appearance of Good

8. The Communism of today, more emphatically than similar movements in the past, conceals in itself a false messianic idea. A pseudo-ideal of justice, of equality and fraternity in labor impregnates all its doctrine and activity with a deceptive mysticism, which communicates a zealous and contagious enthusiasm to the multitudes entrapped by delusive promises. This is especially true in an age like ours, when unusual misery has resulted from the unequal distribution of the goods of this world. This pseudo-ideal is even boastfully advanced as if it were responsible for a certain economic progress. As a matter of fact, when such progress is at all real, its true causes are quite different, as for instance the intensification of industrialism in countries which were formerly almost without it, the exploitation of immense natural resources, and the use of the most brutal methods to insure the achievement of gigantic projects with a minimum of expense.

## *Materialism Is Its Foundation*

9. The doctrine of modern Communism, which is often concealed under the most seductive trappings, is in substance based on the principles of dialectical and historical materialism previously advocated by Marx, of which the theoricians of Bolshevism claim to possess the only genuine interpretation. According to this doctrine there is in the world only one reality, matter, the blind forces of which evolve into plant, animal and man. Even human society is nothing but a phenomenon and form of matter, evolving in the same way. By a law of inexorable necessity and through a perpetual conflict of forces, matter moves towards the final synthesis of a classless society. In such a doctrine, as is evident, there is no room for the idea of God; there is no difference between matter and spirit, between soul and body; there is neither survival of the soul after death nor any hope in a future life. Insisting on the dialectical aspect of their materialism, the Communists claim that the conflict which carries the world towards its final synthesis can be accelerated by man. Hence they endeavor to sharpen the antagonisms which arise between the various classes of society. Thus the class struggle with its consequent violent hate and destruction takes on the aspects of a crusade for the progress of humanity. On the other hand, all other forces whatever, as long as they resist such systematic violence, must be annihilated as hostile to the human race.

## *Individual Personality Is Destroyed*

10. Communism, moreover, strips man of his liberty, robs human personality of all its dignity and removes all the moral restraints that check the eruptions of blind impulse. There is no recognition of any right of the individual in his relations to the collectivity; no natural right is accorded to human personality, which is a mere cog-wheel in the Communist system. In man's relations with other individuals, besides, Communists hold the principle of absolute equality, rejecting all hierarchy and divinely constituted authority, including the authority of parents. What

men call authority and subordination is derived from the community as its first and only font. Nor is the individual granted any property rights over material goods or the means of production, for inasmuch as these are the source of further wealth, their possession would give one man power over another. Precisely on this score, all forms of private property must be eradicated, for they are at the origin of all economic enslavement.

### Marriage and Family Life Are Attacked

11. Refusing to human life any sacred or spiritual character, such a doctrine logically makes of marriage and the family a purely artificial and civil institution, the outcome of a specific economic system. There exists no matrimonial bond of a juridico-moral nature that is not subject to the whim of the individual or of the collectivity. Naturally, therefore, the notion of an indissoluble marriage tie is scoffed at. Communism is particularly characterized by the rejection of any link that binds woman to the family and the home, and her emancipation is proclaimed as a basic principle. She is withdrawn from the family and the care of her children, to be thrust instead into public life and collective production under the same conditions as man. The care of home and children then devolves upon the collectivity. Finally, the right of education is denied to parents, for it is conceived as the exclusive prerogative of the community, in whose name and by whose mandate alone parents may exercise this right.

### A Godless Civilization Results

12. What would be the condition of a human society based on such materialistic tenets? It would be a collectivity with no other hierarchy than that of the economic system. It would have only one mission: the production of material things by means of collective labor, so that the goods of this world might be enjoyed in a paradise where each would "give according to his powers" and would "receive according to his needs." Communism recognizes in the collectivity the right, or rather, unlimited discretion, to draft

individuals for the labor of the collectivity with no regard for their personal welfare; so that even violence could be legitimately exercised to dragoon the recalcitrant against their wills. In the Communistic commonwealth, morality and law would be nothing but a derivation of the existing economic order, purely earthly in origin and unstable in character. In a word, the Communists claim to inaugurate a new era and a new civilization which is the result of blind evolutionary forces culminating in a "humanity without God."

### Communists Manipulate Existing Political Structures

13. When all men have finally acquired the collectivist mentality in this Utopia of a really classless society, the political State, which is now conceived by Communists merely as the instrument by which the proletariat is oppressed by the capitalists, will have lost all reason for its existence and will "wither away." However, until that happy consummation is realized, the State and the powers of the State furnish Communism with the most efficacious and most extensive means for the achievement of its goal.

### Ideas Contrary to Reason and Divine Revelation

14. Such, Venerable Brethren, is the new gospel which bolshevistic and atheistic Communism offers the world as the glad tidings of deliverance and salvation! It is a system full of errors and sophisms. It is in opposition both to reason and to Divine Revelation. It subverts the social order, because it means the destruction of its foundations; because it ignores the true origin and purpose of the State; because it denies the rights, dignity and liberty of human personality.

### Operates on Half-truths and Deceptions

15. How is it possible that such a system, long since rejected scientifically and now proved erroneous by experience, how is it, We ask, that such a system could spread so rapidly in all parts of

the world? The explanation lies in the fact that too few have been able to grasp the nature of Communism. The majority instead succumb to its deception, skillfully concealed by the most extravagant promises. By pretending to desire only the betterment of the condition of the working classes, by urging the removal of the very real abuses chargeable to the liberalistic economic order, and by demanding a more equitable distribution of this world's goods (objectives entirely and undoubtedly legitimate), the Communist takes advantage of the present worldwide economic crisis to draw into the sphere of his influence even those sections of the populace which on principle reject all forms of materialism and terrorism. And as every error contains its element of truth, the partial truths to which We have referred are astutely presented according to the needs of time and place, to conceal, when convenient, the repulsive crudity and inhumanity of Communistic principles and tactics. Thus the Communist ideal wins over many of the better-minded members of the community. These in turn become the apostles of the movement among the younger intelligentsia who are still too immature to recognize the intrinsic errors of the system. The preachers of Communism are also proficient in exploiting racial antagonisms and political divisions and oppositions. They take advantage of the lack of orientation characteristic of modern agnostic science in order to burrow into the universities, where they bolster up the principles of their doctrine with pseudo-scientific arguments.

## Errors Spread Quickly in a De-Christianized World

16. If we would explain the blind acceptance of Communism by so many thousands of workmen, we must remember that the way had been already prepared for it by the religious and moral destitution in which wage-earners had been left by liberal economics. Even on Sundays and holy days, labor shifts were given no time to attend to their essential religious duties. No one thought of building churches within convenient distance of factories, nor of facilitating the work of the priest. On the contrary, laicism[9] was actively and persistently promoted, with the result

that we are now reaping the fruits of the errors so often denounced by Our Predecessors and by Ourselves. It can surprise no one that the Communistic fallacy should be spreading in a world already to a large extent de-Christianized.

## *Propaganda Is Well-Organized*

17. There is another explanation for the rapid diffusion of the Communistic ideas now seeping into every nation, great and small, advanced and backward, so that no corner of the earth is free from them. This explanation is to be found in a propaganda so truly diabolical that the world has perhaps never witnessed its like before. It is directed from one common center. It is shrewdly adapted to the varying conditions of diverse peoples. It has at its disposal great financial resources, gigantic organizations, international congresses and countless trained workers. It makes use of pamphlets and reviews, of cinema, theatre and radio, of schools and even universities. Little by little it penetrates into all classes of the people and even reaches the better-minded groups of the community, with the result that few are aware of the poison which increasingly pervades their minds and hearts.

## *Conspiracy of Silence in the Worldwide Press*

18. A third powerful factor in the diffusion of Communism is the conspiracy of silence on the part of a large section of the non-Catholic press of the world. We say conspiracy, because it is impossible otherwise to explain how a press usually so eager to exploit even the little daily incidents of life has been able to remain silent for so long about the horrors perpetrated in Russia, in Mexico and even in a great part of Spain; and that it should have relatively so little to say concerning a world organization as vast as Russian Communism. This silence is due in part to short-sighted political policy, and is favored by various occult forces which for a long time have been working for the overthrow of the Christian social order.

### Many Catholics Martyred

19. Meanwhile, the sorry effects of this propaganda are before our eyes. Where Communism has been able to assert its power—and here We are thinking with special affection of the people of Russia and Mexico—it has striven by every possible means, as its champions openly boast, to destroy Christian civilization and the Christian religion by banishing every remembrance of them from the hearts of men, especially of the young. Bishops and priests were exiled, condemned to forced labor, shot and done to death in inhuman fashion; laymen suspected of defending their religion were vexed, persecuted, dragged off to trial and thrown into prison.

### All Evidence of Christianity Eradicated

20. Even where the scourge of Communism has not yet had time enough to exercise to the full its logical effect, as witness Our beloved Spain, it has, alas, found compensation in the fiercer violence of its attack. Not only this or that church or isolated monastery was sacked, but as far as possible every church and every monastery was destroyed. Every vestige of the Christian religion was eradicated, even though intimately linked with the rarest monuments of art and science! The fury of Communism has not confined itself to the indiscriminate slaughter of Bishops, of thousands of priests and religious of both sexes; it searches out above all those who have been devoting their lives to the welfare of the working classes and the poor. But the majority of its victims have been laymen of all conditions and classes. Even up to the present moment, masses of them are slain almost daily for no other offense than the fact that they are good Christians or at least opposed to atheistic Communism. And this fearful destruction has been carried out with a hatred and a savage barbarity one would not have believed possible in our age. No man of good sense, nor any statesman conscious of his responsibility can fail to shudder at the thought that what is happening today in Spain may perhaps be repeated tomorrow in other civilized countries.

## A System Lacking All Restraint

21. Nor can it be said that these atrocities are a transitory phenomenon, the usual accompaniment of all great revolutions, the isolated excesses common to every war. No, they are the natural fruit of a system which lacks all inner restraint. Some restraint is necessary for man considered either as an individual or in society. Even the barbaric peoples had this inner check in the natural law written by God in the heart of every man. And where this natural law was held in higher esteem, ancient nations rose to a grandeur that still fascinates—more than it should!—certain superficial students of human history. But tear the very idea of God from the hearts of men, and they are necessarily urged by their passions to the most atrocious barbarity.

## By Its Nature Anti-Religious

22. This, unfortunately, is what we now behold. For the first time in history we are witnessing a struggle, cold-blooded in purpose and mapped out to the least detail, between man and "all that is called God." (Cf. 2 Thess. 2:4). Communism is by its nature anti-religious. It considers religion as "the opiate of the people" because the principles of religion which speak of a life beyond the grave dissuade the proletariat from the dream of a Soviet paradise which is of this world.

## Terrorism Reigns

23. But the law of nature and its Author cannot be flouted with impunity. Communism has not been able, and will not be able, to achieve its objectives even in the merely economic sphere. It is true that in Russia it has been a contributing factor in rousing men and materials from the inertia of centuries, and in obtaining by all manner of means, often without scruple, some measure of material success. Nevertheless We know from reliable and even very recent testimony that not even there, in spite of slavery imposed on millions of men, has Communism reached its promised goal.

After all, even the sphere of economics needs some morality, some moral sense of responsibility, which can find no place in a system so thoroughly materialistic as Communism. Terrorism is the only possible substitute, and it is terrorism that reigns today in Russia, where former comrades in revolution are exterminating each other. Terrorism, having failed despite all to stem the tide of moral corruption, cannot even prevent the dissolution of society itself.

## Not a Condemnation of the Peoples

24. In making these observations it is no part of Our intention to condemn *en masse* the peoples of the Soviet Union. For them We cherish the warmest paternal affection. We are well aware that not a few of them groan beneath the yoke imposed on them by men who in very large part are strangers to the real interests of the country. We recognize that many others were deceived by fallacious hopes. We blame only the system, with its authors and abettors, who considered Russia the best-prepared field for experimenting with a plan elaborated decades ago, and who from there continue to spread it from one end of the world to the other.

## A True Notion of Human Society

25. We have exposed the errors and the violent, deceptive tactics of bolshevistic and atheistic Communism. It is now time, Venerable Brethren, to contrast with it the true notion, already familiar to you, of the *civitas humana* or human society, as taught by reason and Revelation through the mouth of the Church, *Magistra Gentium* (Teacher of Peoples).

## God Is the Supreme Reality

26. Above all other reality there exists one supreme Being: God, the omnipotent Creator of all things, the all-wise and just Judge of all men. This supreme reality, God, is the absolute condemnation of the impudent falsehoods of Communism. In truth, it

is not because men believe in God that He exists; rather, because He exists do all men whose eyes are not deliberately closed to the truth believe in Him and pray to Him.

## God Alone Is Our Last End

27. In the Encyclical on Christian Education[10] We explained the fundamental doctrine concerning man as it may be gathered from reason and Faith. Man has a spiritual and immortal soul. He is a person, marvelously endowed by his Creator with gifts of body and mind. He is a true "microcosm," as the ancients said, a world in miniature, with a value far surpassing that of the vast inanimate cosmos. God alone is his last end, in this life and the next. By Sanctifying Grace he is raised to the dignity of a son of God and incorporated into the Kingdom of God in the Mystical Body of Christ. In consequence, he has been endowed by God with many and varied prerogatives: the right to life, to bodily integrity, to the necessary means of existence; the right to tend toward his ultimate goal in the path marked out for him by God; the right of association and the right to possess and use property.

## Marriage a Divine Institution

28. Just as matrimony and the right to its natural use are of divine origin, so likewise are the constitution and fundamental prerogatives of the family fixed and determined by the Creator. In the Encyclical on Christian Marriage[11] and in Our other Encyclical on Education, cited above, we have treated these topics at considerable length.

## Society Is Made for Man

29. But God has likewise destined man for civil society according to the dictates of his very nature. In the plan of the Creator, society is a natural means which man can and must use to reach his destined end. Society is for man and not vice versa. This must not be understood in the sense of liberalistic individualism,

which subordinates society to the selfish use of the individual; but only in the sense that by means of an organic union with society and by mutual collaboration, the attainment of earthly happiness is placed within the reach of all. In a further sense, it is society which affords the opportunities for the development of all the individual and social gifts bestowed on human nature. These natural gifts have a value surpassing the immediate interests of the moment, for in society they reflect the divine perfection, which would not be true were man to live alone. But on final analysis, even in this latter function society is made for man, that he may recognize this reflection of God's perfection and refer it in praise and adoration to the Creator. Only man, the human person, and not society in any form is endowed with reason and a morally free will.

### Man's Relationship with Society

30. Man cannot be exempted from his divinely imposed obligations toward civil society, and the representatives of authority have the right to coerce him when he refuses without reason to do his duty. Society, on the other hand, cannot defraud man of his God-granted rights, the most important of which We have indicated above. Nor can society systematically void these rights by making their use impossible. It is therefore according to the dictates of reason that ultimately all material things should be ordained to man as a person, that through his mediation they may find their way to the Creator. In this wise we can apply to man, the human person, the words of the Apostle of the Gentiles, who writes to the Corinthians on the Christian economy of salvation: "All are yours; and you are Christ's; and Christ is God's." (*1 Cor.* 3:22-23). While Communism impoverishes human personality by inverting the terms of the relation of man to society, to what lofty heights is man not elevated by reason and Revelation!

### Private Property and the Dignity of Labor

31. The directive principles concerning the social-economic

order have been expounded in the social Encyclical of Leo XIII on the question of labor.[12] Our own Encyclical on the Reconstruction of the Social Order[13] adapted these principles to present needs. Then, insisting anew on the age-old doctrine of the Church concerning the individual and social character of private property, We explained clearly the right and dignity of labor, the relations of mutual aid and collaboration which should exist between those who possess capital and those who work, the salary due in strict justice to the worker for himself and for his family.

## Civil Authority Should Further Social Harmony

32. In this same Encyclical of Ours We have shown that the means of saving the world of today from the lamentable ruin into which amoral Liberalism has plunged us are neither the class-struggle nor terror, nor yet the autocratic abuse of State power, but rather the infusion of social justice and the sentiment of Christian love into the social-economic order. We have indicated how a sound prosperity is to be restored according to the true principles of a sane corporative system which respects the proper hierarchic structure of society; and how all the occupational groups should be fused into an harmonious unity inspired by the principle of the common good. And the genuine and chief function of public and civil authority consists precisely in the efficacious furthering of this harmony and coordination of all social forces.

## Not All Have Equal Rights in Civil Society

33. In view of this organized common effort towards peaceful living, Catholic doctrine vindicates to the State the dignity and authority of a vigilant and provident defender of those divine and human rights on which the Sacred Scriptures and the Fathers of the Church insist so often. It is not true that all have equal rights in civil society. It is not true that there exists no lawful social hierarchy. Let it suffice to refer to the Encyclicals of Leo XIII already cited, especially to that on State power,[14] and to the other on the Christian Constitution of States.[15] In these documents the Catholic

will find the principles of reason and the Faith clearly explained, and these principles will enable him to defend himself against the errors and perils of a Communistic conception of the State. The enslavement of man despoiled of his rights, the denial of the transcendental origin of the State and its authority, the horrible abuse of public power in the service of a collectivistic terrorism, are the very contrary of all that corresponds with natural ethics and the will of the Creator. Both man and civil society derive their origin from the Creator, who has mutually ordained them one to the other. Hence neither can be exempted from their correlative obligations, nor deny or diminish each other's rights. The Creator Himself has regulated this mutual relationship in its fundamental lines, and it is by an unjust usurpation that Communism arrogates to itself the right to enforce, in place of the divine law based on the immutable principles of truth and charity, a partisan political program which derives from the arbitrary human will and is replete with hate.

### The Church Fosters Temporal and Eternal Happiness

34. In teaching this enlightening doctrine the Church has no other intention than to realize the glad tidings sung by the Angels above the cave of Bethlehem at the Redeemer's birth: "Glory to God . . . and . . . peace to men . . ." (*Luke* 2:14), true peace and true happiness, even here below as far as is possible, in preparation for the happiness of Heaven—but to men of good will. This doctrine is equally removed from all extremes of error and all exaggerations of parties or systems which stem from error. It maintains a constant equilibrium of truth and justice, which it vindicates in theory and applies and promotes in practice, bringing into harmony the rights and duties of all parties. Thus authority is reconciled with liberty, the dignity of the individual with that of the State, the human personality of the subject with the divine delegation of the superior; and in this way a balance is struck between the due dependence and well-ordered love of a man for himself, his family and country, and his love of other families and other peoples, founded on the love of God, the Father of all, their

first principle and last end. The Church does not separate a proper regard for temporal welfare from solicitude for the eternal. If she subordinates the former to the latter according to the words of her divine Founder, "Seek ye therefore first the kingdom of God, and His justice, and all these things shall be added unto you" (*Matt.* 6:33), she is nevertheless so far from being unconcerned with human affairs, so far from hindering civil progress and material advancement, that she actually fosters and promotes them in the most sensible and efficacious manner. Thus even in the sphere of social economics, although the Church has never proposed a definite technical system, since this is not her field, she has nevertheless clearly outlined the guiding principles which, while susceptible of varied concrete applications according to the diversified conditions of times and places and peoples, indicate the safe way of securing the happy progress of society.

*Even Non-Christians Value Catholic Social Doctrine*

35. The wisdom and supreme utility of this doctrine are admitted by all who really understand it. With good reason outstanding statesmen have asserted that, after a study of various social systems, they have found nothing sounder than the principles expounded in the Encyclicals *Rerum Novarum* and *Quadragesimo Anno*. In non-Catholic, even in non-Christian countries, men recognize the great value to society of the social doctrine of the Church. Thus, scarcely a month ago, an eminent political figure of the Far East, a non-Christian, did not hesitate to affirm publicly that the Church, with her doctrine of peace and Christian brotherhood, is rendering a signal contribution to the difficult task of establishing and maintaining peace among the nations. Finally, We know from reliable information that flows into this center of Christendom from all parts of the world that the Communists themselves, where they are not utterly depraved, recognize the superiority of the social doctrine of the Church, when once explained to them, over the doctrines of their leaders and their teachers. Only those blinded by passion and hatred close their eyes to the light of truth and obstinately

struggle against it.

### Abolition of Slavery; True Dignity of Manual Labor

36. But the enemies of the Church, though forced to acknowledge the wisdom of her doctrine, accuse her of having failed to act in conformity with her principles, and from this conclude to the necessity of seeking other solutions. The utter falseness and injustice of this accusation is shown by the whole history of Christianity. To refer only to a single typical trait, it was Christianity that first affirmed the real and universal brotherhood of all men of whatever race and condition. This doctrine she proclaimed by a method, and with an amplitude and conviction, unknown to preceding centuries; and with it she potently contributed to the abolition of slavery. Not bloody revolution, but the inner force of her teaching made the proud Roman matron see in her slave a sister in Christ. It is Christianity that adores the Son of God, made Man for love of man, and become not only the "carpenter's son" but Himself a "carpenter." (*Matt.* 13:55; *Mark* 6:3). It was Christianity that raised manual labor to its true dignity, whereas it had hitherto been so despised that even the moderate Cicero did not hesitate to sum up the general opinion of his time in words of which any modern sociologist would be ashamed: "All artisans are engaged in sordid trades, for there can be nothing ennobling about a workshop."[16]

### Charitable Organizations and Guilds

37. Faithful to these principles, the Church has given new life to human society. Under her influence arose prodigious charitable organizations, great guilds of artisans and workingmen of every type. These guilds, ridiculed as "medieval" by the Liberalism of the last century, are today claiming the admiration of our contemporaries in many countries who are endeavoring to revive them in some modern form. And when other systems hindered her work and raised obstacles to the salutary influence of the Church, she was never done warning them of their error. We need but recall

with what constant firmness and energy Our Predecessor, Leo XIII, vindicated for the workingman the right to organize, which the dominant Liberalism of the more powerful States relentlessly denied him. Even today the authority of this Church doctrine is greater than it seems; for the influence of ideas in the realm of facts, though invisible and not easily measured, is surely of predominant importance.

## The Nations Scorn the Church's Teachings

38. It may be said in all truth that the Church, like Christ, goes through the centuries doing good to all. There would be today neither Socialism nor Communism if the rulers of the nations had not scorned the teachings and maternal warnings of the Church. On the bases of Liberalism and laicism they wished to build other social edifices which, powerful and imposing as they seemed at first, all too soon revealed the weakness of their foundations, and today are crumbling one after another before our eyes, as everything must crumble that is not grounded on the one cornerstone which is Christ Jesus.

## Zeal for the Glory of God

39. This, Venerable Brethren, is the doctrine of the Church, which alone in the social as in all other fields can offer real light and assure salvation in the face of Communistic ideology. But this doctrine must be consistently reduced to practice in everyday life, according to the admonition of St. James the Apostle: "But be ye doers of the word, and not hearers only, deceiving your own selves." (*James* 1:22). The most urgent need of the present day is therefore the energetic and timely application of remedies which will effectively ward off the catastrophe that daily grows more threatening. We cherish the firm hope that the fanaticism with which the sons of darkness work day and night at their materialistic and atheistic propaganda will at least serve the holy purpose of stimulating the sons of light to a like and even greater zeal for the honor of the Divine Majesty.

### Our Duties in the Current Crisis

40. What then must be done, what remedies must be employed to defend Christ and Christian civilization from this pernicious enemy? As a father in the midst of his family, We should like to speak quite intimately of those duties which the great struggle of our day imposes on all the children of the Church; and We would address Our paternal admonition even to those sons who have strayed far from her.

### A Renewal of Private and Public Life

41. As in all the stormy periods of the history of the Church, the fundamental remedy today lies in a sincere renewal of private and public life according to the principles of the Gospel by all those who belong to the Fold of Christ, that they may be in truth the salt of the earth to preserve human society from total corruption.

### Spiritual Renewal of All Classes

42. With heart deeply grateful to the Father of Light, from whom descends "every best gift, and every perfect gift" (*James* 1:17), We see on all sides consoling signs of this spiritual renewal. We see it not only in so many singularly chosen souls who in these last years have been elevated to the sublime heights of sanctity, and in so many others who with generous hearts are making their way toward the same luminous goal, but also in the new flowering of a deep and practical piety in all classes of society, even the most cultured, as We pointed out in Our recent Motu Proprio *In multis solaciis* of October 28 last, on the occasion of the reorganization of the Pontifical Academy of Sciences.[17]

### The Faith Must Be Taken Seriously

43. Nevertheless We cannot deny that there is still much to be done in the way of spiritual renovation. Even in Catholic countries

there are still too many who are Catholics hardly more than in name. There are too many who fulfill more or less faithfully the more essential obligations of the religion they boast of professing, but have no desire of knowing it better, of deepening their inward conviction, and still less of bringing into conformity with the external gloss the inner splendor of a right and unsullied conscience that recognizes and performs all its duties under the eye of God. We know how much our Divine Saviour detested this empty pharisaic show, He who wished that all should adore the Father "in spirit and in truth." (*John* 4:23). The Catholic who does not live really and sincerely according to the Faith he professes will not long be master of himself in these days when the winds of strife and persecution blow so fiercely, but will be swept away defenseless in this new deluge which threatens the world. And thus, while he is preparing his own ruin, he is exposing to ridicule the very name of Christian.

### *Blessed Are the Poor in Spirit*

44. And here We wish, Venerable Brethren, to insist more particularly on two teachings of Our Lord which have a special bearing on the present condition of the human race: detachment from earthly goods and the precept of charity. "Blessed are the poor in spirit" were the first words that fell from the lips of the Divine Master in His sermon on the mount. (*Matt.* 5:3). This lesson is more than ever necessary in these days of materialism athirst for the goods and pleasures of this earth. All Christians, rich or poor, must keep their eye fixed on Heaven, remembering that "we have not here a lasting city, but we seek one that is to come." (*Heb.* 13:14). The rich should not place their happiness in things of earth nor spend their best efforts in the acquisition of them. Rather, considering themselves only as stewards of their earthly goods, let them be mindful of the account they must render of them to their Lord and Master, and value them as precious means that God has put into their hands for doing good; let them not fail, besides, to distribute of their abundance to the poor, according to the evangelical precept. (*Luke* 11:41). Otherwise there shall be verified of

them and their riches the harsh condemnation of St. James the Apostle: "Go to now, ye rich men, weep and howl in your miseries, which shall come upon you. Your riches are corrupted: and your garments are moth eaten. Your gold and silver is cankered: and the rust of them shall be for a testimony against you, and shall eat your flesh like fire. You have stored up to yourselves wrath against the last days . . ." (*James* 5:1-3).

### *No Lasting Happiness in This World*

45. But the poor, too, in their turn, while engaged, according to the laws of charity and justice, in acquiring the necessities of life and also in bettering their condition, should always remain "poor in spirit" (*Matt.* 5:3) and hold spiritual goods in higher esteem than earthly property and pleasures. Let them remember that the world will never be able to rid itself of misery, sorrow and tribulation, which are the portion even of those who seem most prosperous. Patience, therefore, is the need of all, that Christian patience which comforts the heart with the divine assurance of eternal happiness. "Be patient therefore, brethren," we repeat with St. James, "until the coming of the Lord. Behold, the husbandman waiteth for the precious fruit of the earth: patiently bearing till he receive the early and latter rain. Be you therefore also patient, and strengthen your hearts: for the coming of the Lord is at hand." (*James* 5:7-8). Only thus will be fulfilled the consoling promise of the Lord: "Blessed are the poor!" These words are no vain consolation, a promise as empty as those of the Communists. They are the words of life, pregnant with a sovereign reality. They are fully verified here on earth, as well as in eternity. Indeed, how many of the poor, in anticipation of the Kingdom of Heaven already proclaimed their own: "for yours is the kingdom of God" (*Luke* 6:20), find in these words a happiness which so many of the wealthy, uneasy with their riches and ever thirsting for more, look for in vain!

## Spiritual and Corporal Works of Mercy

46. Still more important as a remedy for the evil we are considering, or certainly more directly calculated to cure it, is the precept of charity. We have in mind that Christian charity, "patient and kind" (*1 Cor.* 13:4), which avoids all semblance of demeaning paternalism and all ostentation; that charity which from the very beginning of Christianity won to Christ the poorest of the poor, the slaves. And We are grateful to all those members of charitable associations, from the conferences of St. Vincent de Paul to the recent great relief organizations, which are perseveringly practicing the spiritual and corporal works of mercy. The more the working men and the poor realize what the spirit of love animated by the virtue of Christ is doing for them, the more readily will they abandon the false persuasion that Christianity has lost its efficacy and that the Church stands on the side of the exploiters of their labor.

## Charity Is Necessary for Salvation

47. But when on the one hand We see thousands of the needy, victims of real misery for various reasons beyond their control, and on the other so many round about them who spend huge sums of money on useless things and frivolous amusements, We cannot fail to remark with sorrow not only that justice is poorly observed, but that the precept of charity also is not sufficiently appreciated, is not a vital thing in daily life. We desire therefore, Venerable Brethren, that this divine precept, this precious mark of identification left by Christ to His true disciples, be ever more fully explained by pen and word of mouth; this precept which teaches us to see in those who suffer Christ Himself, and would have us love our brothers as our Divine Saviour has loved us, that is, even at the sacrifice of ourselves, and, if need be, of our very life. Let all then frequently meditate on those words of the final sentence, so consoling yet so terrifying, which the Supreme Judge will pronounce on the day of the Last Judgment: "Come, ye blessed of my Father . . . for I was hungry, and you gave me to eat; I was thirsty,

and you gave me to drink . . . Amen I say to you, as long as you did it to one of these my least brethren, you did it to me." (*Matt.* 25:34-40). And the reverse: "Depart from me, you cursed, into everlasting fire . . . for I was hungry, and you gave me not to eat; I was thirsty, and you gave me not to drink . . . Amen I say to you, as long as you did it not to one of these least, neither did you do it to me." (*Matt.* 25:41-45).

### *Return to a More Moderate Way of Life*

48. To be sure of eternal life, therefore, and to be able to help the poor effectively, it is imperative to return to a more moderate way of life, to renounce the joys, often sinful, which the world today holds out in such abundance; to forget self for love of the neighbor. There is a divine regenerating force in this "new commandment" (as Christ called it) of Christian charity. (*John* 13:34). Its faithful observance will pour into the heart an inner peace which the world knows not and will finally cure the ills which oppress humanity.

### *Justice and Charity*

49. But charity will never be true charity unless it takes justice into constant account. The Apostle teaches that "he that loveth his neighbor, hath fulfilled the law" and he gives the reason: "For, *Thou shalt not commit adultery: Thou shalt not kill: Thou shalt not steal* . . . and if there be any other commandment, it is comprised in this word, *Thou shalt love thy neighbor as thyself.*" (*Rom.* 13:8-9). According to the Apostle, then, all the Commandments, including those which are of strict justice, as those which forbid us to kill or to steal, may be reduced to the single precept of true charity. From this it follows that a "charity" which deprives the working man of the salary to which he has a strict title in justice, is not charity at all, but only its empty name and hollow semblance. The wage earner is not to receive as alms what is his due in justice. And let no one attempt with trifling charitable donations to exempt himself from the great duties imposed by justice.

Both justice and charity often dictate obligations touching on the same subject matter, but under different aspects; and the very dignity of the working man makes him justly and acutely sensitive to the duties of others in his regard.

### Hypocritical Catholic Employers

50. Therefore We turn again in a special way to you, Christian employers and industrialists, whose problem is often so difficult for the reason that you are saddled with the heavy heritage of an unjust economic regime whose ruinous influence has been felt through many generations. We bid you be mindful of your responsibility. It is unfortunately true that the manner of acting in certain Catholic circles has done much to shake the faith of the working classes in the religion of Jesus Christ. These groups have refused to understand that Christian charity demands the recognition of certain rights due to the working man, which the Church has explicitly acknowledged. What is to be thought of the action of those Catholic employers who in one place succeeded in preventing the reading of Our Encyclical *Quadragesimo Anno* in their local churches? Or of those Catholic industrialists who even to this day have shown themselves hostile to a labor movement that We Ourselves recommended? Is it not deplorable that the right of private property defended by the Church should so often have been used as a weapon to defraud the working man of his just salary and his social rights?

### Individual and Common Good

51. In reality, besides commutative justice, there is also social justice, with its own set obligations, from which neither employers nor working men can escape. Now it is of the very essence of social justice to demand for each individual all that is necessary for the common good. But just as in the living organism it is impossible to provide for the good of the whole unless each single part and each individual member is given what it needs for the exercise of its proper functions, so it is impossible to care for the

social organism and the good of society as a unit unless each single part and each individual member—that is to say, each individual man in the dignity of his human personality—is supplied with all that is necessary for the exercise of his social functions. If social justice be satisfied, the result will be an intense activity in economic life as a whole, pursued in tranquility and order. This activity will be proof of the health of the social body, just as the health of the human body is recognized in the undisturbed regularity and perfect efficiency of the whole organism.

### Just Wages

52. But social justice cannot be said to have been satisfied as long as working men are denied a salary that will enable them to secure proper sustenance for themselves and for their families; as long as they are denied the opportunity of acquiring a modest fortune and forestalling the plague of universal pauperism; as long as they cannot make suitable provision through public or private insurance for old age, for periods of illness and unemployment. In a word, to repeat what has been said in Our Encyclical *Quadragesimo Anno*: "Then only will the economic and social order be soundly established and attain its ends when it offers, to all and to each, all those goods which the wealth and resources of nature, technical science and the corporate organization of social affairs can give. These goods should be sufficient to supply all necessities and reasonable comforts, and to uplift men to that higher standard of life which, provided it be used with prudence, is not only not a hindrance but is of singular help to virtue."[18]

### Duties of Employers and of Employees

53. It happens all too frequently, however, under the salary system, that individual employers are helpless to ensure justice unless, with a view to its practice, they organize institutions the object of which is to prevent competition incompatible with fair treatment for the workers. Where this is true, it is the duty of contractors and employers to support and promote such necessary

organizations as normal instruments enabling them to fulfill their obligations of justice. But the laborers too must be mindful of their duty to love and deal fairly with their employers and persuade themselves that there is no better means of safeguarding their own interests.

### Organizations to Promote Justice and Charity

54. If, therefore, We consider the whole structure of economic life, as We have already pointed out in Our Encyclical *Quadragesimo Anno*, the reign of mutual collaboration between justice and charity in social-economic relations can only be achieved by a body of professional and inter-professional organizations, built on solidly Christian foundations, working together to effect, under forms adapted to different places and circumstances, what has been called the Corporation.

### Spread Church Social Teaching

55. To give to this social activity a greater efficacy, it is necessary to promote a wider study of social problems in the light of the doctrine of the Church and under the aegis of her constituted authority. If the manner of acting of some Catholics in the social-economic field has left much to be desired, this has often come about because they have not known and pondered sufficiently the teachings of the Sovereign Pontiffs on these questions. Therefore, it is of the utmost importance to foster in all classes of society an intensive program of social education adapted to the varying degrees of intellectual culture. It is necessary with all care and diligence to procure the widest possible diffusion of the teachings of the Church, even among the working classes. The minds of men must be illuminated with the sure light of Catholic teaching, and their wills must be drawn to follow and apply it as the norm of right living in the conscientious fulfillment of their manifold social duties. Thus they will oppose that incoherence and discontinuity in Christian life which We have many times lamented. For there are some who, while exteriorly faithful to the practice of

their religion, yet in the field of labor and industry, in the professions, trade and business, permit a deplorable cleavage in their conscience and live a life too little in conformity with the clear principles of justice and Christian charity. Such lives are a scandal to the weak, and to the malicious a pretext to discredit the Church.

### Role of the Catholic Press

56. In this renewal the Catholic Press can play a prominent part. Its foremost duty is to foster in various attractive ways an ever better understanding of social doctrine. It should, too, supply accurate and complete information on the activity of the enemy and the means of resistance which have been found most effective in various quarters. It should offer useful suggestions and warn against the insidious deceits with which Communists endeavor, all too successfully, to attract even men of good faith.

### Communism in Disguise

57. On this point We have already insisted in Our Allocution of May 12th of last year, but We believe it to be a duty of special urgency, Venerable Brethren, to call your attention to it once again. In the beginning, Communism showed itself for what it was in all its perversity, but very soon it realized that it was thus alienating the people. It has therefore changed its tactics and strives to entice the multitudes by trickery of various forms, hiding its real designs behind ideas that in themselves are good and attractive. Thus, aware of the universal desire for peace, the leaders of Communism pretend to be the most zealous promoters and propagandists in the movement for world amity. Yet at the same time they stir up a class warfare which causes rivers of blood to flow, and, realizing that their system offers no internal guarantee of peace, they have recourse to unlimited armaments. Under various names which do not suggest Communism, they establish organizations and periodicals with the sole purpose of carrying their ideas into quarters otherwise inaccessible. They try perfidiously to worm

their way even into professedly Catholic and religious organizations. Again, without receding an inch from their subversive principles, they invite Catholics to collaborate with them in the realm of so-called humanitarianism and charity, and at times even make proposals that are in perfect harmony with the Christian spirit and the doctrine of the Church. Elsewhere they carry their hypocrisy so far as to encourage the belief that Communism, in countries where faith and culture are more strongly entrenched, will assume another and much milder form. It will not interfere with the practice of religion. It will respect liberty of conscience. There are some even who refer to certain changes recently introduced into Soviet legislation as a proof that Communism is about to abandon its program of war against God.

### Communism Is Intrinsically Wrong

58. See to it, Venerable Brethren, that the Faithful do not allow themselves to be deceived! Communism is intrinsically wrong, and no one who would save Christian civilization may collaborate with it in any undertaking whatsoever. Those who permit themselves to be deceived into lending their aid toward the triumph of Communism in their own country will be the first to fall victims of their error. And the greater the antiquity and grandeur of the Christian civilization in the regions where Communism successfully penetrates, so much more devastating will be the hatred displayed by the godless.

### Necessity of Prayer and Penance

59. But "unless the Lord keep the city, he watcheth in vain that keepeth it." (*Ps.* 126:1). And so, as a final and most efficacious remedy, We recommend, Venerable Brethren, that in your dioceses you use the most practical means to foster and intensify the spirit of prayer joined with Christian penance. When the Apostles asked the Saviour why they had been unable to drive the evil spirit from a demoniac, Our Lord answered: "This kind is not cast out but by prayer and fasting." (*Matt.* 17:20). So, too, the evil which

today torments humanity can be conquered only by a worldwide holy crusade of prayer and penance. We ask especially the contemplative orders, men and women, to redouble their prayers and sacrifices to obtain from Heaven efficacious aid for the Church in the present struggle. Let them implore also the powerful intercession of the Immaculate Virgin who, having crushed the head of the serpent of old, remains the sure protectress and invincible "Help of Christians."

### Role of Priests

60. To apply the remedies thus briefly indicated to the task of saving the world as We have traced it above, Jesus Christ, our Divine King, has chosen priests as the first-line ministers and messengers of His Gospel. Theirs is the duty, assigned to them by a special vocation, under the direction of their Bishops and in filial obedience to the Vicar of Christ on earth, of keeping alight in the world the torch of Faith, and of filling the hearts of the Faithful with that supernatural trust which has aided the Church to fight and win so many other battles in the name of Christ: "This is the victory which overcometh the world, our faith." (*1 John* 5:4).

### Instructing the Working Class

61. To priests in a special way We recommend anew the oft-repeated counsel of Our Predecessor, Leo XIII, to go to the working man. We make this advice Our own, and, faithful to the teachings of Jesus Christ and His Church, We thus complete it: "Go to the working man, especially where he is poor; and in general, go to the poor." The poor are obviously more exposed than others to the wiles of agitators who, taking advantage of their extreme need, kindle their hearts to envy of the rich and urge them to seize by force what fortune seems to have denied them unjustly. If the priest will not go to the working man and to the poor, to warn them or to disabuse them of prejudice and false theory, they will become an easy prey for the apostles of Communism.

## Conversion of the Masses

62. Indisputably much has been done in this direction, especially after the publication of the Encyclicals *Rerum Novarum* and *Quadragesimo Anno*. We are happy to voice Our paternal approval of the zealous pastoral activity manifested by so many Bishops and priests who have with due prudence and caution been planning and applying new methods of apostolate more adapted to modern needs. But for the solution of our present problem, all this effort is still inadequate. When our country is in danger, everything not strictly necessary, everything not bearing directly on the urgent matter of unified defense, takes second place. So we must act in today's crisis. Every other enterprise, however attractive and helpful, must yield before the vital need of protecting the very foundation of the Faith and of Christian civilization. Let our parish priests, therefore, while providing of course for the normal needs of the Faithful, dedicate the better part of their endeavors and their zeal to winning back the laboring masses to Christ and to His Church. Let them work to infuse the Christian spirit into quarters where it is least at home. The willing response of the masses, and results far exceeding their expectations, will not fail to reward them for their strenuous pioneer labor. This has been and continues to be our experience in Rome and in other capitals, where zealous parish communities are being formed as new churches are built in the suburban districts, and real miracles are being worked in the conversion of people whose hostility to religion has been due solely to the fact that they did not know it.

## Priests Must Be a Good Example

63. But the most efficacious means of apostolate among the poor and lowly is the priests' example, the practice of all those sacerdotal virtues which We have described in Our Encyclical *Ad Catholici Sacerdotii*.[19] Especially needful, however, for the present situation is the shining example of a life which is humble, poor and disinterested, in imitation of a Divine Master who could say to the world with divine simplicity: "The foxes have holes,

and the birds of the air nests: but the son of man hath not where to lay his head." (*Matt.* 8:20). A priest who is really poor and disinterested in the Gospel sense may work among his flock marvels recalling a Saint Vincent de Paul, a Curé of Ars, a Cottolengo, a Don Bosco and so many others; while an avaricious and selfish priest, as We have noted in the above-mentioned Encyclical, even though he should not plunge with Judas to the abyss of treason, will never be more than empty "sounding brass" and useless "tinkling cymbal." (*1 Cor.* 13:1). Too often, indeed, he will be a hindrance rather than an instrument of grace in the midst of his people. Furthermore, where a secular priest or religious is obliged by his office to administer temporal property, let him remember that he is not only to observe scrupulously all that charity and justice prescribe, but that he has a special obligation to conduct himself in very truth as a father of the poor.

### The Social Apostolate

64. After this appeal to the clergy, We extend Our paternal invitation to Our beloved sons among the laity who are doing battle in the ranks of Catholic Action.[20] On another occasion[21] We have called this movement so dear to Our heart "a particularly providential assistance" in the work of the Church during these troublous times. Catholic Action is in effect a *social* apostolate also, inasmuch as its object is to spread the Kingdom of Jesus Christ not only among individuals, but also in families and in society. It must, therefore, make it a chief aim to train its members with special care and to prepare them to fight the battles of the Lord. This task of formation, now more urgent and indispensable than ever, which must always precede direct action in the field, will assuredly be served by study circles, conferences, lecture courses and the various other activities undertaken with a view to making known the Christian solution of the social problem.

### Leaders of Catholic Action

65. The militant leaders of Catholic Action, thus properly pre-

pared and armed, will be the first and immediate apostles of their fellow workmen. They will be an invaluable aid to the priest in carrying the torch of truth, and in relieving grave spiritual and material suffering, in many sectors where inveterate anti-clerical prejudice or deplorable religious indifference has proved a constant obstacle to the pastoral activity of God's ministers. In this way they will collaborate, under the direction of especially qualified priests, in that work of spiritual aid to the laboring classes on which We set so much store because it is the means best calculated to save these, Our beloved children, from the snares of Communism.

### Promote Widespread Knowledge of Catholic Teaching

66. In addition to this individual apostolate which, however useful and efficacious, often goes unheralded, Catholic Action must organize propaganda on a large scale to disseminate knowledge of the fundamental principles on which, according to the Pontifical documents, a Christian Social Order must build.

### Auxiliary Forces

67. Ranged with Catholic Action are the groups which We have been happy to call its auxiliary forces. With paternal affection We exhort these valuable organizations also to dedicate themselves to the great mission of which We have been treating, a cause which today transcends all others in vital importance.

### Cultural and Labor Organizations

68. We are thinking likewise of those associations of workmen, farmers, technicians, doctors, employers, students and others of like character, groups of men and women who live in the same cultural atmosphere and share the same way of life. Precisely these groups and organizations are destined to introduce into society that order which We have envisaged in Our Encyclical *Quadragesimo Anno*, and thus to spread in the vast and vari-

ous fields of culture and labor the recognition of the Kingdom of Christ.

## Prudent and Intelligent Participation

69. Even where the State, because of changed social and economic conditions, has felt obliged to intervene directly in order to aid and regulate such organizations by special legislative enactments, supposing always the necessary respect for liberty and private initiative, Catholic Action may not urge the circumstance as an excuse for abandoning the field. Its members should contribute prudently and intelligently to the study of the problems of the hour in the light of Catholic doctrine. They should loyally and generously participate in the formation of the new institutions, bringing to them the Christian spirit which is the basic principle of order wherever men work together in fraternal harmony.

## A Word to Catholic Workmen

70. Here We should like to address a particularly affectionate word to Our Catholic working men, young and old. They have been given, perhaps as a reward for their often heroic fidelity in these trying days, a noble and an arduous mission. Under the guidance of their Bishops and priests, they are to bring back to the Church and to God those immense multitudes of their brother workmen who, because they were not understood or treated with the respect to which they were entitled, in bitterness have strayed far from God. Let Catholic working men show these their wandering brethren, by word and example, that the Church is a tender Mother to all those who labor and suffer, and that she has never failed, and never will fail, in her sacred maternal duty of protecting her children. If this mission, which must be fulfilled in mines, in factories, in shops, wherever they may be laboring, should at times require great sacrifices, Our workmen will remember that the Saviour of the world has given them an example not only of toil but of self-immolation.

## Fraternal Union

71. To all Our children, finally, of every social rank and every nation, to every religious and lay organization in the Church, We make another and more urgent appeal for union. Many times Our paternal heart has been saddened by the divergencies—often idle in their causes, always tragic in their consequences—which array in opposing camps the sons of the same Mother Church. Thus it is that the radicals, who are not so very numerous, profiting by this discord, are able to make it more acute and end by pitting Catholics one against the other. In view of the events of the past few months, Our warning must seem superfluous. We repeat it nevertheless once more, for those who have not understood, or perhaps do not desire to understand. Those who make a practice of spreading dissension among Catholics assume a terrible responsibility before God and the Church.

## An Appeal to All Who Believe in God

72. But in this battle joined by the powers of darkness against the very idea of Divinity, it is Our fond hope that, besides the host which glories in the name of Christ, all those—and they comprise the overwhelming majority of mankind—who still believe in God and pay Him homage may take a decisive part. We therefore renew the invitation extended to them five years ago in Our Encyclical *Caritate Christi*, invoking their loyal and hearty collaboration "in order to ward off from mankind the great danger that threatens all alike." Since, as We then said, "belief in God is the unshakable foundation of all social order and of all responsibility on earth, it follows that all those who do not want anarchy and terrorism ought to take energetic steps to prevent the enemies of religion from attaining the goal they have so brazenly proclaimed to the world."[22]

## Constructing a Christian Society

73. Such is the positive task, embracing at once theory and

practice, which the Church undertakes in virtue of the mission, confided to her by Christ, of constructing a Christian society, and, in our own times, of resisting unto victory the attacks of Communism. It is the duty of the Christian State to concur actively in this spiritual enterprise of the Church, aiding her with the means at its command, which although they be external devices, have nonetheless for their prime object the good of souls.

### Faith Is the Basis of Moral Law

74. This means that all diligence should be exercised by States to prevent within their territories the ravages of an anti-God campaign which shakes society to its very foundations. For there can be no authority on earth unless the authority of the Divine Majesty be recognized; no oath will bind which is not sworn in the Name of the Living God. We repeat what We have said with frequent insistence in the past, especially in Our Encyclical *Caritate Christi*: "How can any contract be maintained, and what value can any treaty have, in which every guarantee of conscience is lacking? And how can there be talk of guarantees of conscience when all faith in God and all fear of God have vanished? Take away this basis, and with it all moral law falls, and there is no remedy left to stop the gradual but inevitable destruction of peoples, families, the State, civilization itself."[23]

### The Wealthy

75. It must likewise be the special care of the State to create those material conditions of life without which an orderly society cannot exist. The State must take every measure necessary to supply employment, particularly for the heads of families and for the young. To achieve this end, demanded by the pressing needs of the common welfare, the wealthy classes must be induced to assume those burdens without which human society cannot be saved nor they themselves remain secure. However, measures taken by the State with this end in view ought to be of such a nature that they will really affect those who actually possess more than their share

of capital resources and who continue to accumulate them to the grievous detriment of others.

## Duties of the State

76. The State itself, mindful of its responsibility before God and society, should be a model of prudence and sobriety in the administration of the commonwealth. Today more than ever the acute world crisis demands that those who dispose of immense funds, built up on the sweat and toil of millions, keep constantly and singly in mind the common good. State functionaries and all employees are obliged in conscience to perform their duties faithfully and unselfishly, imitating the brilliant example of distinguished men of the past and of our own day, who with unremitting labor sacrificed their all for the good of their country. In international trade relations, let all means be sedulously employed for the removal of those artificial barriers to economic life which are the effects of distrust and hatred. All must remember that the peoples of the earth form but one family in God.

## The State Must Allow the Church Full Liberty

77. At the same time the State must allow the Church full liberty to fulfill her divine and spiritual mission, and this in itself will be an effectual contribution to the rescue of nations from the dread torment of the present hour. Everywhere today there is an anxious appeal to moral and spiritual forces; and rightly so, for the evil we must combat is at its origin primarily an evil of the spiritual order. From this polluted source the monstrous emanations of the communistic system flow with satanic logic. Now, the Catholic Church is undoubtedly pre-eminent among the moral and religious forces of today. Therefore the very good of humanity demands that her work be allowed to proceed unhindered.

## Political or Economic Means Are Insufficient

78. Those who act otherwise, and at the same time fondly pre-

tend to attain their objective with purely political or economic means, are in the grip of a dangerous error. When religion is banished from the school, from education and from public life, when the representatives of Christianity and its sacred rites are held up to ridicule, are we not really fostering the materialism which is the fertile soil of Communism? Neither force, however well organized it be, nor earthly ideals, however lofty or noble, can control a movement whose roots lie in the excessive esteem for the goods of this world.

### *Rulers Must Not Hinder the Work of the Church*

79. We trust that those rulers of nations who are at all aware of the extreme danger threatening every people today may be more and more convinced of their supreme duty not to hinder the Church in the fulfillment of her mission. This is the more imperative since, while this mission has in view man's happiness in Heaven, it cannot but promote his true felicity in time.

### *A Plea for the Conversion of Communists*

80. We cannot conclude this Encyclical Letter without addressing some words to those of Our children who are more or less tainted with the Communist plague. We earnestly exhort them to hear the voice of their loving Father. We pray the Lord to enlighten them, that they may abandon the slippery path which will precipitate one and all to ruin and catastrophe, and that they recognize that Jesus Christ, Our Lord, is their only Saviour: "For there is no other name under heaven given to man, whereby we must be saved." (*Acts* 4:12).

### *The Example of St. Joseph*

81. To hasten the advent of that "peace of Christ in the Kingdom of Christ"[24] so ardently desired by all, We place the vast campaign of the Church against world Communism under the standard of St. Joseph, her mighty Protector. He belongs to the

working class, and he bore the burdens of poverty for himself and the Holy Family, whose tender and vigilant head he was. To him was entrusted the Divine Child when Herod loosed his assassins against Him. In a life of faithful performance of everyday duties, he left an example for all those who must gain their bread by the toil of their hands. He won for himself the title of "The Just," serving thus as a living model of that Christian justice which should reign in social life.

### The Promise of Christ

82. With eyes lifted on high, our Faith sees the new heavens and the new earth described by Our first Predecessor, St. Peter. (*2 Ptr.* 3:13; Cf. *Is.* 65:17 and 66:22; *Apoc.* 21:1). While the promises of the false prophets of this earth melt away in blood and tears, the great apocalyptic prophecy of the Redeemer shines forth in heavenly splendor: "Behold, I make all things new." (*Apoc.* 21:5).

Venerable Brethren, nothing remains but to raise Our paternal hands to call down upon you, upon your clergy and people, upon the whole Catholic family, the Apostolic Benediction.

Given at Rome, at St. Peter's, on the feast of St. Joseph, Patron of the Universal Church, on the nineteenth of March, 1937, the sixteenth year of Our Pontificate.

Pius XI, Pope

### NOTES

1. Encycl. *Qui Pluribus*, Nov. 9, 1846 (*Acta Pii IX*, vol. 1, p. 13). Cf. *Syllabus*, § IV (A.A.S., vol. III, p. 170).
2. Encycl. *Quod Apostolici Muneris*, Dec. 28, 1978 (*Acta Leonis XIII*, vol. 1, p. 46).
3. Dec. 18, 1924 (*A.A.S.*, vol. XVI, 1924, pp. 494-495).

4. May 8, 1928 (*A.A.S.*, vol. XX, 1928, pp. 165-178).
5. May 15, 1931 (*A.A.S.*, vol. XXIII, 1931, pp. 177-228).
6. May 3, 1932 (*A.A.S.*, vol. XXIV, 1932, pp. 177-194).
7. Sept. 29, 1932 (*A.A.S.*, vol. XXIV, 1932, pp. 321-332).
8. June 3, 1933 (*A.A.S.*, vol. XXV, 1933, pp. 261-274).
9. Laicism—deprivation by the government of the Church's control over schools and Church property.
10. Encycl. *Divini Illius Magistri*, Dec. 31, 1929 (*A.A.S.*, vol. XXII, 1930, pp. 47-86).
11. Encycl. *Casti Connubii*, Dec. 31, 1930 (*A.A.S.*, vol. XXII, 1930, pp. 539-592).
12. Encycl. *Rerum Novarum*, May 15, 1891 (*Acta Leonis* XIII vol. IV, pp. 177-209).
13. Encycl. *Quadragesimo Anno*, May 15, 1931 (*A.A.S.*, vol. XXIII, 1931, pp. 177-228).
14. Encycl. *Diuturnum Illud*, June 20, 1881 (*Acta Leonis* XIII, vol. I, pp. 210-222).
15. Encycl. *Immortale Dei*, Nov. 1, 1885 (*Acta Leonis* XIII, vol. II, pp. 146-168).
16. Cicero, *De Officiis*, Bk. 1, c. 42.
17. *A.A.S.*, vol. XXVIII (1936), pp. 421-424.
18. Encycl. *Quadragesimo Anno*, May 15, 1931 (*A.A.S.*, vol. XXIII, 1931, p. 202).
19. Dec. 20, 1935 (*A.A.S.*, vol. XXVIII (1936), pp. 5-53).
20. Catholic Action—A general term which was given a specific content and worldwide significance by Pope Pius XI, who defined Catholic Action as "the participation and collaboration of the laity with the apostolic hierarchy." The scope of Catholic Action was broad, and it varied from place to place—from being highly organized to being largely a personal ideal of working for Christ under the direct encouragement of the pastors. It included study, apologetics, corporal works of mercy, etc., etc.—but not political activity, which was absolutely forbidden to Catholic Action. (Cf. Attwater, *A Catholic Dictionary* [New York: Macmillan, 1961; TAN, 1997], p. 81.)
21. May 12, 1936.
22. Encycl. *Caritate Christi*, May 3, 1932 (*A.A.S.*, vol. XXIV, p. 184).
23. *Ibid.*, p. 190.
24. Encycl. *Ubi Arcano*, Dec. 23, 1922 (*A.A.S.*, vol. XIV, 1922, p. 691).

Encyclical Letter of Pope Pius XII

# On Certain False Opinions
## WHICH THREATEN TO UNDERMINE THE
## FOUNDATIONS OF CATHOLIC DOCTRINE
### *(Humani Generis)*

August 12, 1950

To Our Venerable Brethren, Patriarchs, Primates, Archbishops,
Bishops and other local Ordinaries Enjoying Peace and
Communion with the Holy See

Venerable Brethren,
Greetings and Apostolic Benediction

1. Disagreement and error among men on moral and religious
matters have always been a cause of profound sorrow to all good
men, but above all to the true and loyal sons of the Church, especially today, when we see the principles of Christian culture being
attacked on all sides.

*Obstacles to Recognizing Truth*

2. It is not surprising that such discord and error should always
have existed outside the fold of Christ. For though, absolutely
speaking, human reason by its own natural force and light can
arrive at a true and certain knowledge of the one personal God,
who by His providence watches over and governs the world, and
also the natural law, which the Creator has written in our hearts,
still there are not a few obstacles to prevent reason from making

efficient and fruitful use of its natural ability. The truths that have to do with God and the relations between God and men completely surpass the sensible order and demand self-surrender and self-abnegation in order to be put into practice and to influence practical life. Now the human intellect, in gaining the knowledge of such truths, is hampered both by the activity of the senses and the imagination, and by evil passions arising from original sin. Hence men easily persuade themselves in such matters that what they do not wish to believe is false or at least doubtful.

### Divine Revelation Is Morally Necessary

3. It is for this reason that Divine Revelation must be considered morally necessary, so that those religious and moral truths which are not of their nature beyond the reach of reason, in the present condition of the human race may be known by all men readily with a firm certainty and with freedom from all error.[1]

### Man Resists Grace

4. Furthermore, the human intelligence sometimes experiences difficulties in forming a judgment about the credibility of the Catholic Faith, notwithstanding the many wonderful external signs God has given, which are sufficient to prove with certitude by the natural light of reason alone the divine origin of the Christian religion. For man can, whether from prejudice or passion or bad faith, refuse and resist not only the evidence of the external proofs that are available, but also the impulses of actual grace.

### Materialists Promote Evolution

5. If anyone examines the state of affairs outside the Christian fold, he will easily discover the principal trends that not a few learned men are following. Some imprudently and indiscreetly hold that Evolution, which has not been fully proved even in the domain of natural sciences, explains the origin of all things, and audaciously support the monistic and pantheistic opinion that the

world is in continual evolution. Communists gladly subscribe to this opinion so that, when the souls of men have been deprived of every idea of a personal God, they may the more efficaciously defend and propagate their dialectical materialism.

### Existentialism Is an Erroneous Philosophy

6. Such fictitious tenets of evolution which repudiate all that is absolute, firm and immutable have paved the way for the new erroneous philosophy which, rivaling idealism, immanentism and pragmatism, has assumed the name of existentialism, since it concerns itself only with existence of individual things and neglects all consideration of their immutable essences.

### Christian Dogmas Are Rejected

7. There is also a certain historicism which, attributing value only to the events of man's life, overthrows the foundation of all truth and absolute law both in regard to philosophical speculations and especially to Christian dogmas.

### The Teaching Authority of the Church

8. In all this confusion of opinion it is some consolation to Us to see former adherents of rationalism today not uncommonly desiring to return to the fountain of divinely communicated truth and to acknowledge and profess the word of God as contained in Sacred Scripture as the foundation of religious teaching. But at the same time it is a matter of regret that not a few of these, the more firmly they accept the word of God, so much the more do they diminish the value of human reason; and the more they exalt the authority of God the Revealer, the more severely do they spurn the teaching office of the Church, which has been instituted by Christ, Our Lord, to preserve and interpret Divine Revelation. This attitude is not only plainly at variance with Holy Scripture, but is shown to be false by experience also. For often those who disagree with the true Church complain openly of their disagree-

ment in matters of dogma and thus unwillingly bear witness to the necessity of a living Teaching Authority.

## Understanding the Errors

9. Now Catholic theologians and philosophers, whose grave duty it is to defend natural and supernatural truth and instill it in the hearts of men, cannot afford to ignore or neglect these more or less erroneous opinions. Rather they must come to understand these same theories well, both because diseases are not properly treated unless they are rightly diagnosed, and because sometimes even in these false theories a certain amount of truth is contained, and, finally, because these theories provoke more subtle discussion and evaluation of philosophical and theological truths.

## Novel Ideas Infect Some Theologians

10. If philosophers and theologians strive only to derive such profit from the careful examination of these doctrines, there would be no reason for any intervention by the Teaching Authority of the Church. However, although We know that Catholic teachers generally avoid these errors, it is apparent, however, that some today, as in apostolic times, desirous of novelty, and fearing to be considered ignorant of recent scientific findings, try to withdraw themselves from the sacred Teaching Authority and are accordingly in danger of gradually departing from revealed truth and of drawing others along with them into error.

## Some Reject Traditional Theology

11. Another danger is perceived which is all the more serious because it is more concealed beneath the mask of virtue. There are many who, deploring disagreement among men and intellectual confusion, through an imprudent zeal for souls, are urged by a great and ardent desire to do away with the barrier that divides good and honest men; these advocate an "eirenism" according to which, by setting aside the questions which divide men, they aim

not only at joining forces to repel the attacks of atheism, but also at reconciling things opposed to one another in the field of dogma. And as in former times some questioned whether the traditional apologetics of the Church did not constitute an obstacle rather than a help to the winning of souls for Christ, so today some are presumptive enough to question seriously whether theology and theological methods, such as with the approval of ecclesiastical authority are found in our schools, should not only be perfected, but also completely reformed, in order to promote the more efficacious propagation of the Kingdom of Christ everywhere throughout the world among men of every culture and religious opinion.

### Promoting a False Unity

12. Now if these only aimed at adapting ecclesiastical teaching and methods to modern conditions and requirements through the introduction of some new explanations, there would be scarcely any reason for alarm. But some through enthusiasm for an imprudent "eirenism" seem to consider as an obstacle to the restoration of fraternal union, things founded on the laws and principles given by Christ and likewise on institutions founded by Him, or which are the defense and support of the integrity of the Faith, and the removal of which would bring about the union of all, but only to their destruction.

### New Opinions Are Circulated Privately

13. These new opinions, whether they originate from a reprehensible desire for novelty or from a laudable motive, are not always advanced in the same degree, with equal clarity, nor in the same terms, nor always with unanimous agreement of their authors. Theories that today are put forward rather covertly by some, not without cautions and distinctions, tomorrow are openly and without moderation proclaimed by others more audacious, causing scandal to many, especially among the young clergy and to the detriment of ecclesiastical authority. Though they are usu-

ally more cautious in their published works, they express themselves more openly in their writings intended for private circulation and in conferences and lectures. Moreover, these opinions are disseminated not only among members of the clergy and in seminaries and religious institutions, but also among the laity, and especially among those who are engaged in teaching youth.

### A New Approach to Catholic Dogma

14. In theology, some want to reduce to a minimum the meaning of dogmas, and to free dogma itself from terminology long established in the Church and from philosophical concepts held by Catholic teachers, to bring about a return in the explanation of Catholic doctrine to the way of speaking used in Holy Scripture and by the Fathers of the Church. They cherish the hope that when dogma is stripped of the elements which they hold to be extrinsic to Divine Revelation, it will compare advantageously with the dogmatic opinions of those who are separated from the unity of the Church and that in this way they will gradually arrive at a mutual assimilation of Catholic dogma with the tenets of the dissidents.

### Attempts to Express Dogmas by New Concepts

15. Moreover, they assert that when Catholic doctrine has been reduced to this condition, a way will be found to satisfy modern needs that will permit of dogma being expressed also by the concepts of modern philosophy, whether of immanentism or idealism or existentialism or any other system. Some more audacious affirm that this can and must be done, because they hold that the Mysteries of Faith are never expressed by truly adequate concepts, but only by approximate and ever changeable notions, in which the truth is to some extent expressed, but is necessarily distorted. Wherefore they do not consider it absurd, but altogether necessary, that theology should substitute new concepts in place of the old ones in keeping with the various philosophies which in the course of time it uses as its instruments, so that it should give

human expression to divine truths in various ways which are even somewhat opposed, but still equivalent, as they say. They add that the history of dogmas consists in the reporting of the various forms in which revealed truth has been clothed, forms that have succeeded one another in accordance with the different teachings and opinions that have arisen over the course of the centuries.

## Dogmatic Relativism Has Emerged

16. It is evident from what We have already said that such endeavors not only lead to what they call dogmatic relativism, but that they actually contain it. The contempt of doctrine commonly taught, and of the terms in which it is expressed, strongly favor it. Everyone is aware that the terminology employed in the schools and even that used by the Teaching Authority of the Church itself is capable of being perfected and polished; and we know also that the Church itself has not always used the same terms in the same way. It is also manifest that the Church cannot be bound to every system of philosophy that has existed for a short space of time. Nevertheless, the things that have been composed through common effort by Catholic teachers over the course of the centuries to bring about some understanding of dogma are certainly not based on any such weak foundation. These things are based on principles and notions deduced from a true knowledge of created things. In this deductive process, divinely revealed truth, like a star, gave enlightenment to the human mind through the Church. Hence it is not astonishing that some of these notions have not only been used by the Ecumenical Councils, but even sanctioned by them, so that it is wrong to depart from them.

## Scholastic Theology Is Despised

17. Hence to neglect, or to reject, or to devalue so many and such great resources which have been conceived, expressed and perfected so often by the age-old work of men endowed with no common talent and holiness, working under the vigilant supervision of the holy Magisterium and with the light and leadership of

the Holy Ghost in order to state the truths of the Faith ever more accurately—to do this so that these things may be replaced by conjectural notions and by some formless and unstable tenets of a new philosophy, tenets which, like the flowers of the field, are in existence today and die tomorrow—this is supreme imprudence and something that would make dogma itself a reed shaken by the wind. The contempt for the terms and notions habitually used by Scholastic theologians leads of itself to the weakening of what they call speculative theology, a discipline which these men consider devoid of true certitude because it is based on theological reasoning.

## Contempt for Church Teaching Authority

18. Unfortunately these advocates of novelty easily pass from despising Scholastic theology to the neglect of and even contempt for the Teaching Authority of the Church itself, which gives such authoritative approval to Scholastic theology. This Teaching Authority is represented by them as a hindrance to progress and an obstacle in the way of science. Some non-Catholics consider it as an unjust restraint preventing some more qualified theologians from reforming their subject. And although this sacred Office of Teacher in matters of faith and morals must be the proximate and universal criterion of truth for all theologians, since to it has been entrusted by Christ Our Lord the whole Deposit of Faith—Sacred Scripture and divine Tradition—to be preserved, guarded and interpreted, still the duty that is incumbent on the faithful to flee also those errors which more or less approach heresy, and accordingly "to keep also the constitutions and decrees by which such evil opinions are proscribed and forbidden by the Holy See,"[2] is sometimes as little known as if it did not exist. What is expounded in the Encyclical Letters of the Roman Pontiffs concerning the nature and constitution of the Church is deliberately and habitually neglected by some with the idea of giving force to a certain vague notion which they profess to have found in the ancient Fathers, especially the Greeks. The Popes, they assert, do not wish to pass judgment on what is a matter of dispute among theolo-

gians, so recourse must be had to the early sources, and the recent constitutions and decrees of the Teaching Church must be explained from the writings of the ancients.

## Some Matters Not Open to Discussion

19. Although these things seem well said, still they are not free from error. It is true that Popes generally leave theologians free in those matters which are disputed in various ways by men of very high authority in this field; but history teaches that many matters that formerly were open to discussion, no longer now admit of discussion.

## The Weight of Encyclical Letters

20. Nor must it be thought that what is expounded in Encyclical Letters does not of itself demand consent since in writing such Letters the Popes do not exercise the supreme power of their Teaching Authority. For these matters are taught with the ordinary teaching authority, of which it is true to say: "He that heareth you, heareth me" (*Luke* 10:16); and generally what is expounded and inculcated in Encyclical Letters already for other reasons appertains to Catholic doctrine. But if the Supreme Pontiffs in their official documents purposely pass judgment on a matter up to that time under dispute, it is obvious that that matter, according to the mind and will of the same Pontiffs, cannot be any longer considered a question open to discussion among theologians.

## True and False "Return to the Sources"

21. It is also true that theologians must always return to the sources of Divine Revelation: for it belongs to them to point out how the doctrine of the living Teaching Authority is to be found either explicitly or implicitly in the Scriptures and in Tradition.[3] Besides, each source of divinely revealed doctrine contains so many rich treasures of truth that they can really never be exhausted. Hence it is that theology, through the study of its

sacred sources, remains ever fresh; on the other hand, speculation which neglects a deeper search into the Deposit of Faith proves sterile, as we know from experience. But for this reason even positive theology cannot be on a par with merely historical science. For together with the sources of positive theology, God has given to His Church a living Teaching Authority to elucidate and explain what is contained in the Deposit of Faith only obscurely and implicitly. This Deposit of Faith our Divine Redeemer has given for authentic interpretation not to each of the faithful, not even to theologians, but only to the Teaching Authority of the Church. But if the Church does exercise this function of teaching, as she often has through the centuries, either in the ordinary or extraordinary way, it is clear how false is a procedure which would attempt to explain what is clear by means of what is obscure. Indeed the very opposite procedure must be used. Hence Our Predecessor of immortal memory, Pius IX, teaching that the most noble office of theology is to show how a doctrine defined by the Church is contained in the sources of Revelation, added these words, and with very good reason: "in that sense in which it has been defined by the Church."

*Errors Involving Sacred Scripture*

22. To return, however, to the new opinions mentioned above, a number of things are proposed or suggested by some even against the divine authorship of Sacred Scripture. For some go so far as to pervert the sense of the Vatican Council's definition that God is the author of Holy Scripture, and they put forward again the opinion, already often condemned, which asserts that immunity from error extends only to those parts of the Bible that treat of God or of moral and religious matters. They even wrongly speak of a human sense of the Scriptures, beneath which a divine sense, which they say is the only infallible meaning, lies hidden. In interpreting Scripture, they will take no account of the analogy of faith and the Tradition of the Church. Thus they judge the doctrine of the Fathers and of the Teaching Church by the norm of Holy Scripture, interpreted by the purely human reason of

exegetes, instead of explaining Holy Scripture according to the mind of the Church which Christ Our Lord has appointed guardian and interpreter of the whole deposit of divinely revealed truth.

## A New and Erroneous Exegesis

23. Further, according to their fictitious opinions, the literal sense of Holy Scripture and its explanation, carefully worked out under the Church's vigilance by so many great exegetes, should yield now to a new exegesis, which they are pleased to call symbolic or spiritual. By means of this new exegesis the Old Testament, which today in the Church is a sealed book, would finally be thrown open to all the faithful. By this method, they say, all difficulties vanish, difficulties which hinder only those who adhere to the literal meaning of the Scriptures.

## Principles of Interpretation

24. Everyone sees how foreign all this is to the principles and norms of interpretation rightly fixed by Our Predecessors of happy memory, Leo XIII, in his Encyclical *Providentissimus*, and Benedict XV in the Encyclical *Spiritus Paraclitus*, as also by Ourselves in the Encyclical *Divino Afflante Spiritu*.

## Novelties Bear Deadly Fruit in Theology

25. It is not surprising that novelties of this kind have already borne their deadly fruit in almost all branches of theology. It is now doubted that human reason, without Divine Revelation and the help of divine grace, can, by arguments drawn from the created universe, prove the existence of a personal God; it is denied that the world had a beginning; it is argued that the creation of the world is necessary, since it proceeds from the necessary liberality of divine love; it is denied that God has eternal and infallible foreknowedge of the free actions of men—all this in contradiction to the decrees of the Vatican Council.[4]

## Doctrines Are Modified and Perverted

26. Some also question whether Angels are personal beings, and whether matter and spirit differ essentially. Others destroy the gratuity of the supernatural order, since God, they say, cannot create intellectual beings without ordering and calling them to the Beatific Vision. Nor is this all. Disregarding the Council of Trent, some pervert the very concept of Original Sin, along with the concept of sin in general as an offense against God, as well as the idea of satisfaction performed for us by Christ. Some even say that the doctrine of Transubstantiation, based on an antiquated philosophic notion of substance, should be so modified that the Real Presence of Christ in the Holy Eucharist be reduced to a kind of symbolism, whereby the consecrated species would be merely efficacious signs of the spiritual presence of Christ and of His intimate union with the faithful members of His Mystical Body.

## Necessity of Belonging to the True Church to Gain Eternal Salvation

27. Some say they are not bound by the doctrine, explained in Our Encyclical Letter of a few years ago, and based on the sources of Revelation, which teaches that the Mystical Body of Christ and the Roman Catholic Church are one and the same thing.[5] Some reduce to a meaningless formula the necessity of belonging to the true Church in order to gain eternal salvation. Others, finally, belittle the reasonable character of the credibility of Christian faith.

## Clear Errors and Dangers of Error

28. These and like errors, it is clear, have crept in among certain of Our sons who are deceived by imprudent zeal for souls or by false science. To them We are compelled with grief to repeat once again truths already well known, and to point out with solicitude clear errors and dangers of error.

### Reason Must Be Properly Trained

29. It is well known how highly the Church regards human reason, for it falls to reason to demonstrate with certainty the existence of God, personal and one; to prove beyond doubt from divine signs the very foundations of the Christian Faith; to express properly the law which the Creator has imprinted in the hearts of men; and finally to attain to some notion, indeed a very fruitful notion, of mysteries.[6] But reason can perform these functions safely and well only when properly trained, that is, when imbued with that sound philosophy which has long been, as it were, a patrimony handed down by earlier Christian ages, and which moreover possesses an authority of even higher order, since the Teaching Authority of the Church, in the light of Divine Revelation itself, has weighed its fundamental tenets, which have been elaborated and defined little by little by men of great genius. For this philosophy, acknowledged and accepted by the Church, safeguards the genuine validity of human knowledge, the unshakable metaphysical principles of sufficient reason, causality, and finality, and finally the mind's ability to attain certain and unchangeable truth.

### Truth Cannot Change

30. Of course this philosophy deals with much that neither directly nor indirectly touches faith or morals, and which consequently the Church leaves to the free discussion of experts. But this does not hold for many other things, especially those principles and fundamental tenets to which We have just referred. However, even in these fundamental questions, we may clothe our philosophy in a more convenient and richer dress, make it more vigorous with more effective terminology, divest it of certain scholastic aids found less useful, prudently enrich it with the fruits of the progress of the human mind. But never may we overthrow it, or contaminate it with false principles, or regard it as a great but obsolete relic. For truth and its philosophic expression cannot change from day to day, least of all where there is a ques-

tion of the self-evident principles of the human mind or of those propositions which are supported by the wisdom of the ages and by Divine Revelation. Whatever new truth the sincere human mind is able to find certainly cannot be opposed to truth already acquired, since God, the highest Truth, has created and guides the human intellect, not that it may daily oppose new truths to rightly established ones, but rather that, having eliminated errors which may have crept in, it may build truth upon truth in the same order and structure that exist in reality, the source of truth. Let no Christian therefore, whether philosopher or theologian, embrace eagerly and lightly whatever novelty happens to be thought up from day to day, but rather let him weigh it with painstaking care and a balanced judgment, lest he lose or corrupt the truth he already has, with grave danger and damage to his faith.

### Thomistic Philosophy

31. If one considers all this well, he will easily see why the Church demands that future priests be instructed in philosophy "according to the method, doctrine, and principles of the Angelic Doctor,"[7] since, as we well know from the experience of centuries, the method of Aquinas is singularly pre-eminent both for teaching students and for bringing truth to light; his doctrine is in harmony with Divine Revelation and is most effective both for safeguarding the foundation of the Faith and for reaping, safely and usefully, the fruits of sound progress.[8]

### Other Philosophies Replacing Thomism

32. How deplorable it is then that this philosophy, received and honored by the Church, is scorned by some, who shamelessly call it outmoded in form and rationalistic, as they say, in its method of thought. They say that this philosophy upholds the erroneous notion that there can be a metaphysic that is absolutely true; whereas in fact, they say, reality, especially transcendent reality, cannot better be expressed than by disparate teachings which mutually complete each other, although they are in a way mutu-

ally opposed. Our traditional philosophy, then, with its clear exposition and solution of questions, its accurate definition of terms, its clear-cut distinctions, can be, they concede, useful as a preparation for Scholastic theology, a preparation quite in accord with medieval mentality; but this philosophy hardly offers a method of philosophizing suited to the needs of our modern culture. They allege, finally, that our perennial philosophy is only a philosophy of immutable essences, while the contemporary mind must look to the existence of things and to life, which is ever in flux. While scorning our philosophy, they extol other philosophies of all kinds, ancient and modern, oriental and occidental, by which they seem to imply that any kind of philosophy or theory, with a few additions and corrections if need be, can be reconciled with Catholic dogma. No Catholic can doubt how false this is, especially where there is question of those fictitious theories they call immanentism, or idealism, or materialism, whether historic or dialectic, or even existentialism, whether atheistic or simply the type that denies the validity of the reason in the field of metaphysics.

### Role of Will and Emotions in Attaining Knowledge

33. Finally, they reproach this philosophy taught in our schools for regarding only the intellect in the process of cognition, while neglecting the function of the will and the emotions. This is simply not true. Never has Christian philosophy denied the usefulness and efficacy of good dispositions of soul for perceiving and embracing moral and religious truths. In fact, it has always taught that the lack of these dispositions of good will can be the reason why the intellect, influenced by the passions and evil inclinations, can be so obscured that it cannot see clearly. Indeed, St. Thomas holds that the intellect can in some way perceive higher goods of the moral order, whether natural or supernatural, inasmuch as it experiences a certain "connaturality" with these goods, whether this "connaturality" be purely natural, or the result of grace;[9] and it is clear how much even this somewhat obscure perception can help the reason in its investigations. However, it is one thing to

admit the power of the dispositions of the will in helping reason to gain a more certain and firm knowledge of moral truths; it is quite another thing to say, as these innovators do, indiscriminately mingling cognition and act of will, that the appetitive and affective faculties have a certain power of understanding, and that man, since he cannot by using his reason decide with certainty what is true and is to be accepted, turns to his will, by which he freely chooses among opposite opinions.

### Certitude Is Denied

34. It is not surprising that these new opinions endanger the two philosophical sciences which by their very nature are closely connected with the doctrine of faith, that is, theodicy and ethics; they hold that the function of these two sciences is not to prove with certitude anything about God or any other transcendental being, but rather to show that the truths which faith teaches about a personal God and about His precepts are perfectly consistent with the necessities of life and are therefore to be accepted by all, in order to avoid despair and to attain eternal salvation. All these opinions and affirmations are openly contrary to the documents of Our Predecessors Leo XIII and Pius X, and cannot be reconciled with the decrees of the Vatican Council. It would indeed be unnecessary to deplore these aberrations from the truth if all, even in the field of philosophy, directed their attention with the proper reverence to the Teaching Authority of the Church, which by divine institution has the mission not only to guard and interpret the deposit of divinely revealed truth, but also to keep watch over the philosophical sciences themselves, in order that Catholic dogmas may suffer no harm because of erroneous opinions.

### Catholic Doctrine and Scientific Hypotheses

35. It remains for Us now to speak about those questions which, although they pertain to the positive sciences, are nevertheless more or less connected with the truths of the Christian Faith. In fact, not a few insistently demand that the Catholic reli-

gion take these sciences into account as much as possible. This certainly would be praiseworthy in the case of clearly proved facts; but caution must be used when there is rather question of hypotheses, having some sort of scientific foundation, in which the doctrine contained in Sacred Scripture or in Tradition is involved. If such conjectural opinions are directly or indirectly opposed to the doctrine revealed by God, then the demand that they be recognized can in no way be admitted.

### Opinions regarding Evolution of the Human Body

36. For these reasons the Teaching Authority of the Church does not forbid that, in conformity with the present state of human sciences and sacred theology, research and discussions on the part of men experienced in both fields take place with regard to the doctrine of Evolution, in as far as it inquires into the origin of the human body as coming from pre-existent and living matter—for the Catholic Faith obliges us to hold that souls are immediately created by God. However, this must be done in such a way that the reasons for both opinions, that is, those favorable and those unfavorable to Evolution, be weighed and judged with the necessary seriousness, moderation and measure, and provided that all are prepared to submit to the judgment of the Church, to whom Christ has given the mission of interpreting authentically the Sacred Scriptures and of defending the dogmas of faith.[10] Some, however, rashly transgress this liberty of discussion when they act as if the origin of the human body from pre-existing and living matter were already completely certain and proved by the facts which have been discovered up to now and by reasoning on those facts, and as if there were nothing in the sources of Divine Revelation which demands the greatest moderation and caution in this question.

### Polygenism

37. When, however, there is question of another conjectural opinion, namely polygenism, the children of the Church by no

means enjoy such liberty. For the faithful cannot embrace that opinion which maintains either that after Adam there existed on this earth true men who did not take their origin through natural generation from him as from the first parent of all, or that Adam represents a certain number of first parents. Now it is in no way apparent how such an opinion can be reconciled with that which the sources of revealed truth and the documents of the Teaching Authority of the Church propose with regard to Original Sin, which proceeds from a sin actually committed by an individual Adam and which through generation is passed on to all and is in everyone as his own.[11] (*Rom.* 5:12-19).

### Overly Free Interpretations of the Old Testament

38. Just as in the biological and anthropological sciences, so also in the historical sciences there are those who boldly transgress the limits and safeguards established by the Church. In a particular way must be deplored a certain too free interpretation of the historical books of the Old Testament. Those who favor this system, in order to defend their cause, wrongly refer to the Letter which was sent not long ago to the Archbishop of Paris by the Pontifical Commission on Biblical Studies.[12] This Letter, in fact, clearly points out that the first eleven chapters of Genesis, although properly speaking not conforming to the historical method used by the best Greek and Latin writers or by competent authors of our time, do nevertheless pertain to history in a true sense, which, however, must be further studied and determined by exegetes; the same chapters (the Letter points out), in simple and metaphorical language adapted to the mentality of a people but little cultured, both state the principal truths which are fundamental for our salvation, and also give a popular description of the origin of the human race and the chosen people. If, however, the ancient sacred writers have taken anything from popular narrations (and this may be conceded), it must never be forgotten that they did so with the help of divine inspiration, through which they were rendered immune from any error in selecting and evaluating those documents.

## Old Testament Books Are Sacred

39. Therefore, whatever of the popular narrations have been inserted into the Sacred Scriptures must in no way be considered on a par with myths or other such things, which are more the product of an extravagant imagination than of that striving for truth and simplicity which in the Sacred Books, also of the Old Testament, is so apparent that our ancient sacred writers must be admitted to be clearly superior to the ancient profane writers.

## New Opinions Entice the Incautious

40. Truly, We are aware that the majority of Catholic doctors, the fruit of whose studies is being gathered in universities, in seminaries and in the colleges of religious, are far removed from those errors which today, whether through a desire for novelty or through a certain immoderate zeal for the apostolate, are being spread either openly or covertly. But we know also that such new opinions can entice the incautious; and therefore We prefer to withstand the very beginnings rather than to administer the medicine after the disease has grown inveterate.

## Serious Duty of Bishops and Superiors General

41. For this reason, after mature reflection and consideration before God, that We may not be wanting in Our sacred duty, We charge the Bishops and the Superiors General of Religious Orders, binding them most seriously in conscience, to take most diligent care that such opinions be not advanced in schools, in conferences or in writings of any kind, and that they be not taught in any manner whatsoever to the clergy or the faithful.

## Duties of Teachers

42. Let the teachers in ecclesiastical institutions be aware that they cannot with tranquil conscience exercise the office of teaching entrusted to them unless in the instruction of their students

they religiously accept and exactly observe the norms which We have ordained. Let them also instill into the minds and hearts of their students that due reverence and submission which in their unceasing labor they must profess toward the Teaching Authority of the Church.

### Prudence in Study

43. Let them strive with every force and effort to further the progress of the sciences which they teach; but let them also be careful not to transgress the limits which We have established for the protection of the truth of Catholic Faith and doctrine. With regard to new questions which modern culture and progress have brought to the foreground, let them engage in most careful research, but with the necessary prudence and caution; finally, let them not think, indulging in a false "eirenism," that the dissident and erring can happily be brought back to the bosom of the Church if the whole truth found in the Church is not sincerely taught to all without corruption or diminution.

### The Apostolic Blessing

44. Relying on this hope, which will be increased by your pastoral care, as a pledge of celestial gifts and a sign of Our paternal benevolence, We impart with all Our heart to each and all of you, Venerable Brethren, and to your clergy and people, the Apostolic Benediction.

45. Given at Rome, at St. Peter's, August 12, 1950, the twelfth year of Our Pontificate.

Pius XII, Pope

## NOTES

1. Vatican Council I, DB 1786, Dogmatic Constitution *On the Catholic Faith,* Chap. 2, "Revelation."
2. *Code of Canon Law* [1917], can. 1324; cf. Vatican Council I, DB 1820, Dogmatic Constitution *On the Catholic Faith,* Chap. 4, "Faith and Reason," following canons.
3. Pius IX, *Inter Gravissimas,* October 28, 1870, *Acta,* Vol. 1, p. 260.
4. Cf. Vatican Council I, Dogmatic Constitution *On the Catholic Faith,* Chap. 1, "God the Creator of All Things."
5. Cf. Encyclical *The Mystical Body of Christ, A.A.S.,* Vol. XXXV, p. 193f.
6. Cf. Vatican Council I, DB 1796.
7. *Code of Canon Law* [1917], can. 1366, 2.
8. *A.A.S.,* vol. XXXVIII, 1946, p. 387.
9. Cf. St. Thomas, *Summa Theologica,* II-II, Q. 1, art. 4 ad 3; Q. 45, art. 2, in c.
10. Cf. Pontifical Allocution to the Members of the Academy of Science, November 30, 1941 (*A.A.S.,* Vol. XXXIII, p. 506).
11. Cf. Council of Trent, Session V, canons 1-4.
12. January 16, 1948 (*A.A.S.,* Vol. XL, pp. 45-48).